THE SUCCESSFUL BUSINESS LIBRARY

Write Your Own Business Contracts

What Your Attorney Won't Tell You

E. Thorpe Barrett

The Oasis Press®
Grants Pass, Oregon

The Oasis Press
300 North Valley Drive
Grants Pass, Oregon 97526
(541) 479-9464

Second edition

ISBN: 1-55571-196-0 (binder)
1-55571-170-7 (paperback)

This publication is designed to provide accurate and authoritative information in regard to the subject matter covered. It is sold with the understanding that the publisher is not engaged in rendering legal, accounting, or other professional service. If legal advice or other expert assistance is required, the services of a competent professional person should be sought.

- From a Declaration of Principles jointly adopted by a committee of the American Bar Association and a Committee of Publishers.

The Oasis Press is a Registered Trademark of Publishing Services Incorporated, an Oregon corporation doing business as PSI Research.

Printed in the United States of America

To Eva, Ron, and Jon
With All My Love

Contents

Prologue

Fog everywhere. Fog up the river, where it flows among green aits and meadows; fog down the river, where it rolls defiled among the tiers of shipping, and the waterside pollution of a great city. Fog on the Essex marshes, fog on the Kentish heights. Fog creeping into the cabooses of collier-brigs; fog lying out on the yards and hovering in the rigging of great ships; fog drooping on gunwales of barges and small boats. Fog in the eyes and throats of ancient Greenwich pensioners, wheezing by firesides of their wards; fog in the stem and bowl of the afternoon pipe of the wrathful skipper, down in his close cabin; fog cruelly pinching the toes and fingers of his shivering little 'prentice boy on deck. Chance people on bridges peeping over the parapets into a nether sky of fog, with fog all around them, as if they were up in a balloon, and hanging in misty clouds.

Gas looming through the fog in divers places in the streets, much as the sun may, from the spongy fields, be seen to loom by husbandman and ploughboy. Most of the shops lighted two hours before their time—as the gas seems to know, for it has a haggard and unwilling look.

The raw afternoon is rawest, and the dense fog is densest, and the muddy streets are muddiest, near the leaden-headed old obstruction, appropriate ornament for the threshold of a leaden-headed old corporation: Temple Bar. And hard by Temple Bar, in Lincoln's Inn Hall, at the very heart of the fog, sits the Lord High Chancellor in his High Court of Chancery.

Never can there come fog too thick, never can there come mud and mire too deep, to assort with the groping and floundering conditions which this High Court of Chancery, most persistent of hoary sinners, holds, this day, in the sight of heaven and earth.

Charles Dickens,

Bleakhouse, 1852.

Introduction

WHEREAS, the undersigned (hereinafter referred to as "I" or from time to time as "me" as the context may require) being a lawyer in good standing and a member of the Bar of the Commonwealth of Massachusetts, have, as hereinafter set forth, concluded I have been in good standing long enough,

WHEREFORE, I have put my thoughts on paper.

WITNESSETH:

First, let me deny vehemently various statements that have been attributed to me. I deny that I have ever said the expression "stupid lawyer" is redundant, nor have I ever indicated the expression is a single word. I have said, however, that redundancy is the greatest single skill ever developed by the legal profession. I never said lawyers write long contracts because they are incapable of writing shorter ones. I said, contracts are long because fees are higher.

Moreover, I never said lawyers are not needed. What I said is: "If there were no lawyers, we wouldn't need them".

If anyone draws the conclusion that this book was intended to be in any way an indictment of the current legal structure, that person is in error. It wasn't intended—it just worked out that way.

One purpose of this book is to show the typical businessman how to write most of his own contracts or, if he makes use of a lawyer, to show how to do so in a constructive rather than a destructive manner. And that isn't easy. It is also intended to encourage some of the captains of industry to think again about their internal legal departments and find out just how much destruction they are causing. It is plenty.

You may gather from my comments in this book that I hold the legal profession in contempt and regard myself as a superior lawyer. Not true. At least, not entirely. This book is based on several decades of acting as corporate counsel, patent attorney and general handyman for corporate clients. It is also based on long experience in operating commercial business enterprises. I am now just an independent country-town lawyer. I maintain I am more practical than many lawyers and can provide more assistance in putting a deal together. But there are many with far greater skills than I. Nevertheless, it is true that more lawyers are skilled at killing deals than in configuring a deal for the best interests of all parties. I have set forth many examples of contracts proposed by large corporations, written by internal legal departments or word-processed by prestigious law firms. Of course, I picked the worst ones for examples. That was not easy.

Another purpose of this book is to point out the benefits to the ordinary businessman in structuring his own deals and the resulting agreements. I will try to wash away some of the mystery by which the legal profession seeks to preserve its cartel. I will try to provide the basic information for preparing ordinary business contracts. There are practical limits. If a contract involves millions of dollars, you would likely want to obtain the advice and assistance of the best lawyers you can find. Nevertheless, the information presented here will help you make better use of those lawyers and even, perhaps, keep them from killing a desirable deal. This book will not enable you to write your own ticket in certain areas where specialized skills are a necessity, but it will help you make the experts more efficient for your purposes.

Consider two businessmen with a great deal of knowledge about the kind of deal they want to put together and limited legal knowledge. They are generally better off if they negotiate the deal directly and then write the contract than they would be if they turned the negotiating over to two sets of typical lawyers. To understand why this is true, it is helpful to consider the profile of the typical business or corporate attorney. Usually with a modicum of intelligence, or at least a creditable memory, he* made his way through law school and across the bar. Whether he is now a member of a large law firm or a small independent practitioner, he likely went directly from law school to the business of law. Most likely, he never worked in any commercial enterprise other than law. It is even less likely he ever had responsibility for payrolls and bottom line results. It is not surprising to find a lawyer who, even after years of legal activities and advising clients on business problems, has only the faintest understanding of how business operates and those things that are important to the profit objective.

** The sexist words "he", "him" and the like are used here only for purposes of simplification and are intended to include both the male and female gender. Or, as some lawyers might say: "Semper sexus etiam femininum sexum continet."*

In spite of all I have said, attorneys can be useful, both as independent counsel and as "in-house" employees. Hopefully, this book will enable you to make effective use of lawyers and avoid the wide-spread destruction now being visited upon the business community by the legal profession.

This book is more than a form book: actual contracts prepared by large companies and prestigious law firms are analyzed, and in some cases destroyed, provision by provision. By this method, the reader learns how to modify the typical agreements set forth here, which cover many of the most usual business situations, to best suit the particular requirements or preferences of the reader, or even to prepare an agreement of a kind not contemplated by this author.

It is not intended that anyone will merely read this book from cover to cover. Nothing could be more boring. And it wouldn't be very useful. The book is a combination teaching tool and a reference. It is recommended the reader initially read Chapters 1, 2, 13, 14 and 15. From that point, the chapters should be selected in accordance with the particular needs of the moment.

We'll discuss employment contracts, license agreements, distributor agreements, leases, purchase order terms, sales contracts, consulting agreements, non-disclosure and non-competition agreements, and others. We'll also consider specific contractual terms in a more general sense, such as hold-harmless clauses, warranties, representations, and the like.

The reader is specifically cautioned that the agreements used as examples in this book may not be satisfactory, without modification, for a particular situation. The reader is urged in all instances, after preparing his own contract, to have it reviewed by his attorney before making use of it. The purpose of the attorney is to tell you how the proposed agreement might get you into trouble—not to negotiate deals or even prepare the first draft of an agreement.

Lastly, let me express my personal appreciation to my colleagues and friends who reviewed and criticized the manuscript for this book. I express appreciation to my wife, Eva, for her hours of proofreading, to Barbara Duffield for her many editorial contributions, and particularly to the one who said it was "pretty good."

Editor's note:

This book consists of a practical discussion of business contracts interspersed with examples of typical contracts, examples of bad contracts, and the author's suggested alternatives. All examples are set on paper-clipped pages. "Good" and "bad" examples are distinguished by the use of identifying icons in the upper right corner, as follows:

WHEREAS:

This is an example of a typical word-processed, redundancy-ridden, attorney-generated, expensive, costly, and unaffordable contract excerpt...

This is an example of a practical alternative...

Chapter One

The Prerequisites of a "Good" Business Contract

The words "contract" and "agreement" are used interchangeably in this book. They are used to refer to written documents, but this is not intended to imply that all binding agreements must be in writing. Many oral contracts are enforceable. However, it is an important business practice to put all agreements in writing and, to that end, this book is limited to a discussion of written agreements. Perhaps, literally, a written document is only evidence of an agreement between the parties, but we shall refer here to the written document as the agreement or contract.

The objective of a contract should be clearly understood. You may say that a good contract is one that will stand up in court and that armed with it you can be sure of prevailing. But only a small percentage of contracts end up in litigation. Drafting a contract with the primary object of its advantages in a court of law will more often than not result in a killed deal. *The primary object should be to set forth the deal clearly, in words that can be understood by the participants in future years.* The more clearly the contract is written, the less the chance of future disputes or litigation.

The written contract should not even be considered until the principals have agreed upon all of the essential terms of the deal. Once that is accomplished, the terms are reduced to writing so that the parties will have a permanent record of just what was agreed to. To be sure, during the preparation of the written agreement, it may be evident that the parties did not, in fact, reach full agreement on all provisions of the deal and further negotiating may be necessary based on a number of drafts of the agreement. To accomplish the function of providing a permanent record of exactly what the deal is, the agreement must be written in an understandable manner. Sometimes, lawyers write in such obfuscating language the client does not understand what he is asked to sign. In such event, the client should ask the lawyer to explain in plain language just what the particular section means. He will usually do this in an understandable manner. When he does, the obvious question is: "Why don't we say that?"

If you cannot understand a contract while the deal is fresh in your mind, imagine what a quagmire it will be a few months or years in the future. Fix it now. Contract problems arise most often because of vague or indefinite language or because the contract is not complete. A contract should state in the simplest language possible, not complex legalese, exactly what each party is obligated to do. There is no requirement for the use in a contract of archaic words or expressions such as: whereas, wherefore, hereinafter, witnesseth, hereinbefore, inter alia, force majeure, a priori, prima facie, etc. Some of these words may be useful from time to time, but there is no requirement they appear in every other sentence. The contract can be quite enforceable without them. There are commonly used words and phrases that should never be used. The expression "and/or" is one to be avoided; it clouds rather than clarifies the intended meaning. Its use may lead to controversy and/or litigation. It would be nice if attorneys were skilled in the art of writing in a clear and precise manner, but few are. Few understand the sometimes not so subtle differences between which and that, or therefor and therefore, or may and shall, or can and may, or infer and imply, or between and among, or either or, or neither nor, etc., etc. Contracts are most readily understood when written with relatively short sentences using familiar short words. Sometimes it is desirable, or even necessary, to use a longer word for reasons of precision, but the needless replacement of a short word with a longer word, even a Latinized word from the legal jargon, is nonsense. The art of clear writing is beyond the scope of this book, but any effort you make in that direction will result in contracts less likely to result in disputes. It is enough to caution that if legalese continues to multiply, G. M. Young may be proven correct when he said "—civilization will come to an end because no one will understand what anybody else is saying."

The contract should contain all of the terms. If earlier documents or agreements relate to the present one, they should be integrated by reference as exhibits or replaced by language in the new agreement.

There are certain elements that are necessary for a contract to be enforceable —not because you expect to bring legal action, but because you are less likely to have need for legal action if the contract is clearly enforceable.

Do not expect too much from your contract. A client once asked me to write an "air-tight" contract because the other party to the deal could not be trusted. "He'll cheat me if he can, and I want him nailed to the wall so tight he hasn't a chance."

I explained I could not write such a contract. A contract should not be relied upon as an instrument to keep crooks in check. Contracts made under those circumstances are the ones most frequently in court. If you do not have confidence in the other party as a relatively honest individual or company, reconsider whether you want to make the deal.

Going to court is not a viable way to settle disagreements. The courts are expensive, slow, disorganized, and ruled by judges with generally little business knowledge. Dickens was on the mark one hundred years ago when he said, referring to the Court of Chancery, "Suffer any wrong that can be done you, rather than come here!" His advice is yet a suitable warning.

The essential elements of the usual business agreement are:

- identification of the parties to the agreement
- consideration
- terms
- execution
- delivery

We shall now review each of these elements.

The Parties to the Agreement

The parties to the contract should be clearly identified. Usually this will be apparent from the terms of the agreement, but if there is any doubt, individuals should be identified by residence or other descriptive terms in addition to names. A corporation can be positively identified by noting the state in which it is incorporated. There will be no other corporation incorporated in that state with the same name, but there may be other corporations with the identical name incorporated in other states. (If you do not understand clearly the differences among corporations, companies, and partnerships, there is a discussion concerning this in chapter 16.)

Because the names of the parties are repeated several times in a typical agreement, it is convenient to assign a "pet" or shorthand name to each of them. In days past, lawyers sometimes identified the parties as Party of the First Part, Party of the Second Part, etc. That sort of thing doesn't save much, if any, typing, and the agreement may be difficult to understand, because one may have to keep referring to the introduction to recall which party is first, second, or third. But then, some lawyers seem to believe contracts are not supposed to be easy to understand.

It is preferable to assign a name that will make it clear which party is being mentioned. For example, in a sales contract, one party may be referred to as the "seller" and the other party as the "buyer." If so, it is better to capitalize each pet name so that it will not be confused with any generic use of the same word. A contract between Joe Smith and Fred Jones might use "Joe" and "Fred" as the pet names, or "Smith" and "Jones."Corporations can be identified easily by using part of the corporate name or a suitable acronym. The first time the name of a party is used it should be tagged with the pet name. A typical contract might read:

```
The United Amalgamated Conglomerate Corporation,
Inc., a corporation duly incorporated under the laws
of the state of Delaware, (hereinafter referred to
from time to time as "United")...
```

That is unnecessary legalese. It is simpler to say:

```
The United Amalgamated Conglomerate Corporation, a
Delaware corporation, ("United")...
```

The initial paragraph of a contract typically identifies the parties and may or may not include the date of the agreement. Word-processed lawyers might write a first paragraph somewhat like this:

A simpler paragraph is preferable, such as:

```
THIS LICENSE AGREEMENT (hereinafter referred to as the
"Agreement") is entered into as of the Twenty-seventh
day of January in the year of our Lord 1989 by and
between Coproducts Inc., a corporation duly organized
and validly existing under the laws of the state of
California, having a principal place of business at 24
Lawn Street, Venestro, California, (hereinafter
referred to as "CI") and Albert M. Smith, an
individual residing at 2367 Grandview Street,
Malachai, California (hereinafter referred to as
"Smith")

WITNESSETH: ...
```

Consideration for the Agreement

This is an Agreement, effective January 27, 1989, between Coproducts, Inc., a California corporation, ("CI") and Albert M. Smith, an individual residing at 2367 Grandview Street, Malachai, California ("Smith").

"Consideration" means that each party must gain something from the agreement. The something does not need to be much: a peppercorn was held to be sufficient in early English law. But generally there must be something. For instance, I write a promissory note, payable to you for ten thousand dollars. I sign and deliver the note to you. You have done absolutely nothing on my behalf.

The note is probably not enforceable. However, if you have given me, say, an old bookcase for the note, it may well be enforceable. I recall, dimly, a real estate case where an option was given on valuable property, reciting the option to be in consideration of twenty-five cents. Later, the option was held to be unenforceable because the quarter was never actually paid.

Lawyers even today sometimes include a provision something like:

This is not consideration because money is money and neither party receives anything he

"This agreement is in consideration of one dollar each into the hand of the other paid..."

didn't have before. If your agreement recites this kind of consideration, get another lawyer, or even better—write your own contract.

Consideration may be recited in an agreement, but in many cases it is not necessary because in most agreements each party undertakes an obligation to do something. In such instances, the consideration is obvious and need not be recited. In some instances it is desirable to include a provision such as this:

For valuable consideration, the receipt and adequacy of which are acknowledged, the parties agree as follows:...

Mere recitation of consideration, where none exists, may not be sufficient to ensure the enforceability of the contract. If the contract calls for a payment, even one dollar, be sure the money is actually paid if you are relying on that payment as consideration.

Terms of the Agreement

Following any recitation of consideration, comes the body of the agreement where the specific terms are set forth. This is the critical part. We'll be devoting a major part of this book to the preparation of contract terms, so we'll merely summarize some of the more important points here.

Before starting to write an agreement, it is usually best to prepare a list of obligations of each party to the agreement: a list of who does what, when, etc. The next step is to express these undertakings in clear, unambiguous language. In an effort to avoid ambiguity, and to include all possible ramifications, lawyers are prone to say the same, or a similar thing, a number of times. The result is a contract that is long, difficult to understand, and no more enforceable than a shorter version would be. For example, assume the obligation of one party is to sell and deliver a box of gizmos to the other party. The provision might read like this:

```
Joe hereby sells, transfers, sets over,
delivers, gives title, and assigns his entire
right, title, and interest in and to the box
of gizmos to Bill.
```

The following will work just as well:

```
Joe sells the box of gizmos to Bill.
```

These provisions are only satisfactory if we have defined in the agreement exactly what the "box of gizmos" is, but we'll get to that later.

The format of the terms is not particularly important and is very much a matter of personal choice. In a short agreement, say, one or two pages, I seldom use section headings, but in longer agreements, headings are useful in locating a particular part of the agreement. Typical section headings might be:

- Background
- Definitions
- Assignment of Rights
- Payment Terms
- Representations by the Seller
- Representations by the Buyer
- Notices

- Warranties
- Termination
- Execution

There is no magic in the titles, but they should describe with reasonable accuracy the contents of each section. We'll be putting much emphasis on the construction of terms and titles for the various sections.

Execution of the Agreement

The agreement should be signed by each of the parties. If each party is an individual, the signature is usually enough. In some instances it is desirable to have the signature witnessed if there is doubt about the identity of the individual. To be valid, a contract generally does not have to be under seal or be witnessed by a Notary Public. There are special situations, such as in real estate transactions, trusts, etc. where a Notary Public acknowledgment is either necessary or desirable. In preparing documents that are executed only by one party, such as a trust document, it is desirable to have a notarial acknowledgment to establish with some certainty the date on which the instrument was executed.

If one or both parties are corporations, it is important to make sure the party signing for the corporation has, in fact, the power to bind that corporation to the agreement. In some instances, it is necessary for the individual to be empowered by the Board of Directors to execute the agreement. A copy of the minutes authorizing the execution, together with a certification by the secretary of the corporation, may be requested. In some situations, for example the sale of a major part of the assets of a corporation, a vote of the stockholders may be required. In most instances, after satisfying myself the individual does have the power to bind the corporation, I include a paragraph such as:

```
Each party executing this Agreement on
behalf of a corporation personally
represents that he is authorized to
execute this agreement on behalf of such
corporation and that this Agreement is
binding on that corporation.
```

Delivery of the Agreement

To be valid, a contract must be "delivered" to the other party. For example, let's say I am not sure I want to enter into a particular agreement and want to consult an expert before making a final deal. I do, however, sign the agreement and leave it in my private desk drawer. The other party, being a scoundrel, comes into my office in my absence and takes the executed agreement. There was no delivery and it is probable that the agreement cannot be enforced. As a matter of practice, make sure that a copy of the agreement is executed for each party and that each party receives a copy of the executed contract.

The Omnipotent Seal

The "seal" is a subject of mystery on legal documents. It is archaic, but the legal profession hasn't discovered that. Perhaps one reason is that a document looks so official the attorney is able to charge an extra fifty bucks. Maybe not. In any event, the use of the seal goes far back in history in both the East and the West. When few people could write, a signet ring made especially for the owner was impressed in sealing wax or clay to serve as an authenticating signature.

Today, when people and most attorneys can write, the seal would seem to be of no further import. Not so. Banks and lawyers like seals. The lawyers make laws. So we still have laws in some states requiring seals on certain documents, or giving longer life to contracts made "under seal." Many banks will not accept a corporate resolution unless it bears the corporate seal. Somehow, banks seem to think (to whatever extent a bank can think) that the seal is exclusive to a corporation and that it makes the document authentic. It does nothing for it. A corporate seal usually embosses the corporate name into the document. But that proves little; anyone can buy a seal for any corporation for a few dollars. There is no law against making or owning a corporate seal for any corporation. In other words, a seal proves nothing. Moreover, the embossing process is not necessary to create a sealed instrument. Merely including the words "signed under seal" will do as well. Or a scroll, or one half of a postage stamp, or... However, the seal doesn't hurt anything, so if someone is happier with a seal on the document, let him have it.

Before going on to some practical situations, we can get a feel for learning to speak "Legal"—if anyone should ever want to do so—from the following example of how an omelet recipe looks when translated into Legal:

<u>Legal Omelet</u>*

This Agreement between the undersigned (hereinafter referred to as "UNDERSIGNED") and you (hereinafter referred to as "COOK")

WITNESSETH:

WHEREAS: COOK desires to prepare, construct, create and/or make an omelet (hereinafter referred to as "OMELET FRANCAISE"); and

WHEREAS: it is well known that poultry eggs when subjected to elevated temperatures, either Celsius or Fahrenheit, will coagulate to a degree dependent upon both temperature and time of exposure; and

WHEREAS: UNDERSIGNED has skills, talents, know-how, ability, knowledge, dexterity and/or experience in such culinary arts;

NOW, THEREFORE, in consideration of the exchange of the benefits of such skills, talents, know-how, ability, knowledge, dexterity and/or experience by the UNDERSIGNED for participation in the enjoyment of OMELET FRANCAISE prepared, constructed, created and/or made in accordance with the following specifications, the parties have agreed as follows:

continued on page 1-8

**From the author's "Cook Book for Lawyers" a seven hundred-page volume containing twenty-one savory recipes.*

continued from page 1-7

1. EGG PREPARATION

COOK shall remove the shells, by any appropriate means including, but not limited to, breaking, peeling, and/or cracking, from not more than three and not less than two poultry eggs (hereinafter referred to as "EGGS") and place them in a small dish of appropriate size or dimensions. COOK shall then add to said EGGS one teaspoon (approximately one and one-half (1.5) fluid drams) of water and an appropriate amount of salt and pepper. COOK shall then mix said EGGS with a fork by beating said EGGS not less than thirty or more than forty-two strokes.

2. STEP ONE OF COAGULATION PROCEDURE

COOK shall then place approximately six (6) grams of butter, margarine, or saturated or polyunsaturated fat in a seven (7) inch stick-proof skillet (hereinafter called the "PAN") previously heated to a desirable temperature by an appropriate source, including but not limited to gas, electric or nuclear. When the butter, margarine, or saturated or polyunsaturated fat reaches maximum boiling activity and begins to subside, COOK will immediately add said EGGS to said PAN.

3. COMPLETION OF COAGULATION PROCESS

COOK will allow said PAN to continue heating for a period of time not less than thirty or more than fifty-five seconds. COOK will then, by a sharp and practiced flip, turn the most distant half of said OMELET FRANCAISE back onto itself to form a semi-circular cross-sectional shape.

4. SERVING SAID OMELET FRANCAISE

COOK shall promptly slide, slip, skid, and/or tumble said OMELET FRANCAISE onto a preheated substantially circular serving plate having a diameter of not less than eight (8) or more than ten (10) inches.

5. FORCE MAJEURE

Neither COOK nor UNDERSIGNED shall be responsible for damages resulting from riots, floods, strikes, Acts of God and/or other unforseen events including, but not limited to unskilled, awkward, inept,

continued on page 1-9

continued from page 1-8

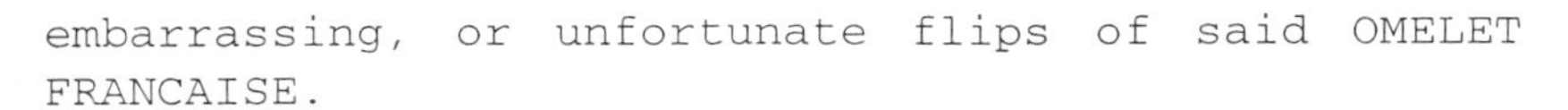

embarrassing, or unfortunate flips of said OMELET FRANCAISE.

6. LIMITED WARRANTY

UNDERSIGNED makes no warranty, implied or express, with respect to said OMELET FRANCAISE and makes no warranty of fitness for any particular purpose. In no event shall UNDERSIGNED be liable for consequential damages.

7. EXECUTION

WHEREFORE, the parties hereto have this seventeenth (17th) day of December in the year of our Lord 1988, set their hands and seals hereonto.

UNDERSIGNED ______________________________

COOK ______________________________

Chapter Two

Clauses…Standard and Dangerous

So-called "boiler plate" has been included in agreements for ages. Such clauses have frequently represented an unforeseen hazard, but with the advent of the wordprocessor, they have become a downright menace. Unfortunately, all too often, the standard clauses are used as a substitute for thinking. Here are some samples and comments on widely-used provisions.

Multiple Copies

```
Counterparts.

This Agreement may be executed in one or more
counterparts, all of which taken together shall
constitute one and the same Agreement.
```

The "Counterparts" clause is generally not required. A signed paper called the "agreement" is technically not the agreement: it is *evidence* of the agreement between the parties. Agreements are usually executed in two or more copies, each signed by each of the parties to the agreement. No special clause is necessary to render each copy an enforceable contract and to prevent the interpretation of the multiple copies as separate instruments. In some instances, there may be a number of individuals that, for example, are required to approve an agreement. For convenience, particularly when signatures must be secured by mail, a duplicate copy of the signature page, along with a copy of the agreement, is sent to each signatory. The final contract will then include a number of separate pages each containing one signature. Under those circumstances, the "Counterparts" clause is appropriate. In most cases, however, it just ain't necessary.

Eliminating Earlier Understandings

```
Entire Agreement; Modification

This Agreement represents the entire understanding
between the parties hereto [with respect to the subject
matter hereof] and this Agreement supersedes any and
all prior agreements, obligations, understandings and
representations, whether written or oral, between the
parties [with respect to the subject matter hereof].
```

continued on page 2-2

continued from page 2-1

```
This Agreement, including without limitation any
Exhibits attached hereto, may only be modified by a
written instrument signed by each of the parties
hereto.
```

The "Entire Agreement" clause is appropriate in many agreements, but it should not be used without considering whether it is applicable to the particular situation at hand. If this is the only agreement between Smith and Jones, the clause is appropriate to wipe out previous oral or written discussions about the proposed agreements along with any representations made by either party.

New agreements are sometimes entered into with no intention to abrogate previous agreements. For example, Jones and Smith may have a non-competition agreement. They now enter into an agreement for Jones to sell his apple crop to Smith. They may not want to cancel the prior agreement, or at least one of them may not want to. If the "Entire Agreement" clause is used under these circumstances, the bracketed phrase "with respect to the subject matter hereof" should be included. The clause may be simplified as follows:

```
Entire Agreement; Modification

This Agreement is the entire understanding between the
parties with respect to the subjects matter hereof and
may only be modified by written agreement.
```

Invalidity of Contract Provisions

```
Severability

In the event any provision of this Agreement is
determined to be invalid or unenforceable, it shall be
adjusted so as to best reflect the intent of the
parties to the maximum extent possible, and the
remainder of this agreement shall be valid and
enforceable to the maximum extent possible.
```

The "Severability" clause is sometimes appropriate, but it is much overused. In most instances it doesn't accomplish anything and in other instances it can be harmful. A client of mine desired to make a gift to certain key employees of a part of any money he might get by selling his business. An agreement was drafted which detailed the procedures by which the money would be divided among the eligible candidates. It also contained provisions excluding anyone who committed fraud toward the business, or engaged in competition with it, or who was fired for flagrant disregard of instructions, etc. A large Boston law firm reviewed the agreement and added a covey of "standard" clauses including the "Severability" clause. Was this in the best interests of the client? He was making a gift to the employees, but he was getting nothing. He would be better off if the agreement provided that if any clause was held to be unenforceable, the entire agreement would be void. For example, an employee is fired for flagrant disregard of his instructions and goes into competition with his former employer. If the clause in the agreement, excluding that person from sharing the returns of the sale is held to be unenforceable, the donor would want the entire contract to be voided and thereby exclude the rascal employee. The lesson is, think about the contents of the "standard" clauses. Do not include any one of them because it is considered unimportant "boiler plate."

Titles for Contract Provisions

```
Headings

The headings at the beginnings of the Sections of this
Agreement are for identification purposes and shall not
affect the interpretation or construction of this
Agreement.
```

The "Headings" clause is used enough to be standard. It is perhaps a matter of preference—my preference is to omit it. If you are too indolent to monitor carefully the drafting of an agreement, then you may want to use the clause. But, of course, no attorney would be so indolent. If the headings are drafted with reasonable care, they may be considered a part of the agreement to the benefit of all. A heading that does not include all of the subjects matter in a particular section, does not invalidate that section. Use reasonable care in drafting your headings and omit the "Headings" clause.

Terms that Outlast the Agreement

The "Survival of Terms" clause is appropriate for many agreements, but there are many where it is unsuitable. In the agreement you may make certain statements that are relied upon by the other party. You may not want to be in a position where those representations survive any termination of the agreement. In fact, you may want to provide that all representations and warranties die with expiration or termination of the agreement and are no longer binding.

```
Survival of Terms

The representations and warranties contained in this
Agreement and all Exhibits hereto shall be continuous
and shall survive the expiration or termination of this
Agreement.
```

A typical use for Survival clauses is in non-disclosure agreements. There are usually two time periods in such agreements: a first time period when confidential information may be exchanged and a second time period when the obligation of confidentiality expires. The agreement may be drafted to expire in, say, one year, but the obligation to maintain confidentiality may survive the expiration of the agreement for a stated period. Another format is to limit the definition of "Confidential Information" to information disclosed within a first time period and provide for a second time period when the agreement expires. Under the latter arrangement no Survival clause is needed.

Survival and other standard clauses sometimes include the words

```
…including without limitation all Exhibits attached
hereto…
```

even in agreements which have no exhibits. This indicates it was the word processor and not the attorney that generated the clause. Even if there are exhibits, the phrase is a bit more conservative than belt and suspenders. The Exhibits are almost always an integral part of the agreement and any separate identification of them is superfluous. It is even more superfluous when there are Exhibits, but the Exhibits contain no warranties or representations. I haven't the faintest idea what the words "without limitation" do for this clause. But as we shall see, those two words are an automatic lawyer reflex. A typical lawyer might even say the expression is banal, hackneyed, trite, musty, stale, tiresome, and worn out.

When a Right to Act is Ignored

```
Waiver

Waiver of any term or condition in this Agreement shall
not be construed as a waiver of a subsequent breach of
the same term or condition or any other term or
condition.
```

Or:

```
Waiver

The failure of either party to enforce any right
accruing under this Agreement shall not be construed as
a waiver of a subsequent right of such party to enforce
the same or any other right, term or condition.
```

The "Waiver" clause may be one you want or it may be one you distinctly do not want. Suppose you have an agreement for the continuing purchase of goods from Jones and the agreement states that no order is considered to be accepted unless it is in writing. In spite of this provision you order goods regularly from Jones by telephone without a purchase order. He consistently ships and submits invoices for the goods. One day, Jones accepts a telephone order from you and agrees to ship within ten days. A month later you have not received the goods. You raise the appropriate ruckus. Jones tells you the price has gone up and you did not order the goods in time to take advantage of the lower price. Jones points to the section of the agreement requiring all orders to be in writing. You point out that you have always placed verbal orders. Jones then points to the "waiver" clause and says the previous waivers of the written-order provision do not apply here.

Waiver clauses are often included in contracts for commercial construction, particularly in those situations where there will be a number of engineering or specification change orders. Usually, the contract will call for the builder to obtain the written consent of the owner before making any deviation in the specifications. If you are the owner, you will likely not want the waiver clause—the contractor will want it. If the owner makes a habit of not signing and returning notices of specification changes, but does not object to them and continues to make payments to the contractor, the waiver clause may prohibit him from later objecting to changes because he did not approve them in advance.

Notifying the Other Party

Notices

All notices shall be in writing and shall be sent by certified mail, return receipt requested, or by facsimile,

if to Jones to:

Robert G. Jones
117 Ashbury Park
Dayton, Ohio 45420
Facsimile: (513) 276-2000

if to Smith to:

Jim Smith
1414 Toronto Road
Dayton Ohio 45420,
Facsimile: (503)295-2000

or to such other address as either party may request by notice. All notices sent by certified mail shall be effective three (3) days after mailing. Notices sent by facsimile shall be immediately confirmed in writing sent by Federal Express or Express Mail for overnight delivery and shall be effective on the date of transmission.

The "Notices" clause is useful. It provides an explicit procedure for giving notice to any party under the agreement and will usually result in a shorter agreement. It is not necessary to even call for a written notice in other parts of the agreement. It is sufficient to say merely that notice shall be given, because the notice provision provides that "all" notices under the agreement shall follow the prescribed procedure. Modern agreements that call for delivery of notices by telegram or registered mail predate even the word processor. It is now appropriate to include notice by facsimile (with appropriate facsimile addresses).

Protection from Legal Claims

Hold Harmless (Indemnity) Clauses

Of all of the dangerous clauses, perhaps the reddest flag is raised by the "Hold Harmless" clause. If there is a general rule, it is: take 'em, don't give 'em. Big corporations have a habit of requiring suppliers, consultants, contractors and the like to sign clauses guaranteeing to hold the big company harmless from any damage resulting from the negligence or workmanship of the other party. Usually, such clauses require the party to protect the company from claims of damage—even if not well-founded. Suppose a supplier desires to sell a machine to a manufacturer and the supplier is asked to sign a clause holding the manufacturer harmless from any claim of patent infringement. Even if the delivered machine does not infringe any patent, but an infringement suit is brought, the supplier must either defend the suit or pay the manufacturer for his expense in defending the suit. If the machine does infringe, the supplier may also have to pay the cost of acquiring a license, revising the machine to avoid infringement, or taking the machine out of use. An ironic situation occurs frequently: a large corporation requires that some individual hold the corporation harmless from this or that which may involve a potential liability of millions of dollars—completely overlooking the fact that the individual doesn't have any assets. A hold harmless is only of value if there are assets to back it up.

Let's consider a real-life situation: An individual entered into negotiations with a San Diego manufacturer to license an optical recording medium. The manufacturer, apparently because he wasn't satisfied with the quality of San Diego lawyers, engaged a medium-size three-name firm in San Francisco to draft the agreement. (The name of the firm is omitted to protect the guilty.) The draft included the following hold harmless clause:

**I told you lawyers are the grand masters of redundancy*

Licensor hereby agrees to indemnify, hold harmless and defend Licensee (and any third party claiming under Licensee and any direct or indirect customer of the Licensee) from and against any claim, action, loss, liability, expense, damage or judgment*, including costs and attorneys' fees, that

(i) arises as a result of the breach of any representation or warranty set forth in Section 6 of this Agreement, or

(ii) arises out of any actual or alleged death of, or injury to, any person, damage to any property, or any other damage or loss by whomsoever suffered, resulting or claimed to result in whole or in part from any actual or alleged defect (whether latent or patent) in the Medium or in the materials as delivered to Licensee by the Licensor, design of the Medium by the Licensor, the failure of the Medium and the Materials as delivered by the Licensor to the Licensee to comply with specifications or with any express or implied warranties of the Licensor, or any unfair trade practices of the Licensor, or

(iii) arises out of any actual or alleged violation of the Medium, or by virtue of the manufacture, possession, use or sale of the Medium, of any law, statute or ordinance, or any governmental order, rule or regulation, or

(iv) arises as a result of any other breach by the Licensor of this Agreement. This obligation of the Licensor to indemnify shall not be affected or limited

continued on page 2-7

continued from page 2-6

in any way by Licensee's extension of express or implied warranties to Licensee's customers. Licensee shall have the right to withhold all Royalty payments and all other payments set forth in this Agreement during the pendency of any claim, action or proceeding for which Licensor may seek indemnity hereunder (but only up to a maximum amount equal to the aggregate amount of such claims plus all reasonably anticipated costs and fees for which Licensor may seek indemnity hereunder) and to set off against such payments any costs, expenses or liabilities incurred by Licensor as a result of any such claim, action or proceeding. Licensee shall promptly notify Licensor of the inception of any such claim, action or proceeding brought by a third party.

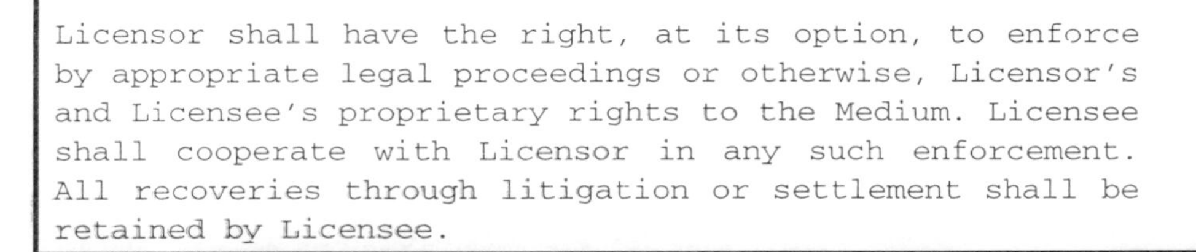

Licensor shall have the right, at its option, to enforce by appropriate legal proceedings or otherwise, Licensor's and Licensee's proprietary rights to the Medium. Licensee shall cooperate with Licensor in any such enforcement. All recoveries through litigation or settlement shall be retained by Licensee.

Whew! Do not be dismayed because you find this gobbledygook unintelligible. It is. But as best we can, let us analyze a few of the clauses and see just what kind of burden is being placed on the licensor.

First, the liability is based on a "claim" of damage, not actual damage. The difference is not trivial. It means the licensor is responsible for all claims coming within the purview of the clause irrespective of whether those claims have any foundation in fact. It means the licensor must defend the action—and defense in our sluggish, inefficient court system can be costly and time consuming. It is bad enough in a hold harmless clause to assume liability for actual damages—but assuming responsibility for claims should be reserved for the very rich and the bankrupt.

Note the clause in reference to liability uses the word "alleged" further exacerbating the liability of the licensor. Consider this scenario: The licensee manufactures the media and sells it with a broad warranty against loss of information recorded on the media. The X Company loses a million dollars worth of its business data. It "alleges" the data was lost because of a defect in the media and "claims" that the licensee is responsible. The licensee in turn claims the defect was "latent" in the sample media delivered to the licensee by the licensor. The licensor is "stuck." He must defend the action by the X Company. Keep in mind that the manufacture, testing, design, quality control, warranty disclaimers, etc. are all under the exclusive control of the licensee.

The licensor may maintain the defect was not present in the sample delivered to the licensee, but he could have great difficulty in positively establishing that defense. The licensor also claims the damage was caused by a defect in the computer of the X Company and not in the media. The fact that the licensee extended an unusually encompassing warranty is not pertinent, since the hold harmless clause specifically states the liability of the licensor is not limited by express or implied warranties. So the case wends its way through the courts for, say, a not unusual period of four years. The licensor pays all expenses. In the final decision, no damages are awarded to the X Company, the court finding the loss was not caused by the media. Too bad. The licensor must lick its wounds and await the next "claim" under the licensee's warranties.

The last paragraph of the hold-harmless clause may be of no consequence—but it could. Suppose the media which is exclusively licensed to the licensee, turns out to be much more important than anticipated. The licensee claims the Mammoth corporation is infringing the patent and settles by giving the company a license for a very large annual fee. The licensor receives no part of this fee, but could well continue to be liable to Mammoth under the hold harmless clause.

There is a vast difference between agreeing to hold someone harmless and agreeing to assume responsibility. In an agreement it is usually quite acceptable for a party to an agreement to assume responsibility for any misrepresentations set forth by him in the agreement, but one should be reluctant to hold another harmless from any damage that may flow from such a misrepresentation. If such an obligation is to be undertaken, it should be limited to "knowing" or "intentional" misrepresentations. We'll have more to say about hold harmless clauses in connection with agreements of various kinds.

All of this is by way of saying once again: hold harmless clauses can be dangerous. Take 'em, don't give 'em!

Defining Terms Used in the Agreement

Whenever the meaning of a term used in an agreement is subject to various interpretations, it should be specifically defined. Typical clauses might be:

Definitions

The term "Previous Agreement" as used herein means the agreement entered into between Jones and The Smith Corporation August 15, 1984, a copy of which is attached hereto as Exhibit A.

"Property" means the premises located at 15 Elm Street in Cincinnati, Ohio as more fully described in Exhibit A hereof.

The term "Milling Machine" means a milling machine that is covered by any claim of U. S. Letters Patent 5,015,274.

It is advisable to capitalize words or phrases that are specifically defined, to prevent the same meaning from being applied to the same or similar words that are used in a generic sense. Caution should be used in constructing the definition, because the dictionary meaning or the meaning accepted in general usage has been ruled out. The term will be strictly interpreted in accordance with the stated definition.

Definitions are useful in contracts and can in many cases appreciably shorten the document, but they are frequently overused. There is little reason to define words that are used with their ordinary dictionary meaning. There are only two reasons for including a definition: either the term is one that could be misconstrued or it is shorthand for a longer term that is repeated several times in the agreement. Cluttering up an agreement with a myriad of useless definitions is best left to attorneys. The following is an actual excerpt from a Compensation Agreement prepared by a large downtown Boston law firm that has a fine reputation among people of limited knowledge. Don't judge a law firm by its size.

Agreement: This Compensation Agreement and all schedules attached thereto.

continued on page 2-9

continued from page 2-8

```
Board: The Board of Directors of the Company

Company: The XYZ Corporation

Employment shall mean the full-time employment of the
Employee by the Company.

Fiscal Year shall mean the fiscal year of the Company.

Market Value shall have the meaning set forth in
paragraph 5(d).

Revenues shall mean the gross revenues of the Company
in any Fiscal Year.

Stockholder means a stockholder of the Company
```

—and on and on for three full pages! Definitions are handy and useful—but most of the above can be eliminated or, more appropriately, set forth the first time the term is used in the agreement. For example, defining Market Value as something defined in another part of the agreement, merely adds legal pollution. We'll talk more about the effective use of definitions in the chapters that follow.

Settling of Out of Court

Because of the incredible inefficiency of the courts (meaning costly, slow, and ineffective), the use of arbitration procedures has become quite popular. A typical arbitration clause might be:

```
Arbitration

In the event of any dispute in connection with this
Agreement, the parties agree that such dispute shall be
settled by arbitration in accordance with the then
existing rules of the American Arbitration Association
in San Francisco, California, and that any decision
resulting therefrom shall be enforceable in any court
of law within the state of California.
```

This has been a useful tool over the years, but it may have passed the limit of its usefulness. The American Arbitration Association has developed a bureaucracy almost as irksome as the courts. It is not unusual for a simple issue to take two or more years to be settled by arbitration. There are situations when it is preferable to provide a complete arbitration procedure in the Agreement and skip the laudatory services of the AAA. Such a provision, in simplified form, might be something like this:

In the event of a dispute between the parties in connection with this Agreement, either party may by notice to the other request arbitration of the dispute. In the event of such notice, each party shall within ten days thereafter appoint an arbitrator. The two arbitrators thus selected shall by agreement within ten additional days select a third arbitrator. The three arbitrators shall within thirty days thereafter review all aspects of the dispute, have a right to examine all documents related to the dispute and shall take sworn testimony from the parties and any other persons designated by the arbitrators. Within thirty days thereafter, the arbitrators shall by majority vote render a disposition of the dispute and such finding shall be enforceable in any court of law within the United States.

Or, [From a lease agreement.] :

If not agreed upon by the Landlord and the Tenant within three (3) months of the date on which the Extension Term is to commence, such Fair Rental Value shall be determined by three (3) appraisers, one selected by the Landlord, one by the Tenant, and a third by the two appraisers first selected. Each appraiser shall independently determine the Fair Rental Value of the Premises. The Fair Rental Value shall be deemed to be the average of the two appraisals arithmetically closest in amount. The cost of the third appraiser shall be borne equally by the Landlord and the Tenant; the cost of each of the other appraisers shall be borne by the party selecting them.

These are not provisions to be copied verbatim into just any agreement. The exact terms will depend upon the particular circumstances and character of the agreement. Considerable more detail may be advisable in any such provision and will be discussed further in connection with specific agreement forms.

Pre-Trial Discovery

One of the many false starts in our litigation procedures is the use of pre-trial "discovery." This is a procedure by which each party may examine and copy all pertinent documents of the other parties and require each party to submit to interrogation under oath. Then, when trial comes, there are no surprises—and the time required to hear the case in court is reduced. Sounds like a great idea. In practice, it has slowed the litigation process and materially increased the cost. Requiring the other party to produce his wife's grocery list, all tax records, and each invoice for the past ten years is a great way to harass the opposition. He may have to produce truckloads of documents. If he objects, he can go to court for a ruling. That delays the case and justly enriches the lawyers. In arbitration proceedings, however, discovery is usually not permitted (unless specifically provided for in the contract). That is one very big plus for arbitration.

Obligations to Perform Under the Agreement

Sometimes as a substitute for an unlimited obligation, it is provided that "best efforts" will be made to achieve the result. Such a clause may relate to a specific obligation or, as in the following example, encompass all obligations of one party under the agreement:

```
Best Efforts

The Distributor agrees to use its best efforts to
comply with all provisions in, and to perform all
obligations of, the Distributor under this agreement.
```

A best-efforts provision appears frequently in consulting agreements in which the consultant is reluctant to guarantee a particular result. For example:

```
The Consultant agrees to use his best efforts to
construct, within the time limit set forth herein, a
whatzit meeting the specifications set forth in Exhibit G.
```

It is usually an acceptable risk for a consultant acting as an individual to agree to a best efforts clause. But the consultant must be prepared to make such an effort that it cannot be said reasonably that he failed to make his "best" efforts. Nevertheless, from the standpoint of the consultant, the following clause is to be preferred.

```
The Consultant agrees to make all reasonable efforts to
construct, within the time limit set forth herein, a
whatzit meeting the specifications set forth in Exhibit G.
```

A corporation or other non-individual entity may be assuming a larger risk in accepting a best efforts requirement. Consider this provision:

```
The ABC Corporation agrees to use its best efforts to
deliver the Products to the Buyer before August 15, 1991.
```

The obligations on the ABC Corporation are not clear. Suppose, for example, that delivery can be made by the specified date only by extreme measures such as working overtime to the extent that the order represents a net loss; or subcontracting the work at a cost far greater than that contemplated when the order was taken; or buying raw materials from an unknown source at a price that would threaten the very existence of the ABC Corporation. If interpreted literally, the ABC Corporation would be required to take any or all of these steps and make on-time delivery. Best efforts may mean anything that is within the power of the corporation—irrespective of losses or long term negative impacts on the corporation. Because one cannot make any reliable prediction of the intensity with which a court would enforce a best-efforts provision, it is much to be preferred to use a provision such as the following.

> The ABC Corporation agrees to make all reasonable efforts to deliver the Products to the Buyer before August 15, 1991.

Which Law to Apply to Interpret the Agreement

In situations where the two parties are from different states, clauses specifying which state law shall be applied in interpreting the agreement are a subject of endless, and mostly useless, arguments between attorneys. Generally, in business agreements, it doesn't matter much, so it is a point where you can allow the opposition to win (hopefully, in exchange for another provision in your favor) without losing much, if anything. The reason why such a clause is not critical in a business agreement is because of something called the Uniform Commercial Code, which we will consider in the next chapter. This is a series of regulations drafted by the American Bar Association that have been adopted in all of the states to govern business transactions. Because the various states have elected to make minor modifications in the statutes, it could more properly be called the Almost Uniform Commercial Code. But generally, the differences are not significant in the interpretation of commercial business agreements. So if the opposing attorney insists the agreement will be governed by the laws of North Dakota—let him. Here is a typical clause:

> Governing Law
>
> This Agreement shall be interpreted and enforced in accordance with the laws of the State of North Dakota.

But avaricious attorneys frequently want more. They want the clause to specify the other party will be subject to the jurisdiction of that state. This is a no-no. Do not agree in advance to be subject to the jurisdiction of any state. In the event of a dispute, the action may be in another state and you may have to travel, hire unknown attorneys, and go to substantial additional expense in prosecuting or defending the action. Give such a request the drug treatment: Just say no.

These Standard Paragraphs represent only a minute sample. Any attorney, with the help of a ten megabyte disk on the wordprocessor, can readily accumulate thousands of such paragraphs, each available on a moment's notice.

This little discussion is included mostly to emphasize the importance of considering the "boiler plate" when "what-iffing" the agreement. (What-iffing is a term we will consider in a later chapter.)

When drafting the terms of a business agreement, it is well to keep in mind an ancient engineering acronym: KISS—keep it simple, stupid.

Chapter Three

Purchase and Sale Agreements

Most agreements for the purchase and sale of movable goods are governed by the Uniform Commercial Code, but those regulations generally can be overridden by a specific agreement between the parties. So it is that all of the fine print, so usual on purchase order forms and invoices, is important. Before getting into the specifics of terms for purchase and sale, let us consider in more detail just what the Uniform Code is all about.

The Uniform Commercial Code

The Uniform Commercial Code has been adopted by most states, with some local variations, to establish a more uniform set of rules under which business transactions are carried out. One important purpose of the Uniform Commercial Code (UCC) is to fill in missing parts in commercial purchase and sale agreements. If the agreement fails to specify one or more conditions, the answer may be found in the UCC. For example, a purchase agreement fails to state when or where the title to the goods is transferred from the seller to the buyer. The UCC may supply the answer. The UCC is longer than this entire book and it is obvious we can review but small parts of it here. It is strongly urged that every businessman obtain a copy of the UCC for his own state. This can usually be obtained from a local legal book store. The UCC with annotations will not only provide valuable insights to business agreements but will also provide a source of rather stilted legalistic forms. The UCC does not apply to other kinds of agreements such as the sale or purchase of real estate, marriage settlements, service agreements, employment contracts, etc.

The Pieces that Make a Purchase Agreement

The basic elements of a purchase agreement are:

- Identification of the parties;
- The dates, or scheduled dates, of the order, acceptance, delivery, etc.;
- The quantities and specifications of the goods to be delivered;
- The place and terms of delivery;
- Warranties and disclaimers; and
- Payment terms.

The Making of a Binding Agreement

When a potential purchaser sends an order to a supplier, in the absence of a previous contractual arrangement, the supplier is under no obligation to do anything. He can toss the order in the waste basket and is liable for nothing. It is necessary for the supplier to accept the purchase order in order for it to become a binding contract. The acceptance may be in the form of a written notice or the acceptance may be implied from the actions of the supplier. If the supplier prepares and ships the goods in accordance with the terms of the purchase order, it has accepted, by implication, all of the terms of the purchase order. If the supplier accepts the purchase order but takes certain exceptions, it is not an acceptance: it is a counter offer. When the buyer receives the notice of acceptance subject to the exceptions, it is under no obligation to do anything. It may, however, by action within a reasonable time, turn the counter offer into a binding contract by notifying the supplier of its acceptance. In other words, before there is a binding purchase order, the buyer and seller must be in agreement on the terms of the purchase.

Purchase and Sale Boiler Plate

The terms conventionally printed on the reverse of purchase order forms are usually the result of grasping attorneys rather than the result of judicious reasoning of what is appropriate. Some otherwise reputable companies have standard purchase order terms that would indeed be onerous if enforced. Here is some boiler plate from printed purchase and sale forms. The clauses headed **[Seller]** appeared, in microscopic print, on the back of an invoice prepared by a supplier: those marked **[Buyer]** appeared, in equally small print, on the back of purchase order forms prepared by a purchaser.

Terms of Delivery of the Goods

[Seller]

Delivery and Freight; Risk of Loss; Security Interest

(a) Title to and risk of loss of all goods sold hereunder shall pass to Buyer upon delivery F.O.B. Supplier's plant to an agent of the Buyer including a common carrier, notwithstanding any prepayment or allowance of freight by Supplier. If Supplier pays the freight, Supplier shall have the right to select the carrier, routing and means of transportation, provided the Buyer may make an alternate selection and pay Supplier additional costs, if any. SUPPLIER SHALL NOT BE LIABLE FOR ANY DELAY IN TRANSPORTATION HOWEVER OCCASIONED.

(b) Supplier reserves, until full payment has been received, a purchase money security interest in the goods sold. Buyer agrees to execute any document appropriate or necessary to perfect the security interest of Supplier, or in the alternative, Supplier may file this Agreement as a financing statement.

[Buyer]

Delivery

Buyer shall pay reasonable shipping costs in accordance with its shipping instructions, but Seller shall be

continued on page 3-3

continued from page 3-2

```
responsible for packing, shipping and safe delivery and
shall bear all risks of damage or loss until the goods
are delivered to the Buyer. Time is of the essence and
delivery must be made in accordance with the schedule
hereon. In the event of failure to make timely
delivery, Buyer shall have the right, after ten days
notice to the Seller, to cancel this Purchase Order, in
its entirety or as to goods not delivered on time, and
shall have no liability for any damage or expenses
resulting from such cancellation, provided if during
such ten-day period, Seller makes all shipments
required as of the end of such period, such notice
shall be of no effect. If accelerated shipping means
are required to meet the delivery set forth herein, or
to minimize the lateness of delivery, excess shipping
charges shall be borne by the Seller.
```

There are two elements of delivery: where and when. Delivery may be specified to be at the address of the buyer, in which case title passes when the goods are delivered to the buyer and the seller takes responsibility for the goods until delivered. Under the Seller's version, because the title passes when the goods are delivered to a common carrier, the risk of loss or damage in shipping is placed on the buyer.

Late delivery can be a problem. In the buyer's version, the risk is placed on the supplier and the buyer can cancel if the goods are late in delivery after a ten-day notice period. The buyer may suffer damages of such extent that he rightfully expects the supplier to assume a substantial risk for failure to make timely delivery. To what extent the supplier should assume the risk depends upon the relative certainty with which it can make delivery. If the purchase order is for a new or modified product that the supplier has little or no experience in building, the delivery penalty should be small. If the product is one routinely delivered by the supplier, the penalty can be substantially larger, provided, an exclusion is made for late delivery caused by events outside the control of the supplier.

Acceptance of the Goods

[Seller]

```
Examination, Suitability and Claims

Buyer shall examine and test each shipment of goods
promptly upon delivery to Buyer and before any part of
the goods has been changed from its original condition
and Buyer hereby waives all claims for any cause after
any part of the goods has been treated, processed or
changed in any manner (except for reasonable test
quantities). Buyer assumes sole responsibility for
determining whether the goods are suitable for their
```

continued on page 3-4

continued from page 3-3

contemplated use (whether or not such use is known to Supplier). Buyer waives all claims of which Supplier is not notified in writing within thirty (30) days after delivery of the goods or in respect of goods disposed of or returned without Supplier's consent.

[Buyer]

INSPECTION: Goods are subject to Buyer's inspection and approval at destination. Rejected goods will be returned at Seller's risk and all handling and transportation, both ways, shall be borne by the Seller.

Again, from the seller's viewpoint, the buyer's terms are subject to question. Sometimes, acceptance is appropriate at the buyer's place of business, but in many occasions the requirement should be for acceptance by the buyer prior to shipment. In addition, the grounds for rejection are not specified. In the next version, we shall see how a seller might rephrase this section.

Warranty of the Goods by the Seller

[Seller]

Warranties, Remedies and Limitations

(a) Supplier warrants to Buyer that at the time of delivery the goods sold hereunder will conform substantially to the description on the face hereof or, if applicable, to the Buyer's applicable drawings or the design standards of Supplier (where designed and built by Supplier). Supplier's liability and Buyer's remedy under this warranty are limited in Supplier's discretion to replacement of goods returned to Supplier which are shown to Supplier's reasonable satisfaction to have been nonconforming or to refund of the purchase price or, if not paid, to a credit in the amount of the purchase price, provided, Supplier shall have no liability hereunder unless Buyer shall have given notice to Supplier of the failure of the goods to so conform with the description within thirty (30) days after delivery. Transportation charges for the return of nonconforming goods to Supplier and the risk of loss thereof will not be borne by Supplier.

continued on page 3-5

continued from page 3-4

(b) Supplier warrants that the goods will not in and of themselves infringe any patent of the United States or Canada. Supplier's liability under this warranty is conditioned upon Buyer's giving prompt written notice of any claim of patent infringement made against Buyer, all information available to Buyer in respect of the claim, and Buyer's granting Supplier exclusive control of its settlement and/or litigation. Supplier may discontinue delivery of goods, without liability, if in Supplier's opinion their manufacture, sale or use would constitute patent infringement. If the use or resale of the goods is finally enjoined, Supplier shall at Supplier's option (i) procure for Buyer the right to use or resell the goods previously delivered, (ii) replace such goods with equivalent non-infringing goods, (iii) modify the goods to be equivalent and non-infringing, or (iv) refund the purchase price (less a reasonable allowance for use, damage and obsolescence). Supplier makes no warranty against any patent infringement arising from the manufacture, use or sale of goods in combination with other matter or in the operation of any process, and if a claim, suit or action is based thereon, Buyer shall defend, indemnify and save harmless Supplier therefrom.

(c) Supplier warrants to Buyer it will convey good title to the goods sold hereunder. Supplier's liability and Buyer's remedy under its warranty are limited to the removal of any title defect or, at the election of Supplier, to the replacement of the goods or any part thereof which are defective in title; provided, the rights and remedies of the parties with respect to patent infringement shall be limited to the provisions of paragraph (b) above.

THE FOREGOING WARRANTIES ARE EXCLUSIVE AND ARE GIVEN AND ACCEPTED IN LIEU OF ANY AND ALL OTHER WARRANTIES, EXPRESS OR IMPLIED, INCLUDING, WITHOUT LIMITATION, ANY IMPLIED WARRANTY OF MERCHANTABILITY. THE REMEDIES OF THE BUYER FOR ANY BREACH OF WARRANTY SHALL BE LIMITED TO THOSE PROVIDED HEREIN, AND FOR DELAY OR NONDELIVERY, WHICH IS NOT THE FAULT OF THE BUYER, TO THE PURCHASE PRICE OF THE GOODS IN RESPECT OF WHICH THE DELAY OR NONDELIVERY IS CLAIMED, TO THE EXCLUSION OF ANY AND ALL OTHER REMEDIES INCLUDING, WITHOUT LIMITATION, INCIDENTAL OR CONSEQUENTIAL DAMAGES. NO AGREEMENT VARYING OR EXTENDING THE FOREGOING WARRANTIES, REMEDIES, OR THIS LIMITATION WILL BE BINDING UPON SUPPLIER UNLESS IN WRITING, SIGNED BY A DULY AUTHORIZED OFFICER OF SUPPLIER.

continued on page 3-6

continued from page 3-5

(d) Supplier warrants the goods will be free from defects in material and workmanship under normal use for a period of one year after the date of delivery, provided, if any of the parts or material supplied by Supplier are subject to a manufacturer's warranty running for a shorter period, such shorter period shall apply to that particular item or material.

[Buyer]

Warranties, Indemnities, and License

Seller warrants all goods delivered: (a) to be free from defects in materials or workmanship; (b) to be of merchantable quality; (c) to conform to the specifications included or referenced herein; and (d) to be fit for the intended purposes, and such warranty shall survive Buyer's acceptance and payment. Seller further warrants that goods delivered hereunder, not of buyer's design, will not infringe any patent and Seller agrees to hold Buyer, its agents and customers, harmless from all costs resulting from any charge of infringement. Seller grants to Buyer and its customers an irrevocable, non-exclusive, royalty-free license under any patent owned by Seller, or under which Seller has license rights: (a) to use and sell any equipment delivered hereunder, and (b) to use and sell any process carried out with the use of such equipment. Seller agrees to hold Buyer, its employees, agents and customers, harmless from claims for personal injury, death or property damage resulting from (a) defects in manufacture, or (b) the performance of this Purchase Order by the Seller, its employees or agents, whether on or off Seller's premises.

Again, there is wide discrepancy between the two sets of terms. The buyer's version clearly favors the buyer and most sellers would want to revise it. The particular revisions would depend upon the nature of the goods being sold. The warranty is without an expressed time limit. Even a warranty against defects in materials or workmanship usually carries a finite time limit. This might be thirty days for a computer or one year for a conference table.

The protection against patent infringement is limited, in the seller's version, to a maximum penalty of a refund of the purchase price. In the buyer's version, the liability is broader than many manufacturers will find acceptable. There is no dollar limit on the liability of the Seller and it could find itself in an impossible position. Note also the license grant. A machine not in itself covered by any patent, might infringe a process performed by the machine. In this example, the seller grants a free license under any patents, under the control of the seller, to use any process carried out by the machine. Whether such a provision is necessary or desirable, again, depends upon the nature of the goods being purchased.

Credit Terms of the Seller

[Seller]

Prices, Credit and Payment

(a) Unless otherwise indicated, the price specified in this Agreement or otherwise quoted is f.o.b. Supplier's plant in Biloxie, Mississippi, and specifically excludes the cost of packaging, crating, shipping, insurance, and taxes. Invoices will be issued as of the date of shipment with terms of net thirty (30) days from date of invoice. Pro rata payment shall become due as deliveries are made. Supplier shall also be entitled to charge Buyer for costs incurred by Supplier prior to delivery in situations where delivery is delayed due to nonreceipt of materials or designs to be furnished by Buyer. Prices are subject to change without notice, provided, orders accepted for shipment within thirty (30) days shall be invoiced at prices in effect at time of acceptance, provided, if shipment is delayed beyond thirty (30) days through no fault of Supplier, Supplier's prices in effect at time of shipment will apply. In the case of any written price quotation either pursuant to this Agreement or any other form, such quotation shall become void unless accepted by Buyer within thirty (30) days or unless sooner rescinded by Supplier. If any invoice is not paid when due: (i) interest will be added to and payable on all overdue amounts at the rate of two percent (2%) per month, or the maximum percentage allowed under applicable laws, whichever is less; and (ii) Buyer shall also pay all costs of collection including without limitation, reasonable attorneys fees.

(b) If Buyer shall fail to fulfill the terms of payment, or if Supplier at any time shall have any doubt as to Buyer's financial responsibility, Supplier, without liability to Buyer, may decline to make further shipments except against cash or satisfactory security.

(c) If Supplier is prevented from revising prices or from continuing any price already in effect by any action of government or by compliance with any request of government, Supplier shall have the right, by written notice to Supplier to terminate this Agreement without liability.

Restrictions on Release of Confidential Information

[Buyer]

PROPRIETARY INFORMATION

Seller agrees for itself, its agents and employees, not to use or divulge to others any information designated by Buyer as proprietary or confidential.

This is a shorthand confidentiality agreement. It is no substitute for the longer agreements of that kind which are covered in Chapter 5. If confidentiality is important in a particular situation, both the supplier and the seller would want a more comprehensive agreement.

Modification of Terms of Purchase

[Buyer]

CHANGES AND TERMINATION

Buyer shall have the right by written order to make changes in the work, specifications, or quantity, provided any change in price or delivery caused thereby shall be adjusted equitably by mutual agreement. If Seller fails to submit a written request for adjustment in price or delivery within ten days after receipt of such change order, it shall be conclusively presumed that no change in price or delivery is to be made. If Seller breaches any provision of the Purchase Order, Buyer shall have the right to cancel this Purchase Order at any time, without liability. Buyer further has the right to cancel all or part of this Purchase Order, for its own convenience, at any time by written notice, and Buyer shall pay reasonable cancellation costs in accordance with industry practice, provided in no event shall the total charges be in excess of the price specified herein or in excess of demonstrable costs.

That provision is fairly reasonable from both viewpoints. A Seller would likely want to insert the word "material" before the word "breach."

Security Protection for Monies Advanced by the Buyer

[Buyer]

SECURITY INTEREST OF BUYER

Seller grants to Buyer a security interest, to the extent any advance payment is made by Buyer, in any goods made or purchased for this order and agrees, promptly upon request of the Buyer, to sign and deliver to Buyer appropriate UCC forms evidencing such security interest.

This is another special situation provision. It doesn't belong in an order for a carload of breakfast cereal. If the buyer advances money to the supplier to buy component parts for an expensive machine, or for direct expenses of the supplier, then the buyer should have a security interest in the machinery being built or parts purchased. This is to prevent the machinery from being confiscated by a creditor of the supplier. The UCC forms are for the purpose of recording with the appropriate state agency, which is a way of giving legal notice to others of the buyer's security interest in the machinery.

Responsibility for Sales and Other Taxes

[Seller]

Taxes, Duties and Excises

In the absence of satisfactory evidence of exemption supplied to Supplier by Buyer, Buyer shall pay, in addition to the price of the goods, all taxes, duties, excises or other charges for which Supplier may be responsible for collection or payment to any government (national, state or local) upon, measured by, or relating to the importation, exportation, production or any phase or part of the production, storage, sale, transportation or use of goods delivered hereunder.

Unforeseen Events that Prevent Performance

[Seller]

Force Majeure

(a) Buyer acknowledges the goods called for hereunder are to be specially manufactured by Supplier to fulfill this Agreement and delivery dates are based on the

continued on page 3-10

continued from page 3-9

assumption there will be no delay due to causes beyond the reasonable control of Supplier. Supplier will not be charged with any liability for delay or non-delivery when caused by delays of suppliers, production problems, acts of God or a public enemy, compliance with any applicable foreign or domestic court order or governmental regulation, order or request whether or not it proves to be invalid, riots, fires, labor disputes, unusually severe weather, or any other cause beyond the reasonable control of Supplier. During the period when deliveries are affected by the matters identified in this paragraph, Supplier may omit delivery during the period of continuance of such circumstances and the Contract quantity shall be reduced by the quantity omitted, but this Agreement shall remain otherwise in effect. Supplier shall endeavor to allocate any available goods among all buyers including its own divisions, departments and affiliates in such manner as it considers fair.

Restrictions on Assignment, Cancellation or Subcontracting

[Buyer]

ASSIGNMENT

This Purchase Order is not assignable and no work called for herein shall be subcontracted without the written permission of the Buyer.

This provision is applicable only for certain classes of goods, for example, where machinery is being manufactured to order and the Buyer wants to keep close control of the project. In most situations, the Seller will be free to subcontract without restriction.

[Seller]

Assignment, Nonwaiver, and Cancellation

(a) This Agreement is not assignable or transferable by Buyer whether voluntary or by operation of law, in whole or in part, without the prior written consent of Supplier.

continued on page 3-11

continued from page 3-10

(b) Supplier's failure to insist upon strict performance of any provisions hereof shall not be deemed to be a waiver of Supplier's rights or remedies or a waiver by Supplier of any subsequent default by Buyer in the performance of or compliance with any of the terms hereof.

(c) Buyer acknowledges this Agreement is binding upon it and all or any portion of it may not be canceled by the Buyer. Upon written request by the Buyer, Supplier, in its sole discretion, may agree to a complete or partial cancellation in which case the Buyer agrees to pay a cancellation charge based upon costs incurred and additional reasonable charges. No such cancellation shall be effective until the receipt of payment of such cancellation charge.

Note there may be a conflict between this provision and the delivery provision of the buyer under which the buyer has a right to cancel for late delivery.

Each Order as a Separate Agreement

[Seller]

Separate Contract

Each delivery shall stand, as a separate and independent contract and payment shall be required for each such shipment. If Buyer fails to fulfill terms of order, purchase, or payment under this or any other contract with Supplier, Supplier, without prejudice to other lawful remedies, may at its option (a) defer further shipments hereunder until such default is cured, (b) treat such default as a breach of this entire Agreement, or (c) terminate this Agreement.

Duty of Seller to Comply with all Laws

[Seller]

Compliance with Fair Labor Standards Act

Supplier certifies that all goods sold hereunder that are produced or manufactured in the United States are produced in compliance with all applicable Sections of

continued on page 3-12

continued from page 3-11

the Fair Labor Standards Act of 1938, as amended, (the "Act") or of any order of the Administration issued under any Section of the Act. All requirements as to the certificate contemplated by the Act, or any amendment thereto, shall be considered satisfied by this certification.

License to Use Purchased Goods

[Seller]

Royalties; Miscellaneous

(a) The purchase of machinery or goods from Supplier confers no license, express or implied, under any patent, provided, when goods delivered hereunder include goods suitable for use under a patent of Supplier, a royalty is deemed to be included in the purchase price and a free license for such use is granted to the Buyer.

(b) Goods delivered hereunder may vary according to Supplier's established limits, sizes and tolerances in effect at the time of delivery.

(c) ANY ADVICE FURNISHED BY SUPPLIER CONCERNING THE USE OF GOODS PURCHASED HEREUNDER SHALL BE GRATUITOUS ADVICE AND REPRESENTS ONLY SUPPLIER'S JUDGMENT AND IS ACTED ON SOLELY AT THE RISK OF THE BUYER.

Purchase Order is the Complete Agreement

[Seller]

Entire Contract and Construction

(a) The Agreement between Buyer and Supplier in connection with goods identified on the face hereof consists in its entirety of the terms and conditions appearing on the face and back of this document in lieu of all others, and supersedes all previous communications, representations and agreements, oral or written, between the parties hereto with respect to the subject matter hereof. No modification shall be

continued on page 3-13

continued from page 3-12

effected by the acknowledgement or acceptance of Buyer's purchase order form, or other documents, containing terms or conditions in addition to or in variance with those set forth here.

(b) Acceptance or use of any goods delivered hereunder shall be an acceptance of these as the only terms and conditions applying to the purchase and sale of goods unless other terms are agreed upon in writing signed by both parties specifically referring to this Agreement.

(c) This Agreement shall be interpreted in accordance with the laws of Mississippi.

(d) Captions as used in these terms are for convenience in reference only and shall not be construed as limiting or extending the language of the provisions.

The buyer should beware of this boiler plate. The provision for disregarding any previous agreements or communications may negate written quotations made by the seller.

Read the Boiler Plate

The above are more or less typical examples of the terms of purchase or sale agreements. They must be modified to apply to your particular business and purchase or sale procedures. Just how they are to be modified depends in large measure on whether you are the buyer or the seller. There is considerable doubt about the wisdom of printing the purchase order terms in print so small that a magnifying glass is necessary to read them. If you do, don't try to enforce them before a judge with failing eyesight. It is far better to simplify the terms and print them in type large enough to be read easily. There is plenty of room on the back of a purchase order for the necessary terms. The face of the purchase order should make reference to the terms on the reverse as an integral part of the purchase order.

Purchase Order with Unacceptable Terms

When you receive a purchase order with unacceptable terms, you should respond immediately with your objections and suggested wording that would be acceptable. You can state that you are not processing the order awaiting the acceptance of your exceptions by the buyer. However, this may not be the most practical approach considering the competitive nature of the business world. Usually, if the terms are not too onerous, you will advise the buyer of your exceptions and state the order is being accepted subject to those changes and ask the buyer to notify you immediately if those terms are not acceptable. This leaves the actual terms to be argued about at a later date if that becomes necessary. However, if the terms are such as to be totally unacceptable, the exceptions should be acknowledged before the order is accepted. What sort of terms should be considered unacceptable? For one, anything that might bankrupt your company. One such provision is included in the above set of terms with respect to consequential damages. If your product has a defect that, say, causes a production machine of the buyer to jam and causes a hiatus in its production for a period of time, the lost profits and other costs could be large and represent a liability much too large to assume except in special circumstances. Or, the jammed machine may cause a fire and burn the factory of the buyer. Here the damages could be even greater. The lesson is simple—always try to obtain a release from consequential damages.

The particular specifications for the goods are a subject for agreement between the buyer and the supplier. About all that can be said here is to caution each party to be certain the specifications are expressed in such clear language that a later dispute will be avoided.

Chapter Four

Consulting and Service Agreements

Agreements for the Performance of Services

One of the more usual business arrangements is for a company to hire a consultant to perform specialized services. This may be an arrangement with an engineer to design a new or improved product, an advertising firm to devise a new sales campaign, or a management consultant to make recommendations with respect to the organization of the company. Because some situations of this kind arise frequently in the operation of most businesses, it is important to understand the basic parameters of consulting and other service agreements. This does not mean you should adopt a standard form and squeeze all consulting situations into the same mold. Unfortunately, many large companies try to do just that: a consulting contract for the design of a new machine may be the same form the company uses for an architect or builder.

Pieces that Make a Consulting Agreement

Each situation will be best served by some tailoring of the agreement in accordance with the particular circumstances. Nevertheless, there are basic elements that will form part of almost all consulting agreements. These include:

- Identification of the parties.
- Precisely what the consultant is to do and when, including specifications and delivery.
- The terms of payment and whether the project is to be done on a fixed price or a time and materials basis.
- Any warranty that is to be given by the consultant.
- The terms under which the consultant is prohibited from disclosing confidential information of the company.
- Any assignment of patent rights, copyrights or software developed by the consultant in the course of work on the project.
- Any agreement by the consultant not to work for competing companies for some period of time.
- An enumeration of any liability to be assumed by the consultant in connection with the work products.

The Digital Proposal

Many companies request that a prospective consultant make certain commitments prior to being given the opportunity to make a proposal to the company. Digital Equipment Corporation (DEC) is one. It proposed the following "standard" agreement to a prospective consultant:

Basic Agreement for Corporate Consultants

THIS BASIC AGREEMENT is made by Digital Equipment Corporation, its successors and its subsidiaries worldwide ("DIGITAL") and ______________________ with its principal office at ________________________ and its agents, servants, employees and subcontractors (collectively the "CONSULTANT"), effective this ______ day of __________, 19_____, for the purpose of setting forth the exclusive terms and conditions by which DIGITAL may acquire CONSULTANT's services on a temporary basis.

In consideration of the mutual obligations specified in this Agreement, and any compensation paid to CONSULTANT for its services, the parties agree to the following:

PURCHASE ORDERS

DIGITAL may issue Purchase Orders which will contain a statement of the work to be performed by CONSULTANT, CONSULTANT's rate of payment for such work, expenses to be paid in connection with such work, the maximum price DIGITAL shall be obligated to pay under each Purchase Order, the specific DIGITAL facilities and work areas which shall be made accessible to CONSULTANT and such other terms and conditions as shall be deemed appropriate or necessary for the performance of the work.

DIGITAL is not obligated to issue any Purchase Orders under this Agreement. CONSULTANT should not commence services without first obtaining an approved purchase order.

II. NONDISCLOSURE AND TRADE SECRETS*

** This section is discussed in the following chapter.*

III. OWNERSHIP OF WORK PRODUCT:

CONSULTANT shall specifically describe and identify in Exhibit A to this Agreement all technology (1) which CONSULTANT intends to use in performing under this Agreement, (2) which is either owned solely by CONSULTANT or licensed to CONSULTANT with a right to sublicense, and (3) which is in existence in the form of a writing or working prototype prior to the effective date of this Agreement ("Background Technology")

continued on page 4-3

continued from page 4-2

CONSULTANT agrees that any and all ideas, improvements and inventions conceived, created or first reduced to practice in the performance of work under this Agreement shall be the sole and exclusive property of DIGITAL.

CONSULTANT further agrees that except for CONSULTANT's rights in Background Technology, DIGITAL is and shall be vested with all rights, title and interests including patent, copyright, trade secret and trademark rights in CONSULTANT's work product under this Agreement. CONSULTANT agrees to grant and hereby grants to DIGITAL a non-exclusive royalty-free and worldwide right to use and sublicense the use of Background Technology for the purpose of developing and marketing DIGITAL products, but not for the purpose of marketing Background Technology separate from DIGITAL products.

CONSULTANT shall execute all papers including patent applications, inventing (sic) assignments, and copyright assignments, and otherwise shall assist DIGITAL at DIGITAL's expense and as reasonably shall be required to perfect in DIGITAL the rights, title and other interests in CONSULTANT's work product expressly granted to DIGITAL under this Agreement.This Section III shall survive the termination of this Agreement for any reason including expiration of term.

IV. INDEMNIFICATION/RELEASE:

CONSULTANT agrees to take all necessary precautions to prevent injury to any persons (including employees of DIGITAL) or damage to property (including DIGITAL's property) during the term of this Agreement and shall indemnify and hold DIGITAL and its officers, agents, directors, and employees harmless against all claims, losses, expenses (including reasonable attorney's fees) and injuries to person or property (including death) resulting in any way, from any act, omission or negligence on the part of CONSULTANT in the performance or failure to perform the Scope of Work under this Agreement, excepting only those losses which are due solely and directly to DIGITAL's negligence.

CONSULTANT warrants that it has good and marketable title to all of the Inventions, Information, Material, work or product made, created, conceived, written, invented or provided by CONSULTANT pursuant to the provisions of this Agreement ("Product"). CONSULTANT further warrants that the Product shall be free and clear of all liens, encumbrances, or demands of third parties, including any claims by any such third parties of any right, title or interest in or to the Product arising out of any trade secret, copyright or patent.

continued on page 4-4

continued from page 4-3

CONSULTANT shall indemnify, defend and hold harmless DIGITAL and its customers from any and all liability, loss, costs, damage, judgment or expense (including reasonable attorney's fees) resulting from or arising in any way out of such claims by any third parties and/or which are based upon or are the result of any breach of the warranties contained in this Subsection IV. In the event of a breach, CONSULTANT shall, at no additional cost to DIGITAL, replace or modify the Product, with a functionally equivalent and conforming Product, obtain for DIGITAL the right to continue using the product and in all other respects use its best efforts to remedy the breach. CONSULTANT shall have no liability under this Subsection IV for any Product created in accordance with details and specific design instructions created by DIGITAL.

Should DIGITAL permit CONSULTANT to use any of DIGITAL's equipment, tools or facilities during the term of this Agreement, such permission will be gratuitous and CONSULTANT shall indemnify and hold harmless DIGITAL and its officers, directors, agents and employees, from and against any claim, loss, expense, or judgment for injury to person or property (including death) arising out of the use of any such equipment, tools or facilities, whether or not such claim is based upon its condition or on alleged negligence of DIGITAL in permitting its use.

CONSULTANT shall maintain appropriate insurance with the following minimum coverage:i. Employer's liability - $100,000.00 per employee.ii. Blanket General Liability - including Contractual Liability, Contractor's Protective Liability and Personal Injury/Property Damage Coverages in a combined single limit of $1,000,000.

A Certificate of Insurance indicating such coverage shall be delivered to DIGITAL upon request. That Certificate shall indicate that the policies will not be changed or terminated without at least ten (10) days' prior notice to DIGITAL, and shall also indicate that the insurer has waived its subrogation rights against DIGITAL.

V. TERMINATION:

Either DIGITAL or CONSULTANT may terminate this Agreement in the event of a material breach of the Agreement which is not cured within thirty (30) days of written notice to the other of such breach. Material breaches include but are not limited to the filing of bankruptcy papers or other similar arrangements due to insolvency, the assignment of CONSULTANT's obligations to perform to third parties or acceptance of employment or consulting arrangements with third parties which are

continued on page 4-5

continued from page 4-4

or may be detrimental to DIGITAL's business interests.

DIGITAL may terminate this Agreement for convenience with thirty (30) days' written notice. In such event CONSULTANT shall cease work immediately after receiving notice from DIGITAL or sending notice to DIGITAL unless otherwise advised by DIGITAL and shall notify DIGITAL of cost incurred up to the termination date.

VI. COMPLIANCE WITH APPLICABLE LAWS:

CONSULTANT warrants that the Material supplied and work performed under this Agreement complies with or will comply with all applicable United States and foreign (sic) laws and regulations.

VII. INDEPENDENT CONTRACTOR:

CONSULTANT is an Independent Contractor, is not an agent or employee of DIGITAL and is not authorized to act on behalf of DIGITAL.

VIII. GENERAL:

This Agreement may not be changed unless mutually agreed upon in writing by both parties.

In the event any provision of this Agreement is found to be legally unenforceable, such unenforceability shall not prevent enforcement of any other provision of the Agreement.

CONSULTANT is responsible to insure that all of its workers adhere to the terms and conditions of this Agreement, and have signed the appropriate non-disclosure Agreement prior to commencing services.

This Agreement shall be governed by the Laws of the Commonwealth of Massachusetts.

IN WITNESS WHEREOF, the parties hereto have executed this Agreement.

DIGITAL EQUIPMENT CORPORATION	______________________________
	CONSULTANT
______________________________	______________________________
Purchasing Representative	Authorized Agent of Corp.
Date______________________	Date______________________

This long and complex agreement is worthy of careful review: If you are a consultant, it is an example of a proposal you should never agree to. If you are a business person who hires consultants, don't let your legal advisers interfere with the opportunity to attract competent consultants. If you adopt an agreement like this one as standard, you are likely to find your choice limited to consultants unable to find work elsewhere or who are so incompetent they do not understand the implications of the proposed agreement. We'll consider just a few of the more important provisions.

The proposed agreement is to be signed by the consultant before being told exactly what the project is all about. Nevertheless, the consultant must list all "Background Information" it intends to use on the project. This is more than a bit difficult. Moreover, consider these two clauses from the agreement:

```
DIGITAL is not obligated to issue any Purchase Orders
under this Agreement.

CONSULTANT agrees to grant and hereby grants to DIGITAL
a non-exclusive royalty free and worldwide right to use
and sublicense the use of Background Technology for the
purpose of developing and marketing DIGITAL products—
```

The consultant grants a free license to DEC under his Background Information. These rights could be worth nothing—but they could be very valuable. In any event, what justifies the consultant giving anything to DEC when DEC doesn't promise to pay one penny to the consultant? No competent consultant would agree to such a giveaway.

Moreover, if a project is undertaken, the consultant assigns to DEC all inventions, ideas, and improvements whether or not reduced to practice on the project. "Reduced to practice" means actually constructed and operated. The filing of a patent application is sometimes said to be a "constructive reduction to practice," but that interpretation is usually limited to matters before the Patent and Trademark Office. In this case, a filing of a patent application might not be considered a reduction to practice if the device has not actually been constructed. The proposed agreement provides that all previous inventions or ideas actually constructed on the job are assigned to DEC.

Suppose the consultant has previously filed a United States patent application on a device. If it first actually builds the device in carrying out the project, it has not just given DEC a free license under any resulting patent, it has assigned the patent application to DEC and the consultant is barred from using or licensing that invention to others. That could be a high price to pay just for doing some consulting work for DEC. The consultant cannot avoid this difficulty by including a reference to the patent application in the Background Technology, because that gives a free license to DEC even if the consultant never does any work for DEC.

As in many cases, there is confusion in the agreement between patentable inventions and unpatentable ideas. A United States patent usually gives the inventor an exclusive right for seventeen years to "make, use and sell" the patented item. But the originator of a new idea that is not patentable, or is not patented, has no exclusive right in that idea (unless it is a writing that is protected by the copyright laws). It follows the consultant has no power to agree with DEC …

> ...that any and all ideas, improvements and inventions conceived, created or first reduced to practice in the performance of work under this Agreement shall be the sole and exclusive property of DIGITAL.

DEC cannot acquire exclusive rights in an unpatented idea and it is no less than silly to put it in this agreement. The provision could, however, have a negative impact on the consultant, for it may be barred from using an idea that is open to the rest of the world. The most that should be asked of the consultant is that it treat such a new idea as confidential information of DEC and not use or disclose the idea until and unless it becomes public knowledge.

Another difficulty with the agreement is that the rights granted to DEC are not limited to DEC's field of activity. Inventions sometimes have applications in different industries. At the very least, any assignment of rights to DEC should exclude areas of activity that do not compete directly with DEC.

Another land mine lurks in the Section IV on Indemnification. This provision can be costly to the consultant, even though it commits no negligent act. The consultant is liable for all "claims" for injury or property damage, including those resulting or claimed to have resulted from structural or design defects in the machinery unless caused "solely and directly" by DEC's negligence. If a claim is made against DEC, the consultant is required to defend it, even if the claim proves to be groundless. By this time you should be aware that lawyers are expensive.

If the claim results from something caused 99 percent by the negligence of DEC and one percent by the consultant, the agreement calls for the consultant to assume full responsibility.

And there are more potential land mines: under the proposed arrangement, the consultant agrees to protect DEC and its customers from all losses caused by patent infringement including the cost of DEC's attorneys. If there is an infringement, the consultant is required at his own expense to modify the product, while maintaining functional equivalence, or obtain for DEC the right for DEC to continue using the product.

This is not a provision requesting the consultant to use due care—it is asking the consultant to provide an insurance policy the likes of which money cannot buy. Consider a hypothetical example: a consulting firm enters into the agreement with DEC. It does an outstanding job building a clever machine that saves DEC tens of thousands of dollars per year. The consultant has given all rights to the machine to DEC. It receives nothing except its direct compensation for services. Then a claim is made against DEC for patent infringement by the machine. The consultant is called and asked to settle the matter. The consultant tries to obtain a license from the patent holder—but that costs more dollars than the consultant has ever seen. The consultant is unable to modify the machine to avoid infringement while maintaining "functional equivalency." What alternatives does the consultant have? Probably only one: bankruptcy. And bankruptcy proceedings are not the greatest advertisement for one who makes his living from consulting work.

Was the consulting firm negligent? Yes—it signed the DEC agreement. The consultant could not be considered negligent because it did not make an infringement search. A patent infringement search is expensive and can easily cost many thousands of dollars. Even if the consultant had paid out that kind of money, it could not be certain there would be no infringement. First, because such searches are not complete and it is always possible something is overlooked. Second, patent applications pending in the Patent and Trademark Office are maintained in secrecy so it is impossible to examine them. A patent could issue even after such a machine is placed in use. Under those conditions, DEC would be infringing and the consultant would be liable.

Notice also that the infringement indemnity is not limited to the United States—infringement in Japan, Germany or elsewhere could trip the land mine for the consultant.

This provision places an unconscionable and unjustified burden on the consultant. There is more justification for a provision in which the contracting company protects the consultant from infringement damages. The most the consultant should be asked to do is warrant that it will not knowingly infringe any patent.

The consultant is required not only to provide a certificate of insurance but to require the insurer to waive its right of subrogation. This means that if DEC is responsible for a loss covered by the insurance held by the consultant, the insurance company is barred from recouping its loss from DEC, the party that caused the loss. Insurance companies do not like such provisions, and the consultant could have difficulty finding an insurer willing to waive its subrogation rights, or there may be a cost attached to the waiver.

There are other provisions that a reasonably prudent consultant should object to. But it is difficult for the usual consultant to argue with the large company with an entrenched legal department.

When it was suggested to the Purchasing Agent that DEC could hardly be serious about this proposed agreement, he assured the potential consultant that it was indeed serious. A request was then made to speak with the legal department to discuss the inequities of the agreement. This, said the agent, was not feasible. It was then explained to the agent that the only consultant who would sign such an agreement either couldn't read or was bankrupt. The agent's reply: "Tell me about it."

The deal died in the arms of the attorneys. The consultant made no proposal to DEC. Situations such as this are unlikely to come to the attention of top management, but the effect on the bottom line is such as to warrant consideration at the highest levels.

An ARCO Solar Development Proposal

Here is another example of a proposed consulting agreement that asks too much of the impossible from the consultant:

**The name of the seller and the description of the EQUIPMENT have been changed—but the proposed agreement is real.*

AGREEMENT FOR PRELIMINARY CONCEPTUAL DESIGN OF AUTOMATED EXTERMINATION EQUIPMENT

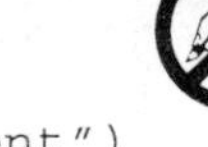

This Agreement (hereinafter referred to as "Agreement") is hereby entered into as of the 9th day of June, 1986 by and between ARCO Solar, Inc., 9351 Deering Avenue, Chatsworth, CA 91311 (hereinafter referred to as the "Buyer") and Ace Development Corporation, incorporated in Texas (hereinafter referred to as the "Seller") to design an automated extermination system (hereinafter referred to as "EQUIPMENT").*

continued on page 4-9

continued from page 4-8

Whereas, Seller is engaged in the development and design of this EQUIPMENT; and

Whereas, Seller has represented to Buyer that it has a proven history in the development and design of quality, high technology automated equipment and that it is qualified to design EQUIPMENT as hereinafter specified and Seller is willing to do so, all on the terms herein contained, and

Whereas, in reliance upon Seller's representations Buyer wishes Seller to design said EQUIPMENT for Buyer; and

Whereas Seller is willing to design the EQUIPMENT and Buyer is willing to purchase said design services.

Now, therefore in consideration of the mutual covenants, representations, warranties, promises and agreements set forth herein, the parties do hereby agree as follows.

The reader will note the handiwork of unnamed attorneys who managed to include even in this short preamble: "hereinafter" four times, "herein" twice, "Whereas" four times, and one redundant "said" referring to EQUIPMENT that has already been defined.

1.0 DEFINITIONS

1.1 The term "Equipment", "Product(s)", "Unit(s)", or "Good(s)" shall mean the "EQUIPMENT" as described in the specifications as set forth in exhibit "A", attached hereto and made a part hereof.

A good example of confusion. There seems to be multiple definitions of EQUIPMENT. It is defined in the opening paragraph and re-defined here. The multiplicity of words said to mean "EQUIPMENT" adds only confusion. A single word should be used throughout the agreement to refer to the system or apparatus to be designed. In this case, "Equipment" is defined to mean "EQUIPMENT." The word "EQUIPMENT" (all capitals) is not used again in the Agreement other than in the title of Section 2.0 and the first sentence of Section 2.3. The word "Equipment" appears once. The words "Products", "Units", and "Goods" are defined, but are not again seen in the agreement.

1.2 The term "Specification(s)" shall mean the documents set forth in Exhibit "A".

The term "Specification(s)" is defined here, but it is not again used throughout the agreement. If it meant to define the use of that word in the preceding Section 1.1, it is redundant. This Section adds nothing other than confusion to the agreement.

1.3 The term "Work" means work performed by the Seller hereunder.

2.0 EQUIPMENT DESIGN

2.1 Seller agrees to provide facilities, all personnel and supervision, supplies, materials, tools, equipment, and services necessary to design the equipment described in Exhibit "A".

Here, the word "EQUIPMENT" could have been used as defined.

2.3 Before undertaking the design of the EQUIPMENT, Seller shall, in the exercise of its expert and professional judgment, examine and verify all information contained in or furnished in connection with this Agreement, and shall at once report in writing to Buyer any error, omission or discrepancy in such information. Seller represents that it has become familiar with the nature and extent of this Agreement, the specifications and local conditions that may affect its performance under this Agreement.

2.4 Seller shall employ sufficient qualified personnel and supervision to complete the Work and furnish the Equipment design by the date specified in this Agreement.

2.5 Seller agrees that the design of the Equipment shall be performed in a professional manner in accordance with generally accepted practices for such Equipment. Any errors or omissions in the design shall be reported to Seller within two (2) years after completion and acceptance of the Equipment and shall be corrected by Seller without charge to Buyer.

The clear intention here is to make the consultant responsible for everything that might go wrong with the equipment. This agreement was drafted in contemplation of a materials and labor contract and was for a new machine that had never been previously designed or built. Obviously, a consultant would be foolish to warrant the performance and delivery date of a new piece of equipment. Too many things can, and usually do, go wrong with a new development. The first three "Whereas" clauses plus Subsections 2.1 - 2.5, are intended to bind the consultant to a statement that it knows all about the design problems—and there aren't any. The first "Whereas" states the seller is already engaged in the design of this equipment. That is most unlikely to be true. The second "Whereas" adds to this by stating that the consultant has done this kind of thing before and is willing to guarantee (in effect) that it can do so again. This is also unlikely to be true. The third "Whereas" points out that the buyer is relying on the representations of the seller that it can do all these things and that is why it is giving the contract to the buyer. Subsection 2.3 passes responsibility to the seller for any errors in information furnished by the buyer. Subsection 2.4 obligates the consultant to hire as many people as necessary to guarantee delivery by the specified date. The design of new machinery is difficult, and guaranteeing a fixed delivery date is a short cut to the poor house. Subsection 2.5 amounts to an unqualified two year warranty—something the buyer could not get from a piece of manufacturing machinery purchased off the shelf. A two-year warranty on a new machine that has not previously been constructed is suicidal.

2.6 Changes in Scope of Work, when proposed by Buyer, shall require that a written request be submitted by the seller to the Buyer summarizing the details for the out-of-scope effort with an estimate of any change in the cost of the equipment. No change in the scope of work shall be made without Buyer's prior written approval.

3.0 PRICE AND PAYMENT [Omitted]

4.0 PROJECT CONTROL [Omitted]

5.0 ARCO SOLAR'S REPRESENTATIVE [Omitted]

6.0 TERMINATION BY BUYER

6.1 Buyer may terminate this Agreement for any reason by giving written notice to the Seller. Seller shall stop all Work on the date specified by Buyer. Buyer shall pay Seller (a) for all Work satisfactorily performed to date of termination, and (b) all actual and reasonable costs incurred by Seller as a consequence of such termination. Upon termination of this Agreement, Seller shall ship to Buyer, pursuant to Buyer's instructions, all drawings, sketches, intellectual property as identified in Section 7.0, plus the equipment at whatever stage of completion on effective date of termination.

This is not only an unacceptable provision for a consultant, it is bad for the buyer. Any consultant that agrees to such a provision isn't likely to do an outstanding job of machine design. The consultant is expected to hire employees to carry out this development project. The buyer has the right to stop it without advance notice. If the consultant cannot immediately assign those employees, to other tasks he may have to pay all salaries without reimbursement from the buyer. Moreover, the buyer is not obligated to pay for any work unless it is "satisfactorily performed." Who is to judge in the middle of a development job just what work is "satisfactory"? This paragraph, in a number of ways, is an open invitation to litigation, which doesn't profit anyone—except us lawyers.

7.0 INTELLECTUAL PROPERTY

7.1 All information, data and the like and all original drawings, plans, schedules, specifications, calculations, rights to inventions, reports, designs and other Work products, products, and all copies thereof, prepared by or obtained by Seller in the performance of the Work, including all patents, copyrights and other legal rights therein, shall be the sole property of the Buyer. All such materials shall be delivered to the Buyer within fifteen (15) days after completion of the Work or upon request. At the buyer's discretion, Seller may maintain one (1) set of all items described in this Section for a period not to exceed that stipulated in Sections 2.5 and 8.2.

We have discussed previously the danger in transferring all ownership of unprotectable information. The consultant may only be barring himself from using information that is unrestricted to everyone else. If the consultant expects to remain in business and to design machines for others that may involve similar design problems, this provision is unacceptable. A more reasonable arrangement from the standpoint of both parties might be: (a) a free non-exclusive license back to the consultant in fields that do not compete directly with the Buyer, and (b) limiting the patent rights assignment to inventions incorporated in the machinery built for the Buyer. Such an arrangement does not completely fence in the future activities of the consulting firm. Companies hiring outside consultants to design machinery should place some reasonable cap on the greed of legal departments.

7.2 Seller agrees not to disclose any information (technical, business or financial) acquired by Seller directly or indirectly from Buyer or developed or otherwise obtained by Seller under this Agreement (hereinafter "Confidential Information"). Seller shall not use the Confidential Information except for the purpose of supplying, start up and furnishing equipment to Buyer. These secrecy and limited use obligations shall not apply to information which:

a) was in Seller's lawful possession prior to disclosure to Seller; or

b) is in or hereafter enters the public domain through no fault or action on the part of the Seller; or

c) is hereafter obtained by Seller from a third party without violation by the third party or any secrecy obligation relating thereto, and without a requirement that Seller hold the information in confidence.

Seller shall limit disclosure of Confidential Information to those of its employees, agents,

continued on page 4-13

continued from page 4-12

```
consultants, subcontractors, suppliers and the like who
need to make use of Confidential Information in
connection with this Agreement and who are bound by the
secrecy and limited use obligations of this Agreement.
```

We have previously considered the reasons why a consultant should not accept those provisions. There is an absolute undertaking of secrecy, that is, absolute liability for unauthorized disclosure irrespective of the way it comes about; no time limit on the period during which secrecy is to be maintained; and no requirement that Confidential Information be in writing or even indicated verbally that it is confidential. Another twist: all information developed by the consultant on the project is Confidential Information. A half dozen agreements like this would put almost any consultant out of business.

```
7.3   Seller shall indemnify, defend and hold Buyer
harmless from all liability for alleged or actual
infringement of any patent, copyright, or trade secret.
Buyer has the right, at its option and expense, to have
counsel of its choice participate in the defense,
compromise or settlement of such claim or action and to
designate such counsel at any stage in the proceeding
it deems desirable.
```

This is again the same old over-reaching patent provision we have seen before. If you are a consultant who is solvent, or even expect to become solvent, never agree to such an unlimited insurance policy. We have already discussed the reasons.

```
7.4   Seller shall not use apparatus, materials or
processes which are known to Seller to be patented or
the subject of patent applications in the design and
fabrication of equipment without the Buyer's prior
written consent. Seller shall advise Buyer in writing
if Seller wishes to use any such apparatus, material,
or process in the design and fabrication of equipment.
Buyer at its sole option, may consent to the use of
such apparatus, material or process. Such consent by
Buyer shall not constitute the furnishing of written
instructions, plans and specifications under Section
7.2 of this Agreement.
```

This might be a reasonable provision were it not for Section 7.3. It is assumed the reference to "equipment" (both occurrences) refers to either EQUIPMENT or Equipment. You might want to ask your attorney about the meaning and implications of the last sentence of Section 7.4. This author isn't at all certain.

7.5 Seller agrees to disclose promptly to Buyer all inventions, developments, innovations, and the like, to cooperate with and assist Buyer in the preparation and prosecution of applications for patents and copyright registrations covering such property, to execute all necessary documents in connection therewith, to assign to Buyer all copyrights in such property and all patent applications and patents issuing on such applications and to aid Buyer in the enforcement of its proprietary rights obtained under this Agreement. Buyer shall pay Seller reasonable fees for time spent in connection with matters under this Paragraph.

The extent to which inventions made on the project are assigned or licensed to the buyer is a matter for negotiation. A policy by the consultant of assigning to the buyer all inventions conceived or first reduced to practice on the project can be damaging to the future finances of the consultant.

7.6 Seller shall not refer in any manner to Buyer or any affiliate of Buyer in any publication, promotional or advertising material, written or oral, in connection with this Agreement without obtaining the prior written consent of Buyer.

This is a useful provision when it is desired to keep secret the association between the parties.

7.7 No Information, including all required documentation provided to Buyer by Seller under this Agreement shall impose any obligation of confidentiality or limited use on Buyer and Buyer shall be free to use, disclose, reproduce and modify all such information as it sees fit.

A paragraph probably added to make the agreement longer. Everything is already assigned to the Buyer, so it is difficult to see what this paragraph adds.

7.8 Seller's obligations under this Section 7.0 shall continue notwithstanding termination of this Agreement and shall not be limited by any other warranty, liability or indemnification provision of this Agreement.

8.0 INTENTIONALLY LEFT BLANK

continued on page 4-15

continued from page 4-14

9.0 APPLICABLE LAW

9.1 The design of the Equipment, pursuant to the terms and conditions of this Agreement shall be governed by all applicable federal, state and local laws, ordinances, rules and regulations, and with applicable requirements of any departments, boards, commissions, or bureaus thereof relating to the performance of the Work hereunder.

This paragraph, aside from being redundant, would seem to require that the design of the machinery conform to all government requirements such as those relating to safety and environment. The consultant should be certain it is familiar with all such requirements before accepting this provision. From the standpoint of the consultant, it is probably preferable to require the buyer to spell out the particular regulations that are to be met.

9.2 Electrical equipment shall comply with the National Electrical Code, current edition, to the extent there is no conflict of applicable statutes, ordinances, regulations or codes, and shall bear an inspection label that indicates listing by Underwriters Laboratory, Inc. (UL); the Los Angeles Testing Laboratory (LATL); the American Gas Association (AGA); Electrical Testing Laboratories (ETL) whichever are applicable, or shall be Factory Mutual (FM) approved.

Complying with the requirements of this paragraph can be time consuming and costly. It should be undertaken only by one familiar with the process of obtaining approval from the listed agencies. The cost may not be trivial.

10.0 WAIVER OF MECHANICS' LIEN

10.1 Seller agrees that no mechanics' liens whatsoever shall be filed against Buyer or Buyer's premises by Seller or any subcontractor or Seller for the supply of any labor, material or both in the performance of the work under this Agreement, and the right to such lien is hereby waived.

One who provides labor or materials used in construction of machinery or the like may have a lien on the machinery until the costs of such labor or material are paid. It may not be sufficient that the buyer paid the seller, if the seller failed to pay a subcontractor. The rights of the subcontractor are not released by the mere statement of the seller that there are no liens. This provision is not particularly important in the agreement because it does not protect the buyer against a claim by a subcontractor, and if the seller has been paid in full, the seller has no right to a lien. It says, in effect, the seller is liable for any liens, but the seller is liable anyway, even without this provision.

```
11.0  EMPLOYMENT OF BUYER'S PERSONNEL BY THE SELLER

11.1  The Seller agrees not to hire, retain, use or
otherwise employ, in any capacity whatsoever, during
the stated period of this Agreement, any employee of
the Buyer who continues in Buyer's employment on a full
time basis. This provision does not in any way limit
Seller's right to hire, retain, use, or otherwise
employ, in any capacity, any individual who, for
whatever reason, is no longer employed by Buyer.
```

There are a number of objections to this provision. Consider: The seller tells one of the buyer's employees that if he leaves his employment, the seller will give him a job. The seller does not hire him while he is employed by the buyer: only after he has left the employment "for whatever reason." The contract refers to an employee who "...continues in buyer's employment on a full time basis." For how long—from when to when? Moreover, the seller is the one who would most often be concerned about the buyer stealing its employees. The obligations could more fairly be on a reciprocal basis and on the basis of "offering" employment. The following provision might be more suitable in most situations: "The parties agree that during this Agreement, and for a period of one year after completion of all work thereunder, neither party shall knowingly employ or offer employment to any individual employed by the other at any time during the term of this Agreement."

```
12.0  PROJECT REVIEWS AND OFFICE SPACE

12.1  Seller hereby grants Buyer's representative the
right to periodically visit Seller's facility for the
purpose of progress reviews of the Equipment design.
Buyer shall advise Seller sufficiently in advance of
said visits, in order that his (sic) normal work
routines are not interrupted.
```

The reader can easily improve upon the wording. It is good practice. Note that "periodically" means at fixed intervals. Is "normal" the best word to mean usual or customary? Note, the seller is a corporation in this Agreement, not a "he." Try rewriting this provision with forty percent fewer words. For starters, scratch "hereby" and "periodically," and change "for the purpose of" to "to." You might want something like this: "Buyer shall have the right to visit Seller's facility to review progress on the EQUIPMENT, and shall give reasonable advance notice of such visits to the Seller." With a little thought you can do better. Does the title of Section 12.0 accurately describe its substance?

13.0 INTENTIONALLY LEFT BLANK

14.0 NOTICES AND PROJECT REPORTING

14.1 All technical questions, requests for approvals and authorizations, and progress reports shall be provided in writing and sent to:

Buyer:	Seller:
ARCO Solar, Inc. Corporation P.O. Box 2105 Chatsworth, CA 91313	Ace Development 2145 Helmsworth Street Waco, Texas 76710

14.2 All written notices shall be delivered in person or shall be sent via certified mail in a securely sealed envelope and shall be effective when deposited in the United States Post Office, postage prepaid and addressed as above. The parties hereto, by like notice in writing may designate another address or office to which notices shall be given pursuant to this Agreement.

Legal gobbledygook. How about this?

"Notices hereunder shall be effective four days after mailing* by certified mail, return receipt requested, to the above address or to such other address as either party may designate by notice hereunder."

*Fairer?

15.0 INDEMNIFICATION

15.1 Seller agrees to fully indemnify, save harmless and defend Buyer, its parent company, subsidiaries and affiliates, their directors, officers, agents and employees from and against any and all loss, cost, damage, injury, liability, claims, demands, penalties, interest or causes of action of every nature or kind whatsoever resulting from damage or destruction to the property (whether the same be that of third persons or of either of the parties hereto), or death of persons or injury to persons (whether they be third persons or employees of Buyer, Seller or subcontractors) in any manner arising out of or incident to or in connection with any defect in the Work.

Aside from the redundancy and the childish language, this provision is a dangerous one for a consultant building a first-of-a-kind machine. It is dangerous even if the consultant makes no design error in the machine. Employees are generally limited in recovery from an employer by the Worker's Compensation statutes. No such limit applies to others. Suppose the consultant provides a safety interlock to guard against injury. The interlock is removed by "somebody" and an employee is injured. The buyer is covered by insurance that limits the recovery of the employee. A suit against the consultant has a good chance of being successful, perhaps because the consultant made the interlock too easy to remove or for some other equally fatuous reason. Even if the consultant successfully defends the suit, the attorneys will clean its pockets of many dollars for the defense. The best advice is never sign any hold harmless clause unless there is an overpowering reason to do so. In this situation where the control, operation, and maintenance of the machine will be solely in the hands of the Buyer, there is no good reason to do so. The best way to revise this paragraph is to draw a line through it.

16.0 INTENTIONALLY LEFT BLANK

17.0 NON-DISCRIMINATION IN EMPLOYMENT—See exhibit "D"

18.0 INTENTIONALLY LEFT BLANK

19.0 SERVICES SCHEDULE

19.1 Seller shall submit to Buyer a proposed Services Schedule for the services specified in Exhibit "A" of this Agreement

19.2 After review and approval of the proposed Services Schedule required in Exhibit "C", the Schedule shall be binding on both parties, and shall be changed only in conformance with the provisions of this Agreement.

20.0 GENERAL

20.1 Seller may not assign this Agreement or any part of this Agreement without the written consent of Buyer.

20.2 No delay or failure on the part of the Buyer in exercising any rights under this Agreement, and partial or single exercise of such rights, shall constitute a waiver of such rights or of any other rights under this Agreement. The guarantees contained in this Agreement shall not be construed to modify or limit in any way, any rights or actions which Buyer may otherwise have against Seller by law or statute or in equity.

Another example of "gouging." If a waiver clause is desirable, it is desirable for both parties. This provision should be deleted or made reciprocal. The last seven words of the provision are nineteenth century fossils.

20.3 In performing the Services, and in furnishing the equipment (sic), Seller is an independent contractor, and not an employee, representative or agent of Buyer.

20.4 No waiver, alteration or modification of any of the provisions of this Agreement shall be binding unless in writing and signed by Buyer.

20.5 The Agreement contains the entire agreement and understanding between Buyer and Seller pertaining to the design of the Equipment and automatically supersedes and terminates all other existing agreements by and between Seller and Buyer covering the Equipment. There are no oral representations, stipulations, warranties, agreements or understandings with respect to the subject matter of this Agreement which are not fully expressed herein.

Okay for subject matter. Too long, too verbose. See the examples in Chapter 2.

In Witness Whereof, Buyer and Seller have executed this Agreement, in duplicate, as of the day and year first above written.*

BUYER SELLER

By___________________________ By___________________________
Title: Title:

No comment.

ARCO Solar should have known better. The deal died in the arms of the attorneys. No bid was made by the consultant receiving this proposed agreement.

Those are real-life situations. Now, let us consider some fictitious ones that may be more useful in your real-life situation.

A Practical Consulting Agreement

Assume the following situation: Polly Pie Corporation manufactures apple pies. Its business has grown to the point where it is desirable to automate the making of the pie crusts, but the company employees are not skilled in the design of such machinery. The company approaches Machine Design Company, Inc., a company that appears to have the requisite skills. The pie company desires to keep all aspects of the project secret from its competitors, even the fact that it is planning such automation. It enters into a non-disclosure agreement so that it can disclose its plans, needs, and present procedures to the prospective consulting company. (The various aspects of non-disclosure agreements are covered in the next chapter.)

Machine Design studies the requirements and believes it can produce a production machine within x months at a cost of y dollars and offers the following agreement to Polly Pie.

CONSULTING AGREEMENT MACHINE DESIGN COMPANY, INC.

This is an agreement, effective July 1, 1988, between Polly Pie Corporation, a Nebraska corporation, ("Polly") and Machine Design Company, Inc., an Illinois corporation, ("MDC").

Background

MDC is in the business of designing and building automated production machinery. Polly desires to retain the services of MDC for the design and construction of automated machinery for the manufacture of pie crusts (the "Field") in accordance with the specifications set forth in Exhibit A. MDC is willing to render such services and the parties agree as follows:

1. The Project

MDC agrees to make all reasonable efforts to design and build automated machinery in accordance with the specifications set forth in Appendix A and to deliver such machinery to Polly on or before May 1, 1990 (the "Project").

2. Basis for Charges

All work is to be done on an accrued charge basis. MDC will invoice Polly monthly for all accrued charges for the Project at MDC's standard hourly rates plus all charges for travel and materials purchased specifically for the Project. All out-of-pocket expenditures will carry a mark-up of twenty percent (20%) to cover the cost of overhead, insurance, financing, etc. Polly agrees to pay such invoices within thirty days after the invoice date. A late payment charge of two percent (2%) per month shall apply to all overdue invoices. MDC shall be under no obligation to continue work when the account is overdue. Polly agrees to pay all sales and use taxes on equipment and services provided by MDC.

3. Termination by Polly

The Project shall be carried out in six Phases as set forth in Exhibit A. Polly shall have the right, by written notice, to terminate the Project at the end of any Phase. If Polly terminates at any other time, MDC will make reasonable efforts to reassign scheduled labor to other projects, but to the extent that MDC is unable to do so, Polly

continued on page 4-21

continued from page 4-20

shall be responsible for scheduled labor charges until such reassignment can be made, but in no event for a period longer than thirty (30) days from the date of the notice of termination. Upon termination, Polly agrees to pay MDC for all accrued Project charges including any non-cancellable commitments for machinery, services, materials or travel.

Upon completion of work authorized under any purchase order for one or more Phases, Polly shall have thirty (30) days to authorize the next subsequent Phase. If no such authorization is received by MDC within such thirty (30) day period, the Project shall be deemed to be terminated.

4. Delivery and Warranty Limitations

Delivery of the machinery and drawings produced on the Project shall be at Peoria, Illinois and shall be subject to payment of all charges owed to MDC. Polly shall approve the machinery before delivery. All rigging and transportation shall be the responsibility of Polly.

MDC warrants Polly shall have clear title to the machinery, free from all liens or other adverse claims of ownership. Polly recognizes the machinery to be constructed is custom-designed under the Project and carries no warranty, express or implied, other than that of clear title. Under no circumstances shall MDC be liable for consequential damages. MDC agrees to pass through to Polly (as possible) all manufacturers' warranties on subsystems and standard components.

5. Operational Responsibility

Polly shall have complete responsibility for the installation, operation and safety of the machinery. Polly agrees to provide insurance relating to the operation of the machinery, or any product made on or processed by it, in sufficient amount and with appropriate terms to protect MDC from all claims of damage, personal injury or death relating in any way to the operation of the machinery. If such insurance is inadequate to protect MDC, Polly agrees to hold MDC, its officers and employees, harmless from liability from any cause, resulting from the operation of the machinery or any product made by or processed on the machinery.

MDC agrees to be responsible for personal injury or property damage resulting, during the term of this Agreement, from acts of an employee of MDC unless such injury or damage is a result of the negligence of Polly or its employ-

continued on page 4-22

continued from page 4-21

ee. MDC agrees to carry reasonably adequate insurance for property damage, public liability, and workmen's compensation for MDC employees while on Polly's premises.

6. Patent License and Infringement

Upon delivery of the machinery produced hereunder, MDC grants to Polly a permanent, exclusive, world-wide, royalty-free license to use the machinery in the Field under all patents owned by MDC whether or not resulting from inventions made on the Project.

MDC warrants it will not knowingly infringe any patent owned by others, but makes no warranty of non-infringement, express or implied.

7. Proprietary Information

In the event either party discloses information, of any sort whatever, to the other that it considers to be secret or proprietary ("Proprietary Information"), the receiving party agrees to make reasonable efforts, for a period of three (3) years after the completion of all work under this Agreement, to maintain the Proprietary Information in confidence and to treat the Proprietary Information with at least the same degree of care and safeguards that it takes with its own proprietary information. Proprietary Information shall be used by the receiving party only in connection with this Agreement and shall be disclosed only to employees as reasonably necessary for the performance of the consulting services.

Proprietary Information shall be limited to information disclosed in writing and suitably marked as "Confidential" or "Proprietary", or if disclosed orally, reduced to writing and delivered, appropriately marked, to the receiving party within twenty (20) days. Proprietary Information shall not be deemed to include any information that:

(a) is in or becomes in the public domain without violation of this Agreement by the receiving party; or

(b) is already in the possession of the receiving party, as evidenced by written documents, prior to the disclosure thereof by the other party; or

(c) is rightfully received from a third entity having no obligation to the disclosing party and without violation of this Agreement by the receiving party.

continued on page 4-23

continued from page 4-22

All information concerning the existence of this Agreement and the existence of any business relationship between the parties shall be deemed to be Confidential Information.

The provisions of this Section 7 shall survive any termination of this Agreement.

8. MDC as Independent Contractor

MDC shall act as an independent contractor and not as an agent of Polly, and neither MDC nor any employee of MDC shall make any representation as an agent of Polly. MDC shall have no authority to bind Polly or incur other obligations on behalf of Polly.

9. Conflict of Interest

MDC warrants that it is under no obligation to any other entity whereby conflicts of interest are or may be created by entering into this Agreement, that it is free to enter into this Agreement and that it has no Agreement to consult for others in the Field.

MDC agrees it will not, during the term of this Agreement, perform consulting services for others in the Field, but shall have the right to perform consulting or other services for others, outside the Field.

10. Complete Agreement

This Agreement shall be attached to, or otherwise made part of, each Purchase Order issued by Polly to MDC and shall be in lieu of all printed terms on the face or reverse of the Purchase Order form and together with the terms typed on the face of the Purchase Order shall constitute the entire agreement between the parties. A "not-to-exceed" price on the Purchase order shall be deemed only to mean that MDC will receive authorization from Polly before incurring charges in excess of such price.

11. This Agreement is not assignable by either party without the consent of the other.

12. Execution

Each individual executing this Agreement on behalf of a party to this Agreement represents and personally warrants that he has authority to enter into this Agreement

continued on page 4-24

continued from page 4-23

on behalf of such party and that this Agreement is binding on such party.

Polly Pie Corporation	Machine Design Corporation
By_________________________	By_________________________
Director of Engineering	President

That agreement is presumed to be the one offered by the machine designer and will, of course, be subject to negotiation of at least some of the terms. It will, however, serve as a starting point for agreements of this kind. This agreement is considered further in Chapter 13 on what-iffing the contract.

A Practical Consulting Agreement

A very different situation is presented when an individual is to do consulting work on a continuing basis for a corporation. The following example will serve as a starting point for such an agreement.

CONSULTING AGREEMENT

This is an agreement, effective as of December 5, 1987, between Warren Rivers, an individual residing at 115 First Avenue, Kansas City, Missouri, ("Warren"), and Northern Electrical Supply Corporation, a Delaware corporation, ("Northern")

Background

Under the terms set forth below, Northern desires to retain the services of Warren to advise and consult with it with respect to its business, and Warren is willing to render such services.

Terms

1. Warren agrees that for a period of twelve (12) months commencing with the effective date of this Agreement, he will, consistent with his other obligations, render to Northern such consulting services as Northern may request relating to the field set forth in Exhibit A, attached, (the "Field"). All such services shall be rendered by Warren or by personnel selected by Warren and approved in advance by Northern. All such personnel, if any, shall be directly supervised by Warren who shall be present with such personnel at such times as he deems reasonably necessary. Warren shall not be required at any time to render services that would conflict with obligations of Warren undertaken prior to the request for such services by Warren.

continued on page 4-25

continued from page 4-24

2. Northern agrees to reimburse Warren for such consulting services at the hourly rates shown in Exhibit B, attached. Warren shall invoice Northern monthly for services rendered and such invoices shall be payable upon receipt. Invoices shall include the hours worked, the hourly rate, and a brief description of the services rendered. Upon adequate substantiation, Northern will reimburse Warren for all travel and related living expenses incurred by Warren in connection with any travel requested by Northern. Prior written approval by Northern shall be required for all travel outside the United States and Canada in connection with this Agreement.

3. Warren shall act as an independent contractor and not as an agent of Northern and Warren shall make no representation as an agent of Northern. Warren shall have no authority to bind Northern or incur other obligations on behalf of Northern.

4. Warren will promptly disclose to Northern each discovery, which he reasonably believes may be new or patentable, conceived by him in carrying out the consulting services under this Agreement. Northern shall have the right to file a patent application, at its own expense, on each such discovery and Warren agrees to cooperate with Northern and to execute all proper documents, at the expense of Northern, to enable Northern to obtain patent protection in the United States and foreign countries. Warren agrees to assign all of his rights to each such patent application and patent to Northern, but Warren shall have a free, non-exclusive, irrevocable license, with the right to sublicense, in all areas except the Field. In the event Northern fails to file a patent application on any such discovery within six (6) months after written disclosure thereof to Northern, Warren shall have the right to file such application, at its own expense, in the United States and foreign countries. On each patent issuing from such application, Northern shall have a free, non-exclusive, irrevocable license, with the right to sublicense, in the Field.

5. In the event Northern discloses information to Warren that it considers to be secret or proprietary ("Proprietary Information"), Warren agrees to maintain the Proprietary Information in confidence and to treat the Proprietary Information with at least the same degree of care and safeguards that he takes with his own proprietary information. Proprietary Information shall be used by Warren only in connection with services rendered under this Agreement.

continued on page 4-26

continued from page 4-25

Proprietary Information shall not be deemed to include information that:

(a) is in or becomes in the public domain without violation of this Agreement by Warren; or

(b) is already in the possession of Warren, as evidenced by written documents, prior to the disclosure thereof by Northern; or

(c) is rightfully received from a third entity having no obligation to Northern and without violation of this Agreement by Warren.

6. Warren warrants that he is under no obligation to any other entity that in any way is in conflict with this Agreement, that he is free to enter into this Agreement, and is under no obligation to consult for others in the Field.

Warren shall not, during the term of this Agreement, perform consulting services for others in the Field, but shall have the right to perform consulting or other services for others, outside the Field.

7. This Agreement may be terminated by Northern at any time on sixty (60) days advance written notice. In the event consulting services requested by Northern hereunder, for immediate performance, shall in any calendar month total less than $2,000.00, then Warren shall have the right to terminate this Agreement by thirty days advance written notice, provided, in the event Northern shall within such thirty day period place sufficient requests with Warren to bring the total for the previous and current month to the minimum amounts set forth above, such notice shall be of no effect.

8. The secrecy provisions of Section 5 hereof shall survive any termination of this Agreement for a period of three (3) years after such termination.

9. This Agreement is not assignable by either party without the consent of the other.

Northern Electrical Supply Corporation

By____________________________
Director of Engineering

____
Warren Rivers

Chapter Five

Confidentiality (Non-disclosure) Agreements

There are many occasions in the business world when it is desirable to disclose information to another party provided such party maintains the information in confidence. It is usual for a corporation soliciting bids on a confidential project to require potential suppliers to sign a non-disclosure agreement before providing them with the information necessary for the preparation of a proposal. Inventors frequently ask for a non-disclosure agreement before disclosing the workings of an invention. Employers routinely ask employees to sign a non-disclosure agreement relating to the affairs of the company. There are many other occasions when the need for such agreements arises.

Unfortunately, such agreements are frequently concocted in the legal departments of large corporations and go far beyond the bounds of decency in what they request. Which is to say, be careful before you sign a non-disclosure agreement for, as we shall see, it may be something more than a mere agreement not to disclose.

Pieces that Make a Non-disclosure Agreement

A non-disclosure agreement should as a minimum include the following elements:

- identification of the parties;
- the nature of the information to be disclosed;
- the procedure for disclosure;
- the scope of responsibility of the receiving party to maintain the confidentiality;
- the term of the agreement;
- the term of the confidentiality obligation; and
- exclusions for information:

  (i) already known to the receiving party, or

  (ii) which is received from a third party without violation of the confidentiality agreement, or

  (iii) which is in or becomes in the public domain.

Illustrative Non-disclosure Agreement

These elements are set forth in the following sample non-disclosure agreement.

NON-DISCLOSURE AGREEMENT

This is an agreement, effective January 1, 1989, between Anathema Corporation, a Colorado corporation, (the "Buyer") and Michael Steel of 121 Foremost Road, Houston, Texas, (the "Seller").

Background

The Buyer desires to have the Seller consider performing certain services for it. To enable the Seller to consider rendering such services, the Buyer has agreed to disclose to the Seller certain information necessary for the Seller to prepare a work proposal which information the Buyer regards as confidential. In consideration of the opportunity to propose performing such services, the Seller agrees as follows:

Terms

"Confidential Information" means information that the Buyer regards as confidential and may include, without limitation, business procedures, customer identities, technical material, and manufacturing plans and procedures. Confidential Information shall include only information disclosed to the Seller within one year from the effective date of this Agreement in writing and appropriately marked as proprietary or confidential or information that is disclosed orally to the Seller and reduced to writing within thirty days thereafter and delivered to the Seller appropriately marked as confidential or proprietary. Confidential Information shall be deemed to exclude information that:

(a) is in or becomes in the public domain without violation of this Agreement by the Seller; or

(b) was known to the Seller prior to disclosure thereof to the Seller by the Buyer as evidenced by written records; or

(c) is disclosed to the Seller by a third party under no obligation of confidentiality to the Buyer and without violation of this Agreement by the Seller.

The Seller agrees to hold in confidence all Confidential Information and not disclose such information to any other party without the written consent of the Buyer and to refrain from making use of the information for his own benefit.

continued on page 5-3

continued from page 5-2

This Agreement shall expire four years from the effective date of this Agreement and the Seller shall thereafter have no obligation of confidentiality with respect to any Confidential Information.

____

Michael Steel (the Seller)

Anathema Corporation

By__________________________

Title:______________________

That is a simple and effective agreement that is suitable for many situations, but there are many other situations where additional or different terms are desirable. We now consider some of the possibilities.

Requirement for Information to be in Writing

The agreement requires all information to be regarded as confidential to be in writing. This can be a controversial provision. If information is included that is provided only orally or which is obtained by observation, it may be difficult or impossible for the receiving party, with the best of intentions, to abide by the agreement. Quite often corporate-type lawyers insist on including all information, however gained by the receiving party. This is apparently based upon the theory that all things about the corporation are secret, when the fact is there are seldom more than a handful of things that are important from a secrecy standpoint. The disclosing corporation may be better served by specifically identifying the items to be kept secret and enabling the receiving party to effectively carry out its obligations. If you are the receiving party, you may want to insist the agreement be limited to disclosures made in writing. The arguments against the requirement for written disclosure includes the practical difficulty of confining the disclosures to written material. The reasonableness of the written requirement depends in large part upon the particular circumstances underlying the interactions between the parties.

I have personally seen more than one deal die in the arms of corporate attorneys insisting that confidential information not be limited to written material. One cannot help but wonder whether top management is aware of the extent to which its in-house lawyers are playing CYA instead of promoting the best interests of the organization. If you are the receiving party and the other party insists on including verbal and visual information, you must make a decision based on the business risk. If you are an individual acting alone, you are in a better position to accept such terms. If you have no substantial assets, you are in a doubly preferred position—lawyers don't sue shallow pockets.

If the agreement does provide that confidential information delivered orally be subsequently reduced to writing, there may yet be a problem for you as the receiving party because of the wording of the subsequent writing. Suppose the disclosure is the workings of a particular oil valve. The subsequent written confirmation states:

> "This is to confirm that on August 17, 1988, oil valve constructions were disclosed to you. In accordance with our non-disclosure agreement, you are now aware that oil valves are a subject of secrecy and you shall disclose no information relating to oil valves to any other party. At the same meeting you were escorted through our production department where you had an opportunity to view our entire set-up. You are also on notice that everything in our production set-up is regarded as confidential and comes within the terms of the agreement."

Such "creeping" (a term we will discuss later in Chapter 14) must be responded to immediately. The response should relate the details of the oil valve that were disclosed and disavow all generalities. The attempt to place all of the production set-up in the secret category should be politely refuted with a request that the specific items to be regarded as confidential be disclosed in writing as required by the agreement.

There is one cogent reason for corporations insisting on verbal disclosures coming within the purview of the secrecy agreement: employees frequently fail to confirm oral disclosures in writing. Once an agreement is signed, the employee freely discloses all information and no one remembers to look at the terms of the agreement. However, this may not be a valid reason for accepting a secrecy commitment based on verbal disclosures.

The above agreement places an absolute obligation of non-disclosure on the receiving party. This is usually an acceptable provision if the receiving party is an individual acting alone. It is usually not a desirable provision for a corporation having a number of employees with access to the restricted information. The corporation may not want to assume liability for a dishonest employee or for one who is negligent.

One possible provision is to the effect:

> The receiver of the confidential information shall use the same degree of care to protect the confidential information that it takes with its own proprietary information, and shall not be liable for inadvertent or accidental disclosure.

Another possibility is to use the word "knowingly", i.e., the disclosee shall not knowingly disclose the confidential information. Or words can be used to the effect that the disclosee corporation shall not be liable for unauthorized disclosure by an employee or other person.

In many instances, the agreement requires the receiving party to obtain a non-disclosure agreement from employees or other parties to whom the information is to be transmitted.

Burden of Proof

Secrecy agreements sometimes place the burden of proof on the disclosee to show that it did not make any unauthorized disclosure of the confidential information. Such clauses can be costly, as negative proof may be difficult or impossible to establish. One such clause reads:

> The foregoing restrictions on Recipients disclosure and use of Confidential Information acquired from Discloser shall not apply to information (i) known to Recipient prior to receipt from Discloser, (ii) of public knowledge without breach of Recipient's obligations hereunder, (iii) rightfully acquired by Recipient from a third party without express restriction on disclosure or use, or (iv) as to which Recipient has received express written consent from an authorized officer of Discloser to disclose or use. Provided, however, that Recipient shall have the burden of proof respecting any of the aforementioned events on which Recipient relies as relieving it of the restrictions hereunder on disclosure or use of such Confidential Information and...

This clause is not as objectionable as a burden of proof clause that places the burden on the disclosee of showing that no disclosure was made. Nevertheless, it shifts a burden to the disclosee that more properly belongs to the discloser. In this case, the Recipient objected to the burden-of-proof clause and the Discloser was adamant in requiring it. As it happened, the parties had previously entered into a non-disclosure agreement in which the positions of the Discloser and Recipient were reversed. The log jam was overcome by an offer to abrogate the previous agreement and to execute a reciprocal agreement using the exact language of the latest proposal.

Time Periods

There are two time periods that are important: the term during which the agreement is in effect for the receiving of confidential information and the period of time during which the information must be retained in confidence. The first is a matter of convenience dependent upon the expected length of the transactions between the parties. The second term is frequently omitted by over-zealous lawyers. If you are the recipient, you should insist there be a time limit on the safeguarding of the information. This is especially true of a corporation that attempts to police and abide by its confidentiality agreements. The policing of agreements represents a real cost and "forever" obligations are expensive. Moreover, the longer the term, the greater the chance of an accidental violation just because of the fallibility of human memory.

The length of the term that is reasonable depends upon the particular industry and circumstances of the disclosure. In high-tech operations, things change so fast that a period of two or three years may be satisfactory. In more sluggish industries such as food processing, steel, mining etc., a longer period of five to ten years may be reasonable. Seldom should you agree to a period of time in excess of ten years. In situations where the relationship is expected to continue for a substantial period of time, the term of confidentiality may run from the date of the disclosure rather than from the date of the agreement as in the above example.

Exclusions from Confidential Information

The exclusions are straightforward and for the most part are based on the premise that the disclosee should not be barred from doing anything that is open to others not under an obligation of confidentiality. Information that is generally known to the public should be excluded, as should information known to the disclosee prior to its disclosure under the confidentiality agreement. If someone else has the information legitimately and brings it to the disclosee, it should not bar the disclosee from taking any action that would be available to one not under the restrictions of confidentiality.

A rather usual provision is one requiring that all documents given to the disclosee during the transactions be returned to the disclosing party:

```
The Seller agrees upon request to return promptly to
the Buyer all documents delivered to him by the Buyer
during the term of this Agreement.
```

A PPG Proposal

It is not unusual for corporations to use a "standard" non-disclosure agreement form that applies to all situations. This usually leads to a document that is longer than required and is not specifically directed to the situation at hand. The following is an agreement proposed by PPG Industries, Inc. to cover a variety of relationships.

```
AGREEMENT OF CONFIDENTIALITY I

The undersigned, an architect, engineer, consultant, a
contractor, subcontractor, or a supplier to PPG
Industries, Inc., or an employee of such architect,
engineer, consultant, contractor, subcontractor or
supplier, in anticipation of rendering services or
supplying materials, machinery or equipment in such
capacity with respect to certain confidential
activities of PPG Industries, Inc. and in consideration
of being given access by PPG Industries, Inc. to
confidential information hereby agrees for the
undersigned and all employees under the control of the
undersigned conditions [sic]:

(1)   All documents of any character including, but not
limited to drawings, designs, plans, specifications,
requisitions, instructions, data, manuals, models,
equipment,* and the like delivered to the undersigned
by PPG Industries, Inc. or produced or developed by or
for the undersigned pursuant to an agreement or
```

Lawyers do love redundancy!

continued on page 5-7

continued from page 5-6

understanding with PPG Industries, Inc. shall be and remain the property of PPG Industries, Inc. and shall be delivered by the undersigned together with all copies thereof to PPG Industries, Inc. promptly upon PPG Industries, Inc.'s request.

(2) The undersigned agrees to refrain except to the extent expressly authorized in writing by PPG Industries, Inc. from using or revealing to any other person or from making copies of or otherwise duplicating or reproducing* any of the above named documents or any equipment, machine or device which is specifically constructed or designed to PPG Industries, Inc. specifications, and to refrain from using or revealing other confidential information or know-how whether written or unwritten, or equipment made known to the undersigned or developed by or for the undersigned for so long as and to the extent that the same shall remain unpublished; provided, however, that nothing herein shall prevent the undersigned or employees responsible to the undersigned from using or disclosing to others information which [sic] is already known to the undersigned or such employee or which is hereafter obtained from some source other than directly or indirectly from PPG Industries, Inc. without an obligation of secrecy provided further that nothing in this agreement shall prevent the undersigned from using or disclosing information acquired under secrecy hereafter from a source other than directly or indirectly from PPG Industries, Inc. in accordance with the rights granted and the obligations imposed (if any) by such source.

**Even if "duplications" and "reproductions" are "copies", redundancy must have its day.*

The terms of this agreement are not perfect but, as we shall see, are not so objectionable as some others. Aside from the awkward wording, the primary objections from the point of view of the one receiving the information are:

(a) The material to be kept confidential is not limited to written material;

(b) The material to be kept secret is not required to be identified by PPG Industries, Inc. as confidential;

(c) There is no time limit on the period of non-disclosure;

(d) The agreement prohibits other use or disclosure of anything made to PPG Industries, Inc.'s specifications.

The extent to which these objections are valid depend to a large extent upon the particular circumstances. An architect designing a building might find the terms less objectionable than a manufacturer of wrapping machines that is considering making a modified machine for PPG Industries, Inc.

The entire agreement could be rewritten to advantage, but sometimes it is difficult to deal with corporate-type lawyers who accept nothing unless written on their paper. It may be more saleable to merely add a couple of paragraphs. Perhaps something like this:

Notwithstanding the above provisions, such documents, equipment or machine delivered to the undersigned by PPG Industries, Inc. shall be considered confidential only if so indicated by PPG Industries, Inc. at the time of such delivery. In the event of any unwritten disclosure to the undersigned by PPG Industries, Inc., such information shall be regarded as confidential only if at the time of disclosure the material is indicated as being confidential and, further, that the information is confirmed in writing and delivered to the undersigned marked as confidential within thirty days after such disclosure.

It is further provided that if no contract subsequent to this Agreement is entered into between PPG Industries, Inc. and the undersigned within three (3) months of the date hereof, all obligations of the undersigned under this Agreement shall terminate two years from the date hereof. If a subsequent contract is entered into between PPG Industries, Inc. and the undersigned, then the term of the obligation of confidentiality by the undersigned and the rights of PPG Industries, Inc. in any developments resulting from such contract shall be exclusively as set forth therein.

Keep it Simple—Simple

The agreement proposed by PPG Industries, Inc. can be simplified while retaining its meaning. If the parties are identified by "pet" names, there is an appreciable simplification. The name PPG Industries, Inc. appears in full twelve times. The full description of the "undersigned" appears twice. The enumeration of the many kinds of consulting services does not seem to be a requirement. The terms might read as follows after incorporating the substance of the paragraphs proposed above:

The undersigned desires to consider providing consulting or other services for PPG Industries, Inc. ("PPG"). In consideration of being given access to certain information that PPG regards as confidential,

continued on page 5-9

continued from page 5-8

which information will assist the undersigned in preparing a work proposal for PPG, the undersigned agrees:

(1) "Confidential Information" means information of every kind that PPG regards as confidential and that is disclosed to the undersigned in writing, appropriately marked as confidential or proprietary, or if disclosed orally is reduced to writing and delivered to the undersigned, appropriately marked as confidential or proprietary, within thirty days after such oral disclosure. All materials belonging to PPG, and all copies of such materials, shall be returned promptly upon request by PPG.

(2) The undersigned agrees to refrain from using Confidential Information or revealing it to any other person (a) for so long as and to the extent the same shall remain unpublished, or (b) unless it is already known to the undersigned, or (c) unless it is later obtained directly or indirectly from a source other than PPG.

(3) It is further provided that if no contract subsequent to this Agreement is entered into between PPG and the undersigned, all obligations of the undersigned under this Agreement shall terminate two years from the date hereof. If a subsequent contract is entered into between PPG and the undersigned, then the term of the obligation of confidentiality by the undersigned and the rights of PPG in any developments resulting from such contract shall be exclusively as set forth therein. The undersigned agrees that each employee of the undersigned having access to Confidential Information will agree in writing to be bound by the terms of this Agreement prior to the disclosure of such Confidential Information to that employee.

Non-disclosure and Invention Assignment Agreements

A non-disclosure agreement should generally be just that. But corporations sometimes put sleepers in the non-disclosure agreements. A frequent example is the assignment of patent rights. Sometimes the title will raise a red flag, but sometimes the title does not refer to the transfer of any intangible rights. The following example of a letter agreement, from Johnson & Johnson Health Care Company, by its very title should have sounded a loud warning to any prospective consultant. Bear in mind, the consultant who is asked to make a proposal to Johnson & Johnson has no assurance of ever receiving one penny.

The first part of the agreement deals with non-disclosure and is reasonable in all respects. The following paragraphs, however, will be resisted by any consultant that desires to remain in business.

The Motley Corporation
Estabrook Creek Road
Miltown, New Jersey 08906

Secrecy and Invention Agreement

...You also agree that all materials, written information, sketches, designs and the like supplied to you by us, or which relates [sic] to the products of the Company and is generated by you for us, will be and remain our property...

Any information which you may choose to disclose to us in connection with this Agreement shall not include any confidential or proprietary information, or be construed to create or imply any obligation on the part of the Company.

Any inventions, improvements or ideas made or conceived by your employees as a result of the performance of services to the Company under this Agreement, insofar as they pertain to the products of the Company which are the subject of this Agreement, shall be owned by the Company and be made available for its unrestricted use. You will, without expense to us other than reasonable payment for time involved and any actual expense incurred, execute, acknowledge and deliver to us all documents required by us to protect such and all countries of the world and to vest title to said patents, [sic] inventions and improvements or ideas in the Company, and further render such assistance to us as may be required in any Patent Office proceeding or litigation involving said inventions, improvements or ideas...

Consider this from the standpoint of a consultant who desires to prepare a technical proposal for the design and construction of machinery for Johnson & Johnson. In order to prevail in such an endeavor, the consultant must put forward sound ideas for solving the problems that will be attractive to the company. The agreement (second paragraph), however, assigns to Johnson & Johnson all "materials, written information, sketches, designs and the like—which relate to the products of the Company." Suppose the consultant discloses in its proposal a new machine that is uniquely adapted to manufacture Johnson & Johnson's products. It would be the desire of any reasonable consultant that if it does not obtain the consulting contract from J&J, that its designs, etc., remain confidential and that J&J make no use of them. But as it stands, Johnson & Johnson may take all the valuable ideas from the proposal, disclose them to a competitor of the consultant, and have someone else manufacture the machinery. J&J could be a big winner while the creator of the wealth gets nothing. Note that all information given by the consultant is barred from being confidential. Even if the consultant puts a notice in its proposal that all of the information is confidential, it still belongs to Johnson & Johnson. The provisions about the assignment of patent rights to the company do not belong in a non-disclosure agreement. They belong in the consulting agreement when and if it is awarded. The consultant's rule should be that nothing is assigned until and unless a contract is awarded and information disclosed to J&J should be treated just as confidentially as information provided by J&J to the consultant. Proposed agreements with provisions like these cost large companies a great deal of money, but it is money that is seldom traced or acknowledged by top management.

Non-disclosure ala Digital Equipment Corporation

Here is an example of a non-disclosure agreement presented by Digital Equipment Corporation (see the preceding chapter) which should give the shakes to any consulting firm considering preparing a proposal for that company:

II. NONDISCLOSURE AND TRADE SECRETS:

The specific technologies which shall be disclosed or otherwise made available to CONSULTANT, and the specific DIGITAL facilities and work areas which shall be accessible to CONSULTANT shall be identified in the Purchase Order issued by DIGITAL. CONSULTANT is hereby expressly prohibited from entering areas other than the designated areas without a DIGITAL escort. Any failure to adhere to this prohibition shall constitute a material breach of this Agreement.

During the term of this Agreement and in the course of CONSULTANT's performances hereunder, CONSULTANT may receive or otherwise be exposed to DIGITAL confidential and proprietary information relating to DIGITAL's business practices, strategies and technologies. Such proprietary and confidential information may include but not be limited to confidential information supplied to the consultant with the legend "Digital Equipment Corporation Confidential and Proprietary" or equivalent, or to provide CONSULTANT with written notice of the confidential nature of such information, DIGITAL's marketing and customer support strategies, to DIGITAL's financial information including sales, costs, profits and pricing methods, to DIGITAL's internal organization, employee lists and customer lists, to DIGITAL's technology including discoveries, inventions, research and development efforts, manufacturing processes, hardware/software design and maintenance tools, and hardware/software product know-how and show-how, and to all derivatives, improvements and enhancements of the above which are created or developed by CONSULTANT under this Agreement (collectively referred to as "Information").

continued on page 5-12

continued from page 5-11

CONSULTANT acknowledges the confidential and secret character of the Information, and agrees that the Information is the sole, exclusive and extremely valuable property of DIGITAL. Accordingly, CONSULTANT agrees not to reproduce any of the Information without DIGITAL's prior written consent, not to use the Information except in the performance of this Agreement, and not to divulge all or any part of the Information in any form to any third party, either during or after the term of this Agreement. Upon termination of this Agreement for any reason including the expiration of term, CONSULTANT agrees to cease using and return to DIGITAL all whole and partial copies and derivatives of DIGITAL's confidential and proprietary information, whether in CONSULTANT's possession or under CONSULTANT's direct or indirect control, including any computer access nodes and/or codes.

DIGITAL shall exercise reasonable care either to prominently and legibly mark all corporeal form of DIGITAL confidential and proprietary information supplied to CONSULTANT with the legend "Digital Equipment Corporation Confidential and Proprietary" or equivalent, or to provide CONSULTANT with written notice of the confidential nature of such information.

CONSULTANT shall not disclose or otherwise make available to DIGITAL in any manner any confidential information received by CONSULTANT from third parties.

Notwithstanding any other provisions of this Agreement, CONSULTANT agrees not to export, directly or indirectly, any U.S. source technical data acquired from DIGITAL or any products utilizing such data to any countries outside the United States which export may be in violation of the United States Export Laws or Regulations. Nothing in this section releases CONSULTANT from any obligation stated elsewhere in this Agreement not to disclose such data.

This Section II shall survive termination of this Agreement for any reason, including expiration of term.

There are many objections to these provisions and the consultant is well advised to refuse to enter into any such unconscionable and burdensome obligation. There is no requirement that confidential information be in writing. The reference to "corporeal" information bearing a legend, does not exclude confidential information acquired orally or by observation.

There is no time limit on the non-disclosure obligations, placing an unreasonable burden on the consultant. It is a particularly expensive burden if the consultant has a number of employees who are privy to the information.

Before the consultant receives the information, it is asked to acknowledge the secret and confidential nature of the information and to agree that it is "extremely valuable property of Digital." The consultant will have to be skilled in ESP to justify making that statement.

The obligation of non-disclosure is not limited to reasonable care or the exercise of the same degree of care exercised in connection with the consultant's own proprietary information. The consultant is burdened with an absolute liability for unauthorized disclosure by an employee. This is a potential liability that the consultant is powerless to avoid.

The proposed DEC agreement does not provide any of the usual caveats. It does not exclude information that (a) was known to the consultant prior to its disclosure by DEC; or (b) is in or becomes in the public domain without fault of the consultant; or (c) is received from a third party under no obligation of secrecy to DEC.

When faced with the choice of signing an agreement such as that proposed by DEC or looking for work elsewhere, look elsewhere.

A Polaroid Non-disclosure Proposal

Polaroid Corporation is not quite so harsh in one set of terms included in a proposed non-disclosure agreement:

> You [meaning the supplier] additionally agree to grant to Polaroid or any company controlled by, controlling or under common control with Polaroid, a royalty-free, nonexclusive, irrevocable license without the right to sublicense, throughout the world to make, have made, use, sell or otherwise dispose of, any and all photographic film products, components, and subassemblies thereof, and manufacturing equipment therefor, which either embody or are derived from inventions, discoveries, or improvements, whether or not patentable, which you, your officers, or employees or others subject to your control, conceive or make during the period covered by this agreement and which result from information provided to you by Polaroid in the course of these collaborations. However, it is expressly understood that Polaroid shall obtain no rights under this agreement in any inventions, discoveries or improvements conceived or made by you prior to the effective date of this agreement.

The agreement further states:

> This agreement does not obligate Polaroid to deliver a purchase order to you for performance of any service or for the supply of any article whatsoever...

The proposed terms are objectionable from the standpoint of the supplier for a number of reasons. First, it could result in a license worth millions of dollars to Polaroid without any compensation to the inventor. It is so worded as to be an invitation to disputes and litigation. As we shall see presently, the provision could be costly to the supplier even if he made an invention that did not seem to come within the purview of the terms of the grant to Polaroid.

Assume this situation: The supplier is a manufacturer of high-speed production equipment. In order to be permitted to make a proposal to Polaroid, the supplier signs a non-disclosure agreement containing the above provisions. The machine desired by Polaroid (this is a fictitious example) is a machine for winding plastic sheet material at high speeds on small tubes. The supplier and its engineers expend time and money devising a novel machine, incorporating a number of inventions, to meet the desired objectives. Polaroid reviews the proposed construction and decides to take the project to another vendor.

At some later time, another film company comes to the same supplier and desires a machine for the same purpose. The supplier shows its previous proposal to the new customer. The customer is ready to place an order for the development when it learns about the Polaroid license provision. The question arises: Did the inventions in the machine arise from the disclosure by Polaroid of its objectives? The agreement provides that Polaroid has free license to inventions that "result from information provided...by Polaroid." Clearly, if Polaroid had not disclosed its objectives, the inventions would not have been made. Although it is arguable whether Polaroid does in fact have a free license, the customer elects to take no chances. He takes the project to another supplier under no obligation to Polaroid.

If a supplier is competent in its field, it should consider rejecting the proposed terms. A provision that might be more acceptable to a supplier, and one that would protect the essential interests of Polaroid, might provide that Polaroid has a right to buy a license under the subject inventions at a reasonable royalty or at a royalty not to exceed some specified amount or percentage. But who can blame Polaroid for trying?

In fairness to Polaroid, however, it must be stated that the remainder of the non-disclosure agreement is not as onerous as some. For example, it contains the following provision:

> You additionally agree to take all reasonable precautions to safeguard the confidential nature of the foregoing information, provided, however, that if such precautions are taken, you will not be liable for any disclosure which is inadvertent or unauthorized or is required by any judicial order or decree or by any governmental law or regulation.

Don't be Fooled by the Title

Because of the frequency with which agreements labeled "Confidentiality Agreements" or the like include material that goes far beyond confidentiality, the "standard" agreement should be examined carefully before acceptance. For example, an agreement labeled "Confidentiality Agreement" provided by Reynolds Metals Company appears at first glance to be merely a requirement for the "Recipient" to maintain Reynolds information in secrecy. But it turns out to be more. Consider this paragraph:

Recipient shall disclose promptly to Reynolds, and shall not use otherwise than for Reynold's benefit or disclose to another party, all inventions, improvements, designs, software and developments derived from Reynolds Information subject to an obligation of Recipient under paragraph I or conceived in the course of work Recipient performs for Reynolds. They and all patent rights and copying rights for them shall belong to Reynolds.

For information disclosed to the Recipient by Reynolds, the usual caveats appear with respect to public information, information from another source, a five-year time limitation, etc. But those limitations do not apply to innovations and information conceived in the course of work for Reynolds—they go on forever and the recipient is not released by public disclosure. From a casual reading, it may not seem unreasonable to assign all work product to Reynolds, but that may not be advisable, as we discussed in Chapter 4.

And I pay an additional salute to the Polaroid and Reynolds attorneys who drafted those non-disclosure agreements: There is not a single "Whereas," "Witnesseth," or "herein-before" in either document. Those attorneys will never make it in any six-name law firm.

A Steelcase Confidential Disclosure Agreement

Here is another example of an agreement that failed to provide for the actual needs of the parties and another promising business deal that died in the arms of the attorneys. This is a confidential disclosure agreement offered by Steelcase, Inc. (its so-called Standard Agreement 5.2B).

CONFIDENTIAL DISCLOSURE AGREEMENT RE:STEELCASE PROPRIETARY INFORMATION

STEELCASE INC. has certain concepts and/or information which the undersigned disclosee is desirous of acquiring for the purpose of determining the extent of any further interest which disclosee may have in becoming involved in the manufacture, possibly including supply of components, or marketing of concepts, products or processes based thereon.

To facilitate disclosure of such information, the undersigned disclosee agrees to maintain all information disclosed in confidence and agrees not to use such information for any purpose without the express written consent of STEELCASE INC. It is understood that these obligations shall not apply to any information which:

continued on page 5-16

continued from page 5-15

(A) is already disclosed through public use or in printed publications;

(B) after disclosure becomes in public use or is disclosed in printed publications through no fault of the disclosee; except that the obligation of confidentiality and nonuse will continue for three (3) years after public disclosure in any form by STEELCASE INC. or its agents, licensees or assignees.

(C) the receiving party can show by written documents was in his or its possession at the time of disclosure.

Nor shall the undersigned disclosee be obligated to obtain permission to use information disclosed to him or it in confidence by third parties who have no obligation of confidentiality to STEELCASE INC. with respect to same, even though such information may previously have been disclosed hereunder.

[!] Disclosee is under no obligation to make any suggestions or disclose information to STEELCASE. However it must be understood and agreed that STEELCASE will own all rights to any suggestions made as applied to any products or processes disclosed by STEELCASE hereunder. Disclosee should not suggest any idea to which it wishes to retain title.

Nothing in this Agreement shall be deemed by implication or otherwise to convey to disclosee any rights under any patents, patent applications or inventions owned by STEELCASE INC. or anyone associated with it. Nor shall this Agreement be deemed a commitment of any kind by either party hereto to enter into any further Agreement with the other party.

Any written documents given to disclosee by STEELCASE INC. shall be returned to STEELCASE INC. upon request. Disclosee assumes responsibility for the acts of any others to whom disclosee discloses information acquired hereunder.

______________________	______________________
Date	Disclosing Party
______________________	______________________
Date	Disclosee

The reader might wish to consider at this point what his reaction would be if the STEELCASE agreement were offered to his company for signature. Compare your conclusions with those offered below.

Aside from some obvious ragged points in the drafting of the agreement, the proposed disclosee in this case took exception to the following conditions:

(1) In Paragraph (B), an obligation is imposed on the disclosee to maintain the information in confidence for three years after public disclosure by Steelcase. This would mean the whole world would be free to use the information except for the disclosee. The part of the Paragraph (B) beginning with "...except that..." should be deleted.

(2) The agreement has no time limit. Agreements that go on forever are difficult or impossible to police. The disclosee is asked to assume this "forever" burden without any assurance that Steelcase will ever do any business with the disclosee. The following paragraph was suggested for addition to the agreement:

```
This Agreement shall expire two years from the date
hereof, provided, if disclosee becomes a supplier for
Steelcase Inc. as evidenced by substantial orders
accepted by the disclosee within six months from the
date hereof, this Agreement shall expire two years after
the latest calendar year in which no substantial orders
from STEELCASE INC. are accepted by the disclosee. *
```

**A dollar amount may be substituted for "substantial" in both instances.*

(3) The agreement provides that information disclosed to Steelcase belongs to Steelcase, at least with respect to Steelcase products. There is no provision for confidential information to be in writing and there may be a high probability of the inadvertent disclosure of confidential information to Steelcase by an employee of the disclosee. Suppose an employee of disclosee tells a Steelcase employee about a patented product or method of the disclosee. The agreement would appear to give Steelcase a free license under the patent. And maybe it is even exclusive as applied to Steelcase products. The disclosee suggested adding the following to the end of the paragraph introduced with "[!]":

```
No information disclosed to STEELCASE INC. shall be
deemed to transfer any rights to STEELCASE INC. unless
such information is in writing accompanied by a written
consent to such transfer signed by an officer of the
disclosee.
```

(4) It was suggested also that the next to last paragraph be made reciprocal, to read:

```
Nothing in this Agreement, or the disclosure of any
information by either party, shall be deemed by
implication or otherwise to convey to disclosee or to
STEELCASE INC. any rights under any patents, patent
applications or inventions owned by either STEELCASE
INC. or the disclosee or anyone associated with either
```

continued on page 5-18

continued from page 5-17

```
of them. This Agreement shall not be deemed a
commitment of any kind by either party to enter into
any further agreement with the other.
```

(5) Finally, the last line of the proposed agreement carries a major threat. Under that provision, the disclosee assumes absolute liability for the misconduct of others. Suppose the disclosee discloses Steelcase confidential information to one of its employees. That employee then leaves the employ of the disclosee and inadvertently or deliberately reveals the information to the detriment of Steelcase. The damages assessed against the disclosee could far exceed any hoped-for profits from doing business with Steelcase.

As in so many cases, the deal died in the arms of the attorneys, no agreement was reached between the parties, and no business was conducted. Another corpse on the doorstep of the lawyers.

The lesson is clear: Don't assume an agreement is a non-disclosure agreement just because the title says it is. Read it carefully before you accept it.

Non-disclosure Agreement with Unauthorized Representative

Sometimes a representative of another company visits a plant with the expectation of being privy to confidential information, but lacks the necessary power to bind his company to a secrecy agreement. Assume this situation: The Real Corporation develops and manufactures communication equipment. Frequently it develops a new product to meet a customer's specifications and bears part of the development costs. It requires the customer to execute the following agreement before disclosing the proposed construction. The last paragraph permits the agreement to be executed by an individual without authority to bind his company.

```
NON-DISCLOSURE AGREEMENT

REAL CORPORATION

This is an agreement, effective ________________________
19___, between Real Corporation, a Massachusetts corpor-
ation, ("Real") and _________________, a _______________
corporation, (the "Customer").

Background

The Customer desires that Real develop one or more
prototypes in accordance with objectives to be agreed
upon later. Real is willing to consider developing such
a prototype at a fixed price, to be agreed upon, under
```

continued on page 5-19

continued from page 5-18

which Real would share in the development cost of the original prototype. To facilitate such consideration by Real and to allow Real to set forth proposed designs for such prototypes, the Customer agrees as follows:

(1) "Confidential Information" means information disclosed by Real to any agent or employee of the Customer, directly or indirectly, which Real regards as proprietary and wishes to protect from unauthorized disclosure. Confidential Information does not include information that:

(a) is in or becomes in the public domain through no fault of the Customer; or

(b) can be shown by written documents to have been in the possession of the Customer prior to the disclosure by Real; or

(c) is disclosed in writing to the Customer by a third party under no obligation of confidentiality to Real and without violation of this Agreement by the Customer.

Confidential Information may include, without restriction, technical information and data; product designs; problem solving methods; business and financial information related to Real; customer names and lists; business or technical plans; and designs and circuits incorporated in any hardware sold or delivered to the Customer.

(2) The Customer agrees for itself and its officers, employees and agents to maintain all Confidential Information in confidence and not use or disclose Confidential Information to any person or entity other than employees or agents of the Customer and then only to the extent necessary for carrying out the purposes of this Agreement.

(3) The Customer agrees that prior to disclosing any Confidential Information to any employee or agent, it will obtain a binding agreement from such person to protect the confidentiality of Confidential Information as set forth herein.

(4) This Agreement, unless sooner terminated as provided, shall terminate one year from the effective date hereof, provided, either party may terminate this Agreement by thirty (30) days advance notice to the other.

continued on page 5-20

continued from page 5-19

(5) The provisions of Sections 1, 2 and 3 hereof shall survive any termination of this Agreement for a period of three (3) years after the date of such termination.

(6) This Agreement supersedes and replaces all previous understandings and agreements between the parties with respect to the subject matter hereof.

(7) Each individual executing this Agreement on behalf of a corporation personally warrants that he or she is authorized to execute this Agreement on behalf of such corporation and that this Agreement is binding on that corporation and on the individual executing this Agreement.

Customer

By__________________________

Real Corporation

By__________________________

If the individual executing this Agreement is an employee of the Customer and is not authorized to execute this agreement on behalf of the Customer, that individual, by signing below in lieu of a corporate signature above, undertakes personally to abide by each of the provisions of this Agreement and not to disclose Confidential Information to any employee or officer of the Customer until an authorized officer of the Customer has executed this Agreement on behalf of the Customer and delivered a copy thereof to Real.

By__________________________

A Mutual Non-disclosure Agreement

Frequently it is desired that each of the parties assume a non-disclosure obligation. Not surprisingly, terms are usually more easily agreed upon in a mutual non-disclosure agreement. Here is an example of such a non-disclosure agreement:

MUTUAL CONFIDENTIAL DISCLOSURE AGREEMENT

This Confidential Disclosure Agreement is entered into on June 14, 1989 between IMACK Corporation, a Delaware

continued on page 5-21

continued from page 5-20

corporation ("IMACK") and Benson Development Inc., a Massachusetts corporation ("Vendor").

RECITALS

1. This Agreement is to establish an understanding of confidence with respect to certain planned disclosures to Vendor by IMACK of confidential information relating to IMACK assembly procedures for the purpose of evaluation by the Vendor and to permit it to make recommendations for automating the assembly process.

2. It is anticipated also that Vendor may disclose confidential information to IMACK and such disclosures are also a subject of this Agreement.

3. It is important to both IMACK and the Vendor that these disclosures be maintained in confidence and both parties recognize that any disclosure to a third party could have a serious adverse financial impact on the party possessing the confidential information.

AGREEMENT

1. For the purpose of this Agreement, the party disclosing confidential information shall be called the "Disclosing Party" and the party receiving the confidential information shall be called the "Recipient".

"Confidential Information" means information of either party that is disclosed to the other relating to existing or new products, processes, materials and components therefor; business, product and components developments; manufacturing processes and techniques; and other information that the Disclosing Party clearly indicates it regards as confidential. Confidential Information shall be in writing and marked as confidential or, if disclosed orally, shall be reduced to writing, marked as confidential, and delivered to the Recipient within thirty (30) days after the oral disclosure. Confidential Information does not include information that is:

a) in or becomes in the public domain without violation of this Agreement by the Recipient; or

b) known to the Recipient, as shown by written records, prior to disclosure by the Disclosing Party; or

c) received by the Recipient from a third party having no obligation of confidentiality to the Disclosing Party.

continued on page 5-22

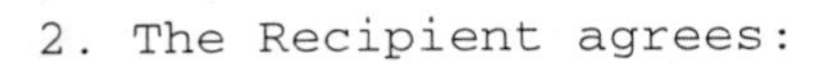
continued from page 5-21

2. The Recipient agrees:

a) It will use Confidential Information for its internal purposes only and shall not disclose it to anyone other than its employees who have a need to know for the benefit of the Disclosing Party;

b) Confidential Information shall be used by the Recipient only for the benefit of the Disclosing Party;

c) Written forms of Confidential Information shall remain the property of the Disclosing Party and shall be returned upon request to the Disclosing Party; and

d) It will enter into a written non-disclosure agreement essentially incorporating the terms of this Agreement with each employee prior to disclosing any Confidential Information to such employee.

3. The Recipient shall not be liable for inadvertent or unauthorized disclosure of Confidential Information provided the Recipient takes at least the same degree of care in safeguarding Confidential Information that it takes with its own proprietary information.

4. No license under any patent or proprietary information is granted or implied to either party by this Agreement or the disclosure of Confidential Information in pursuance thereof.

5. This Agreement shall terminate one year from the date it was entered into, provided, the obligations of confidentiality of each party hereto shall survive expiration of this Agreement for a period of three (3) years after the date of termination.

6. This is the entire agreement between the parties with respect to the subject matter hereof.

7. This Agreement will be binding upon and inure to the benefit of the successors and assigns of the parties, but this Agreement shall not be assignable by either party.

IMACK Corporation	Benson Development Corporation
By______________________	By______________________
Title:	Title

Non-Confidential Agreements

Frequently it is desirable to agree that information to be disclosed is not to be treated as confidential. Such agreements are used mostly by companies that receive voluntary submissions from inventors and others who are interested in receiving royalties or other payment in exchange for good ideas. If such submissions are accepted without an agreement of non-confidentiality, there is a real danger that a confidential relationship may be held to exist and the company forced to pay damages to the one submitting the information, sometimes even when the same or similar information was previously in the hands of the company receiving the submission. Such an agreement is often in the form of a letter from the one making the submission. The company receiving an unsolicited proposal, or an offer to submit such a proposal, usually responds with a letter stating the company cannot consider the proposal unless there is an agreement that nothing submitted establishes a confidential relationship and the one submitting the information will rely wholly on any valid patents for all reimbursement. The following sample letter meets the requirements of the company:

To Able Manufacturing Company, Inc.

Gentlemen,

I desire to submit ideas or products, entirely in writing, (the "Submission") to you for your consideration. Because my submission may be similar to ideas or products previously known to you, I realize that your company must protect itself from unwarranted claims by refusing to examine any Submission unless it is agreed that I will rely solely on my patent rights for any claim against your company.

In return for the opportunity of having you consider my Submission, I agree as follows:

1. I will rely solely upon a validly obtained United States Patent for the protection of my Submission.

2. No confidential or other unusual relationship or agreement to compensate me shall be established by or implied from the presentation of the Submission or by any appraisal thereof made by you.

3. The presentation of the Submission is not made in confidence and shall create no obligation on your company to keep the Submission secret.

4. No obligation of any kind is assumed or imputed to your company by receiving and examining the Submission until and unless a subsequent formal written agreement is entered into between us and then the only obligations of your company will be as set forth in that agreement.

continued on page 5-24

continued from page 5-23

5. If no subsequent agreement is entered into between us, I will rely solely on such rights as I may have under the United States patent laws.

6. I warrant I have the right to disclose all information pertaining to the Submission and no agreements, oral or written, exist which are inconsistent herewith. I warrant no other party has a property interest in the Submission.

7. Unless this agreement is replaced by a subsequent formal written agreement between us, I will make no claim against your company, or any company affiliated with you, with respect to any possible use of the Submission, other than may accrue as a result of rights under the United States patent laws.

8. Your company shall have no obligation to disclose to me any information of its own which may or may not relate to the subject matter of the Submission.

9. If your company rejects my Submission, you shall have no obligation to make any explanation to me.

10. You shall be under no duty to return any part of the Submission to me.

11. The conditions herein shall apply to any subsequent submission by me of additional or other information relating to the subject matter of the Submission.

12. No other understanding or agreement exists between myself and you other than as set forth herein.

Very truly yours,

____
My Signature

Date________________________

Chapter Six

Employer-Employee Agreements

The Usual Provisions

An employment agreement sets forth certain of the obligations of the employer and the employee. The particular provisions vary widely among companies and even among employees within the same company. The more usual provisions include an agreement by the employee:

(a) not to disclose any confidential information of the company either during or subsequent to employment;

(b) to return all materials belonging to the company at the time of termination of employment;

(c) not to enter into any other business during the period of employment without the consent of the company;

(d) not to compete with the company for a period of time subsequent to employment; and

(e) to disclose and assign to the company all inventions made by the employee in the course of employment.

An option plan for the employee to acquire stock of the employer company is quite common. However, the tax and other considerations related to option plans make it preferable to handle those in an agreement separate from the general employment agreement. Employee option plans are covered in the following chapter.

Employment agreements form a special class because an element of coercion is always present. The employee, and even the courts, may assume that because the employer presents an agreement for signature, the employee has little choice but to sign it. The choice for the employee may be to sign or seek employment elsewhere, and this may present a situation where the employee feels he has no practical alternative. When an employer attempts to enforce an employment agreement, the sympathies of the court usually lie with the employee. Seldom will a court enforce an employment agreement if it deprives the ex-employee of a means of making a living comparable to the standard he enjoyed while employed.

For these reasons, employment agreements should be drafted with care and should not give the appearance of an overly greedy employer. It is by all means preferable to have each prospective employee read and agree to the employment terms prior to actual employment as one step in removing the coercion element. With existing employees, it is preferable to have the employee execute a first or revised employment agreement at the time of an increase in compensation which can be part of the consideration for the agreement.

An ideal employment agreement serves as an incentive for the employee and provides protection against the employee damaging the company subsequent to employment. The incentives may include stock options, payments for inventions, bonuses for exceptional contributions, etc.

Different Agreements for Different Employees

Generally, it is not desirable to have a uniform agreement for all classes of employees. For those employees who are hired with any expectation they may make an invention in the field of the company, an invention assignment provision is important. However, generally such a provision should not be included for employees who are not expected to make such a contribution, for example, production workers, secretaries, personnel managers, clerical help, etc. The likelihood of enforcement of the assignment provisions is enhanced if those provisions are limited to employees who are presumably being compensated in part because of their ability to make worthwhile inventive contributions. Sales personnel may have special provisions relating to base salaries, travel and entertainment expenses, commissions, etc. We will now consider some of the alternatives in connection with each of the major provisions mentioned.

General Provisions

Usually the agreement will include some statement of what is expected of the employee. This will include a recitation that the employee is expected to contribute to the economic welfare and growth of the company and will not knowingly take any action that will be to the detriment of the company. Such clauses are optional, but can aid in establishing the fairness of the agreement.

If the employment is not for a specific term, it should be clear from the document that no particular period of employment is contemplated. It can be stated that either the employer or the employee have the unrestricted right to terminate the employment at any time.

If it is contemplated the employee will devote substantially full time to the employment, it is well to include a provision that prohibits the employee from engaging in any outside commercial activity or business without the consent of the employer. To avoid the appearance of being over-reaching, it is well to modify the provision with a statement that the consent will not be unreasonably withheld.

It is important that the agreement not be in violation of any previous agreement of the employee. The new employee should make a representation that no such violation exists and that the employee will not disclose to the company any information which the employee is obligated to retain in secrecy by virtue of a previous agreement.

Invention and Copyright Assignment

If the employee is expected to make innovative contributions, an assignment of inventions is in order. The employee should be required to disclose promptly in writing to the company all inventions made during the period of employment. However, in most cases, it is preferable to limit the actual assignment of inventions to those that relate to the business of the company. The employee should be required to execute all documents necessary to secure to the company all rights in the inventions. This requirement should extend beyond the period of employment, but should then be at the expense of the company.

Agreements sometimes include provisions paying the employee a stipulated sum upon the filing of an application based on the employee's invention and another, perhaps larger, sum on the issuance of a patent. Less often, the agreement may provide for a sharing of royalties with the inventor.

If the employee is expected to do any substantial amount of writing for the company, it is well to include a statement that all rights in the written material are the property of the company and that all material written by the employee is to be considered as "works for hire". (A technical phrase that facilitates registration of the copyright in the name of the company.)

If the employee is expected to generate computer software, an assignment provision for the software, in addition to the copyright clause, should be included.

Non-competition

This is perhaps the trickiest clause of all. The intention is to keep the employee from taking advantage of information gained while in the employment of the company to damage the company after the employment is terminated. The clause is usually constructed carefully with emphasis on the enforceability. Another entirely different approach is to ignore enforceability and set forth clearly just what restrictions are placed on the employee. This is done with the thought that most employees will not violate an obligation they have undertaken irrespective of whether a court would enforce it. Which approach is taken depends upon the particular circumstances. The legal department will, without question, opt for the enforceable provision. For example, a clause such as the following could be included following the non-competition provision:

> The Employee recognizes that the foregoing non-competition provisions may not be legally enforceable and that they may, for a period of time, reduce the income available to the Employee, nevertheless, the Employee accepts those provisions as an ethical and personal obligation.

It is important for the non-competition provision to be limited in two ways: time and geographical area. The period of non-competition should be limited to some reasonable period, say, typically a year or two. It should also be limited to the geographical area in which the company does business or in which it has made specific plans for doing business in the immediate future. These elements are important if there is to be any hope of enforceability.

Companies are most frequently damaged by competition from a group of employees that leave together to join a competitor or to start a new enterprise. A provision can be included prohibiting the employee from engaging in business with a fellow employee for some specified period following termination of employment. The enforceability of such a provision is a question mark.

In recent years there has been much litigation in the high-tech fields resulting from groups of employees resigning from a company to start a competing business. Generally, the courts have been reluctant to enforce the non-competition provisions of the employment agreements. California is one state with a statute that makes post-employment non-competition agreements unenforceable. This is one instance in which it is desirable for the agreement to state that it is to be construed and enforced in accordance with the laws of some state other than California. This likely won't buy much if the agreement is made in California, and is less likely to be meaningful if the competing venture is also in California.

Because of the possibility the non-competition clause will not be enforceable, a severability clause is appropriate.

The attitude of the courts is more favorable toward the protection of confidential materials. If a competing venture violates the clear wording of previous employment agreements, but the enterprise takes care that it makes no use of confidential information from the previous employer, the courts may be lenient in the interpretation of the employment agreement. It may be different if it can be shown the new enterprise is profiting from the use of confidential information.

The surest way of writing an enforceable non-competition agreement is for the employer to have the option of continuing to pay the employee. In this case, the employee cannot argue that he is being denied an opportunity to make a living. The agreement can provide in the event of termination of employment:

(a) the ex-employee will, for a specified period, exert his best efforts to find employment that does not compete with the company;

(b) the company will have the option to pay the ex-employee, for all or part of the period, an amount equal to the difference between what the ex-employee earns and the salary previously paid by the company; and

(c) if the company elects to make such payments, the ex-employee will not engage in any competitive enterprise. If the company elects not to make such payments or to discontinue them, the ex-employee is free to work without restriction as to competitive activities.

A Typical Employment Agreement

The following is a more or less typical employment agreement for supervisory and engineering-type employees:

*
1 *name of employer*
2 *state of incorporation*
3 *name of employee*
4 *home address of employee*

EMPLOYMENT AGREEMENT

This is an agreement, effective ______________ 19____, *between [1]____________________, a [2]____________ company, (the "Company"), and [3]_____________________________, an individual residing at [4]____________________________, (the "Employee").

continued on page 6-5

continued from page 6-4

Background

The Company is in the business of *_____________________ _____________________and desires to employ the Employee for the purpose of advancing the business interests of the Company [or: and the Employee is in the employment of the Company]. In the regular course of its business the Company enters into confidential relationships with its customers and suppliers in which all aspects of information relating to the business or projects of the customer or supplier and services performed for the customer or by the supplier are to be kept secret.

** short description of the nature of the business*

The Company is from time to time required to assign to its customers inventions, or licenses under inventions, and to enter into and maintain agreements with its employees to do all things necessary to effect such assignments and to facilitate procuring letters patent or other protection thereon. Further, the Company desires to advance its competitive position by reserving all rights to inventions made by its employees and which it is not required to assign to its customers.

The Company desires the services of the Employee to contribute to and advance the competitive and financial positions of the Company by innovation and full-time directed efforts. The Employee in the course of such employment is expected to have access to trade secrets, customer names, actual and proposed developments and projects, financial and pricing information, and to other matters, including sales procedures and techniques, whose secrecy the Company desires to preserve. The Company is in a highly competitive business and could be irremediably damaged by disclosure of its trade secrets, developments, techniques, methods, names of customers or prospective customers, sales methods, pricing procedures, and other aspects of its business.

In consideration of the mutual undertakings relating to the employment of the Employee, the parties have agreed as follows:

(1) "Employment" means the period during which the Employee is employed by the Company and extends from the date when employment begins or the date of this Agreement, whichever is later, to the last day for which the Employee receives compensation from the Company as a full time employee.

continued on page 6-6

continued from page 6-5

(2) "Termination" means the last day of employment of the Employee by the Company irrespective of the reason for termination and whether voluntary or involuntary on the part of the Employee.

(3) "Innovations" means inventions, improvements, procedures, and techniques conceived or constructed by the Employee during Employment, which reasonably relate to the business or contemplated business of the Company at the time of the conception or construction, whether produced alone or in concert with others, and irrespective of whether made during or outside the usual working hours of the Employee or with or without the use of Company facilities or materials.

(4) The Employee agrees to use his [or her] best efforts to promote and advance the financial, technical, and competitive positions of the Company throughout the Employment and thereafter to the extent provided herein.

(5) The Employee agrees to keep complete and accurate records of all Innovations and to date and have witnessed all such records in an appropriate manner, as designated by the Company, so as to preserve and protect all legal rights therein. The Employee further agrees to disclose all Innovations promptly and fully to the Company, or to its designated representative.

(6) The Employee agrees to, and hereby does, assign to the Company each Innovation and agrees to execute and deliver to the Company, promptly upon request, whether during or subsequent to the Employment, all proper documents as the Company may reasonably deem necessary or desirable to obtain patent, copyright, or other legal protection in the United States and elsewhere and to vest legal ownership thereof in the Company.

(7) The Company agrees to pay to the Employee, in addition to other compensation, $______________ for each United States patent application filed by the Company on any invention made by the Employee during the Employment and assigned to the Company under the terms of this Agreement. The Company further agrees to pay to the Employee $________________ upon the issuance of each United States Letters Patent resulting from each such application, whether such issuance is during or subsequent to the Employment.

continued on page 6-7

continued from page 6-6

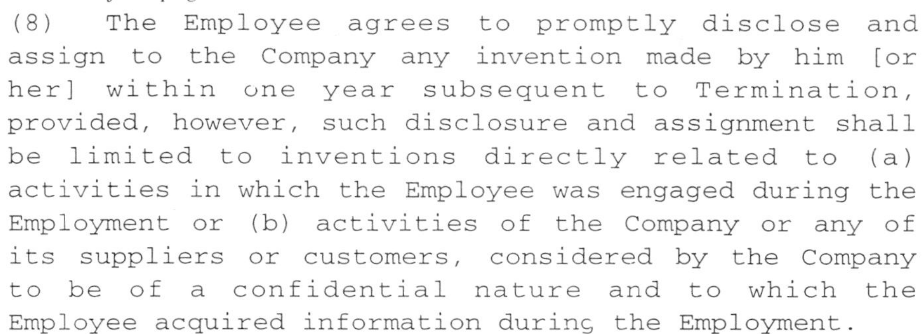

(8) The Employee agrees to promptly disclose and assign to the Company any invention made by him [or her] within one year subsequent to Termination, provided, however, such disclosure and assignment shall be limited to inventions directly related to (a) activities in which the Employee was engaged during the Employment or (b) activities of the Company or any of its suppliers or customers, considered by the Company to be of a confidential nature and to which the Employee acquired information during the Employment.

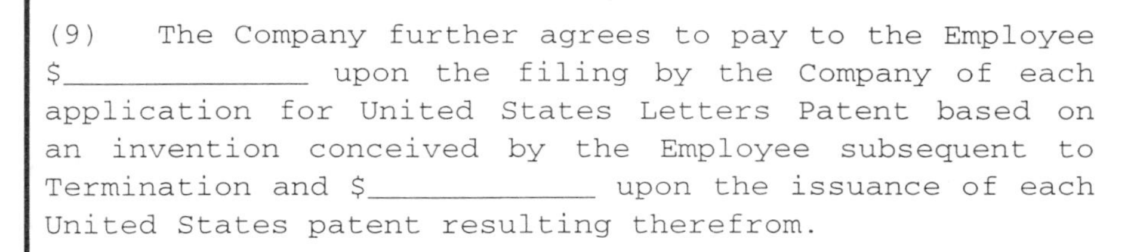

(9) The Company further agrees to pay to the Employee $_____________ upon the filing by the Company of each application for United States Letters Patent based on an invention conceived by the Employee subsequent to Termination and $_____________ upon the issuance of each United States patent resulting therefrom.

(10) The Employee agrees not to engage in any other employment or business venture during the Employment without the written consent of the Company, which consent shall not be unreasonably withheld.

(11) The Employee agrees that he [or she] will during the Employment, and for a period of _______ years subsequent to Termination, maintain in secrecy all information acquired by the Employee during the Employment concerning finances, business procedures, names and lists of customers and prospective customers, sales letters, proposals, trade secrets, and innovations relating to the Company or any of its customers or suppliers, or other matters of a confidential nature or which are designated by a representative of the Company to be among those matters to be regarded as confidential.

(12) The Employee acknowledges that the relationships between the Company and its customers and suppliers, and prospective customers and suppliers, are confidential, whether or not evidenced by a written instrument, and that the Company is under certain obligations to refrain from making use of or revealing information gained from its customers or suppliers, or resulting from work done for its customers, and the Employee agrees to and hereby does adopt all such obligations of the Company as his [or her] own and agrees to personally abide by all such obligations of the Company.

(13) The Employee acknowledges that he [or she] has no power to bind the Company and agrees not to attempt to

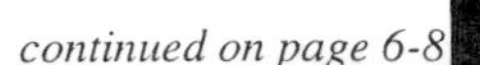

continued on page 6-8

continued from page 6-7

bind the Company to any obligation not authorized in writing by the Company.

(14) The Company agrees that all innovations made by the Employee prior to the Employment are to be excluded from this Agreement, provided all such excluded inventions are identified and described in writing, attached hereto and acknowledged by the signature of an authorized representative of the Company. The Employee agrees that all innovations not so disclosed and acknowledged shall be deemed to have been made subsequent to the beginning of the Employment.

(15) The Employee further agrees, upon Termination, to deliver to the Company all property of the Company including all originals and copies of documents and photographs, models, prototypes, tools, supplies and all other property of the Company of every kind. The Employee agrees that all documents relating to the Company, whether or not originated by the Employee, are the property of the Company.

(16) The Employee acknowledges that during the Employment he [or she] can reasonably expect to acquire information which if applied to a competitive endeavor would be harmful to the Company. Accordingly, the Employee agrees that for a period of ________ years subsequent to Termination, he [or she] will not engage in any activities directly competitive to the activities or business interests of the Company or advise or be employed by any company or other entity engaged in the design, manufacture or sale of products or services of the kinds performed, made or sold by the Company during the Employment. This prohibition of competitive activity is limited to the geographical areas in which the Company shall have done business during the Employment and those areas which, at the time of Termination, the Company has specific genuine intention to do business. The competitive restriction is further limited to those activities which the Company reasonably deems to be financially harmful to its interests.

The Employee acknowledges that the provisions of this Agreement may, for a limited period subsequent to Termination result in a decrease in earning capacity. However, the Employee represents that he [or she] has demonstrated abilities to earn substantial income from business activities non-competitive with the Company and has accepted the restrictions imposed here as a

continued on page 6-9

continued from page 6-8

result of his [or her] considered judgment of the benefits that may accrue from the Employment.

(17) The Employee, by initialing this Paragraph, asserts and affirms that he [or she]: (a) has read and understands each provision of this Agreement; (b) undertakes to perform each duty hereunder without reservation of any kind; and (c) is aware that the provisions herein can cause, for a limited time, a diminution of income and limit the scope of business opportunities. _______________

(18) The Employee warrants that he [or she] is under no obligation to any other entity that would in any way conflict with any obligation of the Employee hereunder. The Employee further warrants that he [or she] will not disclose to the Company any information with respect to which the Employee is under any obligation of confidentiality.

(19) This Agreement shall be construed and enforced in accordance with the laws of the state of [state of incorporation or business home of the Company, but not California] .

(20) This Agreement supersedes and replaces all former agreements or understandings with respect to the subjects matter hereof.

(21) If any provision hereof is determined to be invalid or unenforceable, the remainder of this Agreement shall be unaffected thereby and shall be enforceable against either party.

(22) This Agreement shall inure to the benefit of any successor, assignee or nominee of the Company as fully as if it had been an original party hereto.

____
[Company Name]

By_________________________
Title

____
Date

____
Employee

The Current Trend on Termination

The absolute right to fire an employee at any time for any reason, or no reason, is coming under increasing judicial fire. As usual, California leads the way. There have been a number of cases in which an ex-employee has sued the former employer for wrongful discharge, and an increasing number have been successful. The large awards, some in the six figures, have caused employers to include provisions in the employee contracts by which the employee acknowledges the employer's right to terminate the employment at any time. Probably more effective is the inclusion of "right-to-fire" provisions in the applications for employment.

Some employers have included in the employment agreements a provision providing for some dispute resolution mechanism. This is one situation in which arbitration seems to have a clear advantage over the court procedure. If the arbitration provision is constructed with reasonable care, such disputes can be settled within a month or two. This means the employee can, in most instances, continue employment until a settlement is reached. The company avoids the possibility of a large penalty such as it might incur from a case that lingers in the court system for four or five years. Quick arbitration can make a major reduction in legal costs and in the amount of an award.

The importance of this trend to an employer depends in large measure upon the business policies and size of the employing company. The company that is enlightened enough to recognize that its employees are as important to the success of the company as are its customers will likely have only minor problems in this area. But employers who still think that management is one part of the company, and a competing part of the company is represented by the employees, had better give serious consideration to an arbitration provision in the employment agreement.

In California, during the 1970's, there were practically no legal actions based on wrongful discharge. But those cases have grown exponentially throughout the 1980's. There were nearly one hundred cases filed in California in 1987 and the growth rate seems to be more than 30% per year. Other states seem destined to follow the trend in California.

For some selected situations, a provision somewhat as follows may be helpful.

If the employment of the Employee is terminated by the Company and the Employee believes that such termination is unjustified, the Employee shall have the right to arbitration, as set forth below, which the Employee agrees shall be the only remedial procedure.

The Employee shall notify the Company, within three business days after the termination, of his or her election to seek arbitration. The Employee and the Company shall each within five (5) days after such notice, designate one arbitrator and the two arbitrators shall by agreement select a third arbitrator. As a precondition to serving, each arbitrator shall execute an agreement to keep secret all confidential information relating to the Company.

continued on page 6-11

continued from page 6-10

The arbitrators shall have the right to take sworn testimony from the parties and shall have access to all pertinent Company records. The arbitrators shall, by majority vote, render a decision in the matter within thirty days after the selection of the third arbitrator. The employment of the Employee may, at the option of the Company, be continued during the period of arbitration.

Any award by the arbitrators in favor of the Employee shall not be for an amount greater than the compensation paid to the Employee during the six months previous to the termination except by unanimous approval of all three arbitrators. No award by the arbitrators shall require continued employment of the Employee. The compensation of the arbitrators shall be paid by the Company, provided, if no award is made in favor of the Employee, the compensation for the arbitrators shall be paid by the Employee. The decision of the arbitrators shall be enforceable in any appropriate court.

Chapter Seven

Stock Options and Stock Purchase Agreements

To provide added incentives for obtaining and keeping the services of selected skilled employees, many companies provide for an equity interest in the employing company. This is usually in the form of common stock or options to acquire common stock; for example stock could be given or sold to the employee at a discount from the market price. However, this may create an immediate tax liability for the employee. An alternative is to provide a qualified stock option plan under which selected employees receive options to purchase stock in the company. Qualified stock options are restricted to employees of the company and cannot be made available to others. The word "qualified" indicates the plan is qualified for certain tax benefits under Section 422A of the Internal Revenue Code of 1986. Under such an arrangement, the employee pays no tax at the time the option is granted. Another feature of the option plan is that the ownership of the options can vest over a period of years, so that if the employee is terminated prior to the full term, only a portion of the options are received by the employee.

Statutory Requirements

A qualified employee stock option plan must meet certain statutory requirements. Some of the most important are:

- A "plan" must be adopted by the Board of Directors and approved by the stockholders of the company. The Board can adopt the plan and put it into effect subject to approval by the stockholders at the next annual or other meeting within twelve months.

- The plan must state the aggregate number of shares being set aside for the options and the employees or class of employees (for example, "Key Employees") for which options will be made available.

- No options may be granted more than ten years after the plan is put into effect.

- The option period may not be longer than ten years.

- The option price must be no less than the actual market value of the stock at the time the option is granted. In the case of an employee who is the beneficial owner of ten percent or more of the outstanding stock of the corporation granting the option: (i) the option period must not be for more than five years and (ii) the option price must be at least 110 percent of the fair market value of the stock at the time the option is issued.

- The option must not be transferable other than by will or the laws of descent and distribution and is exercisable during the lifetime of the employee only by him.

- The plan must limit the aggregate fair market value of the stock for which one employee's options are exercisable for the first time, determined at the time the option is granted, to not more than $100,000 in any year. There are carryover provisions applicable in special cases.

The Option Plan

An option plan can be a powerful incentive, particularly in a start-up situation. There is a minimum of red tape in establishing such a plan and you can prepare your own documents. Generally, neither the grant nor the exercise of a qualified option subjects the employee to regular income tax. It is advisable to have your tax accountant review the proposed plan before its adoption to make sure it meets the statutory requirements to qualify for the tax benefits.

Two documents are necessary to put the plan into effect: a Master Plan and a model of the Individual Stock Option Agreement. The following is an example of a simple plan and an individual agreement suitable for many situations. There are, however, situations that are not provided for, such as the granting of non-qualifying stock options or grants of stock, and the like. A more complex agreement can include non-qualifying options along with qualified options in the same plan. But, remember KISS. Do not complicate the documents by attempting to cover all of the situations that might arise in the future. The original plan can be amended at any time. Later, we'll consider a more complex agreement, covering both qualified and unqualified options, that is "standard" with a particular Boston law firm.

PETROL, INC.

1987 INCENTIVE STOCK OPTION PLAN (THE "Plan")

1. Purpose of the Plan

The purpose of this Plan is to provide a means whereby Petrol, Inc. (the "Company") may, through the grant of incentive stock options (the "Options"), within the meaning of Section 422A of the Internal Revenue Code of 1986 as now in effect or hereafter amended, (the "Code") attract and retain employees of the Company (including officers and directors who are also employees of the Company) who, in the judgment of the Stock Option Committee (the "Committee") appointed by the Board of Directors to be responsible for the administration of the Plan, are considered especially important to the future of the Company ("Key Employees").

2. Shares Subject to the Plan

Options may be granted by the Company from time to time to Key Employees to purchase an aggregate of up to Two Hundred Thousand (200,000) shares of common stock of the Company par value $0.01 (the "Stock"), and such amount of shares shall be reserved for Options under the Plan (subject to adjustment as provided in Section

continued on page 7-3

continued from page 7-2

5(g)). The shares issued upon exercise of the Options may be authorized and unissued shares or shares held by the Company in its treasury. If any Option shall terminate, expire or, with the consent of the optionee, be canceled as to any shares, new Options may thereafter be granted covering such shares.

3. Administration of the Plan

The Plan shall be administered by the Committee, consisting of not less than three members appointed by the Board of Directors (the "Board") and serving at the Board's pleasure. Each member of the Committee shall be a "disinterested person" within the meaning of Rule 16b-3 under the Securities Act of 1933 or successor rule or regulation. Any vacancy occurring in the membership of the Committee shall be filled by appointment by the Board. The Committee may interpret the Plan, prescribe, amend, and rescind any rules and regulations necessary or appropriate for the administration of the Plan, or for the continued qualification of any Options, and make such other determinations and take such other action as it deems necessary or advisable, except as otherwise expressly reserved to the Board under the Plan. Any interpretation, determination or other action taken by the Committee shall be final, binding and conclusive.

4. Grant of Options

Subject to the provisions of the Plan, the Committee shall (a) determine and designate those Key Employees to whom Options are to be granted; (b) determine the number of shares subject to each Option; and (c) determine the time or times when and the manner in which each Option shall be exercisable and the duration of the exercise period; provided, however, that (i) no Option shall be granted after the expiration of ten years from the effective date of the Plan specified in Section 10 below, and (ii) the aggregate fair market value (determined as of the date an Option is granted) of all Stock for which any employee may be granted Options under the Plan exercisable for the first time in any calendar year shall not exceed $100,000. No director of the Company who is not also an employee shall be entitled to receive any Option.

5. Terms and Conditions of Options

Each Option shall be evidenced by an agreement in a

continued on page 7-4

continued from page 7-3

form approved by the Committee. Such agreement shall be subject to the following express terms and conditions and to such other terms and conditions as the Committee may deem appropriate:

(a) Option Period. Each option agreement shall specify the period for which the Option evidenced thereby is granted and shall provide that the Option shall expire at the end of such period. The Committee may extend such period provided such extension shall not in any way disqualify the Option as an incentive stock option. In no case shall such period, including any extensions, exceed ten years from the date of the grant, provided, however, that, in the case of an Option granted to a Key Employee who, at the time of the grant, is the beneficial owner of stock possessing more than ten (10) percent of the total combined voting power of all classes of stock of the Company (a "Ten Percent Stockholder"), such period, including extensions, shall not exceed five years from the date of the grant.

(b) Option Price. The option price per share shall be determined by the Committee at the time the option is granted, and shall not be less than (i) the fair market value per share of stock or (ii) in the case of an option granted to a Ten Percent Stockholder, One Hundred Ten Percent (110%) of the fair market value per share of stock on the date the Option is granted, as determined by the Committee.

(c) Exercise of Option. No part of any Option may be exercised until the optionee shall have remained in the employ of the Company for such period, which shall be no less than one year, after the date on which the Option is granted as the Committee may specify in the Option agreement, and the Option agreement may provide for exercisability in installments.

(d) Payment of Purchase Price upon Exercise. Each option agreement shall provide that the purchase price of the shares as to which an Option shall be exercised shall be paid to the Company at the time of exercise either in cash, or in such other consideration as the committee deems appropriate, including, but not limited to, common stock of the Company already owned by the optionee, having a total fair market value, as determined by the Committee, equal to the purchase price, or a combination of cash and such other consideration having a fair market value, as so determined, equal to the purchase price.

continued on page 7-5

continued from page 7-4

(e) Exercise in the Event of Death or Termination of Employment.

(i) If an optionee shall die (i) while in the employment of the Company or (ii) within three months after the termination of employment because of disability of the optionee, the optionee's Option may be exercised to the extent the optionee would have been entitled to do so on the date of the optionee's death or such termination of employment, by the person or persons to whom the optionee's rights under the Option pass by will or otherwise, or if no such person has such right, by the optionee's executors or administrators, at any time, or from time to time, within twelve months after the date of the death of the optionee but in no event after the expiration date set forth in the option agreement.

(ii) If the employment of an optionee by the Company is terminated (a) because of the disability of the optionee; or (b) involuntarily for other than cause; or (c) by reason of the retirement of the optionee in accordance with any Company tax-qualified plan or with consent of the Company, then the Optionee shall be entitled to exercise this option, to the extent the optionee would have been entitled to do so on the date of termination of the optionee, at any time, or from time to time, within three months after such date of termination of employment, but not later than the expiration date set forth in the option agreement.

(iii) If the optionee's employment by the Company is terminated voluntarily by the optionee, or by the Company for cause, the optionee's right to exercise this option shall expire on the earlier of the date of termination or the expiration date set forth in the option agreement. For this purpose, termination for cause shall mean termination of employment by reason of the optionee's willful breach or habitual neglect of his or her duties as an officer or employee of the Company, or the optionee's commission of a felony, fraud or willful misconduct that has resulted, or is likely to result, in material damage to the Company, all as the Committee in its sole discretion may determine.

(f) Nontransferability. No Option shall be transferable other than by will or by the laws of descent and distribution. During the lifetime of the optionee, an Option shall be exercisable only by the optionee.

continued on page 7-6

continued from page 7-5

(g) Adjustment. In the event of any change in the Stock by reason of any stock dividend, recapitalization, reorganization, merger, consolidation, split-up, combination or exchange of shares, or any rights offering to purchase Stock at a price substantially below market value, or of any similar change affecting the Stock, then the number and kind of shares which may thereafter be optioned and sold under the Plan and the number and kind of shares subject to option in outstanding option agreements and the purchase price per share shall be adjusted appropriately consistent with such change in such manner as the Committee may deem equitable to prevent substantial dilution or enlargement of the rights granted to, or available for, participants in the Plan.

(h) No Rights as Stockholder. No optionee shall have any rights as a shareholder with respect to any shares of stock subject to an Option prior to the date of issuance of a certificate for such shares.

(i) No Right to Continued Employment. The Plan and any Option granted under the plan shall not confer upon any optionee any right with respect to continuance of employment by the Company, nor shall it interfere in any way with the right of the Company to terminate employment at any time.

6. Compliance with Laws and Regulations

The Plan, the grant and exercise of Options, and the obligations of the Company to sell and deliver shares under Options, shall be subject to all applicable federal and state laws, rules and regulations and to such approvals by any government agency that may be required. The Company shall not be required to issue or deliver any certificates for shares of Stock prior to (i) the listing of such shares on any stock exchange on which the Stock may then be listed and (ii) the completion of any registration or qualification of such shares under any federal or state law, or any rule or regulation of any governmental body which the Company shall, in its sole discretion, determine to be necessary or advisable.

7. Investment Representation

The Committee may require the optionee to furnish to the Company, prior to and as a condition precedent to the issuance of any shares hereunder, an agreement, in

continued on page 7-7

continued from page 7-6

such form as the Committee may specify, in which the optionee represents the shares acquired by the optionee are being acquired for investment and not with a view to the sale or distribution thereof.

8. Restrictions on Disposition of Shares

The Company shall have a right of first refusal, in accordance with terms to be established by the Committee, on any resale of shares of stock acquired by exercise of an Option and each stock certificate shall bear a legend to that effect. All certificates for Stock delivered under the Plan shall also be subject to stop-transfer orders and other restrictions as the Committee may deem advisable under the rules, regulations, and other requirements of the Securities and Exchange Commission, any stock exchange upon which the stock is then listed and any applicable state and federal securities laws, and the Committee may cause a legend to be placed on such certificates to make appropriate reference to such restrictions. If the optionee desires to sell or transfer any Stock and receives a bona fide offer, the optionee shall submit in writing to the Company the identity of the offeror and all details of the terms of the offer. The Company shall have thirty (30) days from the receipt of the terms of the offer to elect to acquire the stock on identical terms. If the Company fails to exercise its purchase option, the optionee shall have the right, for a period of ten (10) business days after refusal of the option or the expiration of the option period, whichever is earlier, to sell the Stock to the original offeror on the identical terms submitted to the Company. With respect to any Stock not sold within the specified period, this option provision shall remain in full force and effect. The foregoing provisions of this Section 8 shall not be effective if and to the extent the Stock delivered under the Plan is covered by an effective registration statement under the Securities Act of 1933, or if such provisions are no longer required or desirable. In making such determination, the Committee may rely upon an opinion of counsel for the Company.

9. Amendment and Discontinuance

The Board may from time to time amend, suspend or discontinue the Plan, provided, however, subject to the provisions of Section 5(g), no action of the Board or of the Committee may (i) increase the number of shares

continued on page 7-8

continued from page 7-7

reserved for Options pursuant to Section 2, (ii) permit the granting of any Option at an option price less than that determined in accordance with Section 5(b), (iii) shorten the period provided for in Section 5(c) which must elapse between the date of granting an Option and the date on which any part of the Option may be exercised, or (iv) permit the granting of Options which expire beyond the period provided for in Section 5(a). Without the written consent of the optionee in each case, no amendment or suspension of the Plan shall alter or impair any Option previously granted under the Plan

10. Effective Date of the Plan

The effective date of the Plan shall be November 1, 1987, subject to approval of the stockholders of the Company holding not less than a majority of the outstanding shares.

The Plan shall terminate ten years from November 1, 1987 and no Option shall be granted after that date.

CONFIRMATION

I, John Doe, secretary of Petrol, Inc., certify that on October 6, 1987, the Board of Directors of Petrol, Inc. approved and adopted the foregoing Plan. The following individuals were appointed to the Committee:

Albert H. Taylor

Mary Anne Grobus

Raymond Lee

I further certify that on October 6, 1987, the stockholders of Petrol, Inc., by unanimous vote, approved and adopted the foregoing Plan.

____

John Doe, Secretary

Here is an individual option agreement that might be issued under the above plan.

PETROL, INC.

INCENTIVE STOCK OPTION AGREEMENT

This is an agreement between Petrol, Inc., Inc. (the "Company") and Michael Greenberg (the "Employee") and is effective as of June 1, 1988 (the "Date of Grant").

1. Option Grant

Pursuant to the provisions of the 1987 Incentive Stock Option Plan of the Company (the "Plan"), the Company hereby grants to the Employee, subject to the conditions set forth herein and in the Plan, an option to purchase from the Company all or any part of an aggregate of Two Hundred (200) shares of common stock (no par value) of the Company (the "Stock") at a purchase price of Twenty-five Dollars ($25.00) per share.

2. Expiration Date

This option shall expire six (6) years from the Date of Grant, which date is referred to as the "Expiration Date", and under no circumstances can any portion of this option be exercised after the Expiration Date.

3. Exercise of Option

Subject to the other terms and conditions herein, the percentages of total shares of this option shown below may be exercised on or after the indicated annual anniversaries of the Date of Grant:

Anniversary of the Date of Grant	Percentage Exercisable
First	10
Second	15
Third	20
Fourth	25
Fifth	30

Each exercise of any part of this option shall be pursuant to a written notice from the Employee to the Company, specifying the number of shares for which the option is being exercised, accompanied by the full payment of the purchase price for such shares. The purchase price shall be paid in cash, or in the discretion of the Committee (as defined in the Plan), in such other consideration as the committee deems appropriate, including, but not limited to, common stock of the Company already owned by the Employee, having a fair market value, as determined by the

continued on page 7-10

continued from page 7-9

Committee, equal to the purchase price, or a combination of cash and such other consideration having a fair market value, as so determined, equal to the purchase price. Notation of each partial exercise of this option shall be noted by the Company on Schedule I hereof.

4. Exercise in the Event of Death or Termination of Employment

(a) If the Employee shall die (i) while in the employment of the Company or (ii) within three months after the termination of employment because of disability of the Employee, this option may be exercised to the extent the Employee would have been entitled to do so on the date of the Employee's death or such termination of employment, by the person or persons to whom the Employee's rights under this option pass by will or otherwise, or if no such person has such right, by the Employee's executors or administrators, at any time, or from time to time, within twelve months after the earlier of the date of termination or death of the Employee, but in no event later than the Expiration Date.

(b) If the employment of the Employee by the Company is terminated (i) because of the disability of the Employee; or (ii) involuntarily for other than cause; or (iii) by reason of the retirement of the Employee in accordance with any Company tax-qualified plan or with consent of the Company, then the Employee shall be entitled to exercise this option, to the extent the Employee would have been entitled to do so on the date of termination of the Employee, at any time, or from time to time, within three months after such date of termination of employment, but not later than the Expiration Date.

(c) If the Employee's employment by the Company is terminated voluntarily by the Employee, or by the Company for cause, the Employee's right to exercise this option shall expire on the earlier of the date of termination or the Expiration Date. For this purpose, termination for cause shall mean termination of employment by reason of the Employee's willful breach or habitual neglect of his or her duties as an officer or employee of the Company, or the Employee's commission of a felony, fraud or willful misconduct that has resulted, or is likely to result, in material damage to the Company, all as the Committee in its sole discretion may determine.

5. Nontransferability

This option is not transferable other than by will or by the laws of descent and distribution. During the

continued on page 7-11

continued from page 7-10

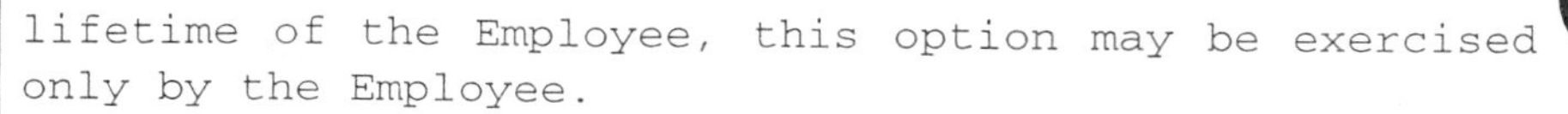

lifetime of the Employee, this option may be exercised only by the Employee.

6. Adjustment

In the event of any change in the Stock by reason of any stock dividend, recapitalization, reorganization, merger, consolidation, split-up, combination or exchange of shares, or any rights offering to purchase stock at a price substantially below market value, or of any similar change affecting the Stock, then the number and kind of shares subject to this option and their purchase shall be adjusted appropriately consistent with such change in such manner as the Committee may deem equitable to the Employee hereunder. Any adjustment so made shall be final and binding on the Employee.

7. No Rights as Stockholder

The Employee shall have no rights as a stockholder with respect to any shares of stock subject to this option prior to the date of issuance of a certificate for such shares.

8. No Right to Continued Employment

This option does not confer upon the Employee any right with respect to continuance of employment by the Company, and shall not interfere in any way with the right of the Company to terminate employment at any time.

9. Compliance with Laws and Regulations

This option and obligation of the Company to sell and deliver shares hereunder shall be subject to all applicable federal and state laws, rules and regulations and to such approvals by any government agency that may be required. The Company shall not be required to issue or deliver any certificates for shares of Stock prior to (i) the listing of such shares on any stock exchange on which the Stock may then be listed and (ii) the completion of any registration or qualification of such shares under any federal or state law, or any rule or regulation of any governmental body which the Company shall, in its sole discretion, determine to be necessary or advisable. Moreover, this option may not be exercised if its exercise, or the receipt of shares of Stock pursuant thereto, would be contrary to applicable law.

10. Restrictions on Disposition of Shares

Each certificate representing shares of Stock acquired upon the exercise of this option shall bear a legend giving effect to the restrictions set forth in the preceding Section 9. Each certificate for Stock

continued on page 7-12

continued from page 7-11

delivered upon exercise of this option shall also be subject to stop-transfer orders and other restrictions as the Committee may deem advisable under the rules, regulations or other requirements of the Securities and Exchange Commission, any stock exchange upon which the Stock is then listed, or any applicable federal or state securities laws, and the Committee may cause a legend to be placed on any such certificates to make appropriate reference to such restrictions. If the Employee desires to sell or transfer any Stock and receives a bona fide offer, the Employee shall submit in writing to the Company the identity of the offeror and all details of the terms of the offer. The Company shall have thirty (30) days from the receipt of the terms of the offer to elect to acquire the stock on identical terms. If the Company fails to exercise its purchase option, the Employee shall have the right, for a period of ten (10) business days after refusal of the option or the expiration of the option period, whichever is earlier, to sell the Stock to the original offeror on the identical terms submitted to the Company. With respect to any Stock not sold within the specified period, this option provision shall remain in full force and effect. The foregoing provisions of this Section 10 shall not be effective if and to the extent the shares of Stock delivered upon exercise of this option are covered by an effective and current registration statement under the Securities Act of 1933, or if and so long as the Committee determines that application of such provisions is no longer required or desirable.

11. Investment Representation

The Committee may require the Employee to furnish to the Company, prior to and as a condition precedent to the issuance of any shares hereunder, an agreement, in such form as the Committee may specify, in which the Employee represents the shares acquired by the Employee are being acquired for investment and not with a view to the sale or distribution thereof.

12. Employee Bound by the Plan

The employee hereby acknowledges receipt of a copy of the Plan and agrees to be bound by all of the terms and provisions thereof.

continued on page 7-13

continued from page 7-12

13. Notices

Any notice hereunder to the Company shall be addressed to it at:

248 Tremont Street
Boston, MA 02118

and any notice to the Employee shall be addressed to him at:

19 Williams Street
Cambridge, MA 02139

subject to the right of either party to designate in writing at any time some other address.

14. Counterparts

This Agreement may be executed in duplicate and the copies together or separately shall constitute one and the same instrument.

Petrol, Inc.

By__________________________

Title:

____

Employee

SCHEDULE I

DATE	NO. OF SHARES ISSUED	AUTHORIZED BY:

This plan calls for vesting over a five-year period which is more or less typical. In addition, the vesting percentages are non-linear. Only 10 percent of the options are exercisable at the end of the first year, and the final 30 percent do not vest until the end of the fifth year. If the employee leaves or is terminated at the end of the first year, only ten percent of the total number of options can be exercised by the employee. If the employee leaves at the end of the fourth year, only 70 percent of the options can be exercised. Additional options can be granted to any employee at any time.

An alternative arrangement, suggested by an aggressive start-up company in California, provides that all of the options vest in one year. A smaller number of options are granted than would usually be the case in a five-year vesting plan and each year the performance of each employee is evaluated and a new award made. This is considered a more effective incentive system than providing for a larger amount of stock to vest over five or more years.

Comprehensive Option Plan

The following is an example of an option agreement that covers both qualified and unqualified options.

TAILORMAID CORPORATION

1987 LONG-TERM INCENTIVE OPTION PLAN

1. Purposes of the Plan

The Tailormaid Corporation 1987 Long-Term Incentive Option Plan (the "Plan") shall be effective as of January 1, 1987. The purposes of the Plan are (i) to associate more closely the interest of key employees with those of shareholders of Tailormaid Corporation (the "Company") (ii) to assist the Company in attracting and retaining management personnel with outstanding experience and ability, and (iii) to motivate key employees toward the achievement of long-term business success.

2. Administration of the Plan

The Plan shall be administered by the Personnel and Compensation Committee (the "Committee") of the Company's Board of Directors. Members of the Committee shall not be eligible to participate in the Plan.

The Committee shall have power to administer and interpret the Plan and to adopt such rules and regulations as the Committee deems desirable. The Committee's interpretations of the Plan and all actions taken and determinations made by the Committee, within the powers vested herein in the Committee, shall be conclusive and binding on all parties, including the Company, its shareholders and participating employees of the Company.

3. Eligibility for Participation

Participants in the Plan shall be recommended by the Chief Executive Officer of the Company and approved by the Committee. Participation shall be limited to key employees (including officers and directors who are also employees) of the Company who, in the opinion of the Committee, have an opportunity and potential to

continued on page 7-15

continued from page 7-14

contribute significantly to the sound growth and profitability of the Company and to influence the long-term success of the Company.

4. Shares of Stock Subject to the Plan

The shares which may be delivered under the Plan pursuant to Stock Options shall not exceed an aggregate of 500,000 shares of the common stock of the Company (the "Stock"). Any shares subject to an option which for any reason expires or is terminated unexercised may again be the subject of an option or right under the Plan.

The shares of Stock that may be delivered under the Plan pursuant to Restricted Stock Awards shall not exceed 250,000 shares. Any shares awarded under the Plan which for any reason are forfeited by the terms of the Plan shall be deemed not to have been awarded and shall be available for other awards.

All of such Stock may be either shares of authorized but unissued Stock or treasury shares.

5. Awards Under the Plan

Awards under the Plan may be in the form of (i) non-qualified stock options ("NQSO's"), (ii) incentive stock options ("ISO's"), (NQSO's and ISO's, individually or collectively, are also referred to as "Stock Options"), or (iii) grants of Stock ("Restricted Stock Awards").

6. Stock Options

All Stock Options granted under the Plan shall be on the following terms and conditions together with such other terms and conditions as the Committee may establish consistent with the Plan:

(a) Election. Prior to receiving a Stock Option award, an employee shall be notified that he or she has been selected to receive an award and will be asked to elect to receive the award either in the form of NQSO's or ISO's. Such election shall be irrevocable and shall be made prior to the date on which the Stock Option grant is made and the option price determined. An employee who fails to make such election shall receive the award in the form of NQSO's.

(b) Price. (i) The option exercise price for Stock covered by ISO's shall be not less than the fair market value of the optioned Stock as of the date of grant. (ii) The option exercise price of Stock covered by

continued on page 7-16

continued from page 7-15

NQSO's shall be not less than 85% of the fair market value of the optioned Stock as of the date of grant.

(c) Award Size and Frequency. The maximum number of shares available for any grant and the frequency of grants to participants shall be determined by the Committee, provided, the aggregate fair market value (determined as of the date of the option grant) of the shares for which any one employee may be granted ISO's in any calendar year (under all plans of the Company) shall not exceed $100,000 plus any unused limit carryover as determined by Section 422A of the Internal Revenue Code.

(d) Term and Exercise of Stock Options. ISO's shall expire five years after the date of grant. NQSO's shall expire ten years after the date of grant. Stock Options shall be exercisable at the rate of 50% per year commencing one year after the date of grant. To the extent that Stock Options are not exercised when they become initially exercisable, they shall be carried forward and be exercised at any time until the expiration of such Stock Options.

(e) Termination of Stock Options.

(i) "Normal Retirement Age" has the meaning as defined in the then current Company Retirement Plan. "Retirement" means the retirement of a participant in the Plan pursuant to the Company's Retirement Plan as then in effect. "Disability" means the inability to engage in any substantial gainful activity by reason of any medically determinable physical or mental impairment which can be expected to result in death or to be of long, continued and indefinite duration. If an optionee reaches Normal Retirement Age or his or her employment with the Company is terminated prior to the expiration of an NQSO by reason of death, Retirement or Disability, then all outstanding NQSO's granted hereunder to that optionee shall terminate twelve (12) months after the reaching of Normal retirement Age or such termination of employment, whichever is earlier. The same shall apply to the termination of ISO's except, if the termination of employment is by reason of Retirement, all outstanding ISO's granted to that optionee shall terminate three (3) months after Retirement.

(ii) If an optionee dies during the twelve-month period (or the three-month period in the case of ISO's) set forth above, then the optionees heirs or legal representatives shall have the right, for an additional

continued on page 7-17

continued from page 7-16

twelve (12) months from the date of death to exercise outstanding Stock Options to the extent they were exercisable by the optionee prior to his or her death.

(iii) If the employment of an optionee by the Company is terminated for any reason other than those stated in paragraph 6(e)(i), then all outstanding Stock Options held by such optionee shall terminate as of the date of termination of employment.

(iv) No provision of this Plan, or anything in this paragraph 6(e), shall be deemed to permit the exercise of any Stock Option after the expiration date thereof or prior to one year after the date of grant thereof.

7. Restricted Stock Awards

All Restricted Stock Awards granted under the Plan shall be on the following terms and any other terms adopted by the Committee consistent with the Plan:

(a) Award Size and Frequency. The maximum number of shares of Stock available for any Restricted Stock grant and the frequency of grants to participants shall be determined by the Chief Executive Officer, subject to the approval of the Committee, provided the total fair market value of Restricted Stock Awards to any one individual in any one calendar year shall not exceed 50% of the annual salary (excluding all fringe benefits) of that individual in effect at the beginning of that calendar year.

(b) Restriction Period. Ownership of the Restricted Stock and the enjoyment of all rights appurtenant thereto are subject to restrictions as set forth herein for a period of five years from the date of grant ("Restriction Period").

(c) Retention by the Company of Restricted Stock. Restricted stock when issued will be represented by a certificate of Stock registered in the name of the participant to whom the Restricted Stock Award has been made. During the Restriction Period, certificates representing the Restricted Stock shall be retained by the Secretary of the Company, together with stock powers or other instruments of assignment, each to be endorsed in blank by the participant, which will permit transfer to the Company all or any portion of the Restricted Stock that shall be forfeited or that shall not become vested in accordance with the Plan.

(d) Rights of Participants. Each participant holding Restricted Stock shall have the right to vote the Restricted Stock, to receive and retain all cash

continued on page 7-18

continued from page 7-17

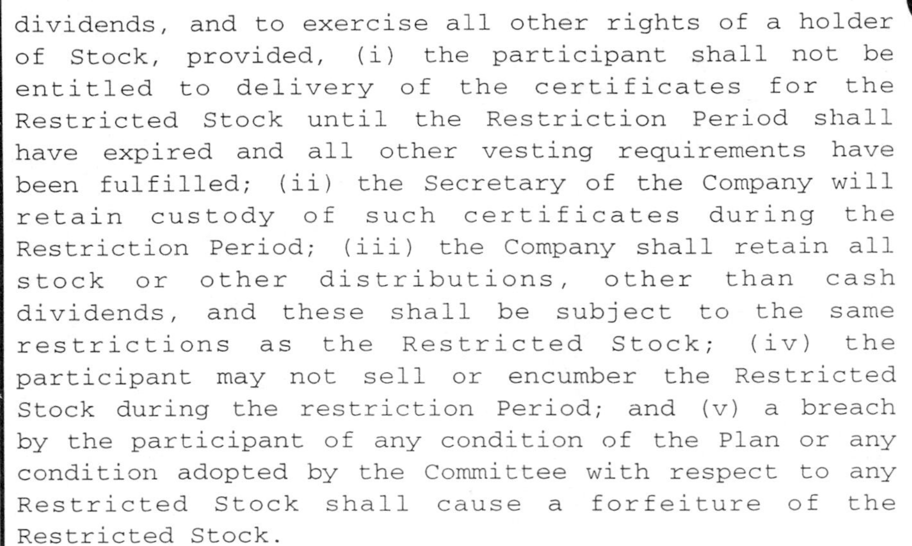

dividends, and to exercise all other rights of a holder of Stock, provided, (i) the participant shall not be entitled to delivery of the certificates for the Restricted Stock until the Restriction Period shall have expired and all other vesting requirements have been fulfilled; (ii) the Secretary of the Company will retain custody of such certificates during the Restriction Period; (iii) the Company shall retain all stock or other distributions, other than cash dividends, and these shall be subject to the same restrictions as the Restricted Stock; (iv) the participant may not sell or encumber the Restricted Stock during the restriction Period; and (v) a breach by the participant of any condition of the Plan or any condition adopted by the Committee with respect to any Restricted Stock shall cause a forfeiture of the Restricted Stock.

(e) Delivery of Restricted Stock. Subject to the following paragraph (f) of this Section, at the end of the Restricted Period the certificates representing Restricted Stock shall be delivered to the participant.

(f) Forfeiture of Restricted Stock Awards. If the employment of a recipient of a Restricted Stock Award is terminated because of death, Retirement or Disability, then a pro rata portion of the Restricted Stock, equal to the number of months since the grant of the Restricted Stock Award divided by sixty, shall be delivered to the participant or such participant's heirs or legal representatives. Upon termination of employment for any other reason of an employee holding a Restricted Stock Award, such Restricted Stock Award shall be forfeited and the certificates representing such Stock shall be immediately cancelled.

8. Dilution and Other Adjustments.

(a) In the event of any change in the outstanding shares of Stock of the Company by reason of any stock dividend, split, recapitalization, merger, consolidation, combination or exchange of shares or other similar corporate change, an equitable adjustment shall be made, as determined by the Committee, in the maximum number of shares issuable under the Plan, and in the number of shares subject to outstanding Stock Options or in the option price of such shares. Such adjustments made by the Committee shall be conclusive.

continued on page 7-19

continued from page 7-18

9. Miscellaneous Provisions.

(a) Notwithstanding any other provision of this Plan, if the Committee becomes aware that a participant of the Plan for any reason has (i) used for profit or disclosed confidential information or trade secrets of the Company to unauthorized persons; (ii) breached any contract with or violated any legal obligations to the Company, (iii) committed any fraud which harms, or threatens to harm, the Company; or (iv) engaged in any activity, or omitted any duty, that would have constituted grounds for discharge for cause by the Company, such participant shall forfeit all undelivered portions of all awards under the Plan.

(b) The award of Stock Options shall convey no rights as a stockholder of the Company to the holder.

(c) No Stock Options or Restricted Stock Awards, or any right or interest therein, shall be assignable or transferable by the participant except by will or the laws of descent and distribution. During the lifetime of the participant, the Stock Options shall be exercisable only by the participant.

(d) All Stock Options and Restricted Stock Awards under the Plan shall be evidenced by agreements in such form, and containing such terms and conditions, consistent with the Plan, as the Committee shall approve.

(e) Shares of Stock pursuant to a Stock Option or a Restricted Stock Award shall be conditioned upon conformance with all requirements of law including the Securities Act of 1933 and all other applicable state and federal laws and regulations, and the Company shall be under no obligation to issue any Stock that would cause it to be in violation of any such law or regulation. As a condition precedent to the transfer of any Stock to a participant, that participant may be required to undertake in writing, in a form acceptable to the Committee, to comply with legal restrictions related to the participant's subsequent disposition of the Stock as the Committee or the Company shall deem necessary or advisable as a result of any applicable law or regulation. Stock certificates delivered to any participant may carry legends reflecting any restrictions or agreements related to the Stock.

continued on page 7-20

continued from page 7-19

(f) No employee or other person shall have any claim or right to be granted an award under this Plan. Neither this Plan or any action taken in pursuance thereof shall be construed to give any right to be retained as an employee of the Company.

I, John Doe, Secretary of Tailormaid Corporation, certify the foregoing Option Plan was adopted by the Board of Directors of Tailormaid Corporation on August 31, 1986 and was approved by the stockholders of Tailormaid Corporation on February 5, 1987.

____
Secretary, Tailormaid Corporation

A participant-company agreement will be required for carrying out the Plan. It will be based on the provisions of the above plan and can be modeled after the participant agreement already discussed. The plan can also be modified to include awards dependent upon the particular performance of the employee or upon the profit growth of the overall enterprise. Note, however, that the special tax benefits relate only to the qualified stock option plan that meets the requirements of Section 422A of the Internal Revenue Code. Generally, it is this author's preference to have a separate plan for each kind of award. This results in simpler documents more easily understood by each class of participants.

Non-qualified Option Agreement

If stock options are to be given to someone who is not a bona fide employee of the company granting the option, the option will not qualify for favored tax treatment. Here is an example of such a non-qualified option that is suitable for a non-employee or, with some modification, for an employee:

NON-QUALIFIED OPTION AGREEMENT

This is an Agreement, effective July 1, 1988, between Orleans Banks, Inc., a Delaware corporation, ("OBI") and George Leander, an individual residing at 68 Beacon Street, Boston, Massachusetts, ("George").

1. Background

OBI desires to have George serve on its Board of Directors and assist in the management of OBI and George desires to participate in both management and ownership of OBI. The parties agree as follows:

continued on page 7-21

continued from page 7-20

2. Option Grant

For valuable consideration, the receipt and adequacy of which are acknowledged, OBI grants to George, subject to the conditions set forth herein, an option to purchase from OBI all or any part of an aggregate of 2000 shares of common stock (no par value) of OBI (the "Stock") at a purchase price of Twenty-five Dollars ($25.00) per share.

3. Expiration Date

This option shall expire five years from the effective date of this Agreement.

4. Exercise of Option

Each exercise of this option shall be pursuant to a written notice from George to OBI, specifying the number of shares for which the option is being exercised, accompanied by the full payment of the purchase price for such shares.

5. Nontransferability

This option may be transferred only by will or by the laws of descent and distribution or with the written consent of OBI.

6. Adjustment

In the event of any change in the Stock by reason of any stock dividend, recapitalization, reorganization, merger, consolidation, split-up, combination or exchange of shares, or any rights offering to purchase stock at a price substantially below market value, or of any similar change affecting the Stock, then the number and kind of shares subject to this option and their purchase shall be adjusted appropriately consistent with such change in such manner as OBI shall reasonably deem equitable.

7. No Rights as a Stockholder

George shall have no rights as a stockholder with respect to any shares of stock subject to this option prior to the date of issuance of a certificate for such shares.

continued on page 7-22

continued from page 7-21

8. Representations by George

George represents that he has been given access to the books and records of OBI, knows the kinds and numbers of shares of OBI stock authorized and outstanding, and understands the risks involved in exercising any part of this option. George further represents that any Stock acquired hereunder is acquired for the purposes of investment and not with a view to distribution. George further represents that he understands the Stock has not been registered under the Securities Act of 1933, has not been registered under the laws of any state, and is subject to restriction as to sale or transfer.

9. Compliance with Laws and Regulations

This option and obligation of OBI to sell and deliver shares shall be subject to all federal and state laws, rules and regulations and to such approvals of any government agency that may be required. OBI shall not be required to issue or deliver any certificates for shares of Stock prior to (i) the listing of such shares on any exchange on which the Stock may then be listed and (ii) the completion of any registration or qualification of such shares under any federal or state law, or any rule or regulation of any governmental body which OBI, in its sole discretion, may determine to be necessary or advisable.

10. Restrictions on Disposition of Shares

Each certificate representing shares of Stock acquired upon the exercise of this option shall bear a legend giving effect to the restrictions set forth in the preceding Section 9. Each certificate for Stock delivered upon exercise of this option shall also be subject to stop-transfer orders and other restrictions as OBI may reasonably deem advisable under the rules, regulations or other requirements of the Securities and Exchange Commission, any stock exchange upon which the stock is listed, or any applicable federal or state securities laws, and OBI may cause a legend to be placed on such certificates to make appropriate reference to such restrictions. The foregoing provisions of this Section 10 shall not be effective if and to the extent the shares of Stock delivered upon exercise of this option are covered by an effective and current registration statement under the Securities Act

continued on page 7-23

continued from page 7-22

of 1933, or if and so long as OBI determines that application of such provisions is no longer required or desirable.

Orleans Banks, Inc.

By______________________________

Title:

____

Sale of Unregistered Stock

There are complex legal restrictions on the sale of stock in a corporation, both federal and in the individual states. If the stock has not been subjected to the rigors of a registration with the Securities and Exchange Commission, the stock cannot be sold "publicly." The following is an example of a private sale of stock in which the company has a first right of refusal to repurchase the stock.

STOCK PURCHASE AGREEMENT

This is an Agreement, effective ________________________, 1988, between Krystal Inc., a Delaware corporation (the "Company"), and George Smith (the "Purchaser"). The parties agree as follows:

1. Sale of Stock.

The Company agrees to sell and deliver herewith to the Purchaser Two Hundred Thousand shares of its $0.01 par value common stock (the "Stock") at a price of ten cents ($0.10) per share.

2. Restrictions on Transferability.

The Purchaser warrants that he (i) is purchasing the stock for purposes of investment and with no view to resale or distribution; (ii) is familiar with the financial and other circumstances of the Company; (iii) recognizes the risks represented by this purchase of the Stock; and (iv) is in a financial position such that loss of this investment will not present any undue hardship on the Purchaser. The Stock has not been

continued on page 7-24

continued from page 7-23

registered under the Securities Act of 1933 and, accordingly, may not be offered for sale, sold or otherwise transferred except (i) upon effective registration of the securities under the Securities Act of 1933, or (ii) upon acceptance by the Company of an opinion of counsel in such form and by such counsel, or other documentation, as shall be satisfactory to counsel for the Company that such registration is not required.

3. First Right of Refusal by the Company.

In the event the Purchaser desires to sell or transfer any Stock and receives a bona fide offer, the Purchaser agrees to submit in writing to the Company the identity of the offeror and all details of the terms of such offer. The Company shall have thirty (30) days from the receipt of the terms of the offer to elect to acquire the Stock on identical terms. In the event the Company fails to exercise its purchase option, the Purchaser shall have the right, for a period of ten (10) business days after refusal of the option or the expiration of the option period, whichever is earlier, to sell the Stock to the original offeror on the identical terms submitted to the Company. With respect to any Stock not sold within the specified period, this provision shall remain in full force and effect.

4. Legends on Stock Certificates.

Each stock certificate issued by the Company to the Purchaser shall bear an appropriate legend stating the restrictions on transfer of the Stock and referencing this Agreement.

____

George Smith, Purchaser

Krystal Inc.

By___________________________

Legend for Stock Certificate

The following is a typical legend for use on a stock certificate issued on unregistered stock and which is subject to a buy-back or other agreement with the company.

These securities have not been registered under the Securities Act of 1933 or any state securities laws. They may not be sold or offered for sale in the absence of an effective registration statement as to the securities under said Act and any applicable state securities laws or an opinion of counsel satisfactory to the issuer that such registration is not required.

Any disposition of any interest in the securities represented by this Certificate is subject to restrictions, and the securities represented by this Certificate are subject to a right of first refusal contained in a certain agreement between the record holder hereof and the corporation, a copy of which will be mailed to any holder of this Certificate without charge within five (5) days of receipt by the issuer of a written request.

A Note of Caution

The preceding comments and examples are of general utility when issuing stock or stock options; however, the reader is cautioned that the regulations governing the legal transfer of unregistered stock are complex. No options should be granted or stock sold prior to consultation with an individual familiar with both federal and state laws and regulations.

Chapter Eight

Representative and Distributor Sales Agreements

Sales Representation Agreements

Sales may be handled directly by sales employees, through distributors, through independent sales representatives or by some combination of them. In any situation there should be a definitive agreement between the sales entity and the company. The kinds of agreements needed are quite different, but the following elements should be considered in drafting a typical sales representative agreement:

Provisions of Sales Representative Agreements

- The precise duties the representative is expected to perform, and whether the representative is full- or part-time.
- The territory in which the representative is to devote his efforts.
- Sales commissions payable to the representative.
- Allocation of Sales Expenses.
- Payment Terms.
- Expenses.
- Authority granted to the representative.
- Confidentiality and non-competition by the representative.
- What, if any, other products the representative may sell.
- Use of other individuals as salesmen or representatives.
- Reporting activities to the company.
- Termination.

Duties of the Representative

The sales representative is an independent contractor and is not an employee of the company. This must be made clear both in explicit words and in the nature of the relationship. Irrespective of the words used in the agreement, if the sales person is in fact treated as an employee, there is a risk the company may be held liable for failure to withhold income tax and for other violations. The sales representative must be free as a general rule to select his own working hours and to arrange his own schedule of activities. The company can, of course, make it clear the sales task is a full time activity and prohibit the sales representative from engaging in other businesses. This is not always appropriate, because sales representatives frequently represent several non-competing companies.

Sales Territory

Generally, sales representatives are assigned specific geographical areas in which to carry on their own activities. Even if the areas are clearly defined, there is likely to be a certain amount of overlap. A sales representative may take an order from a customer in his territory and the goods are delivered to the same or another customer in the territory of another representative. A sale may be made to a division of a company having a home office in another territory. If the purchase order is actually issued from the parent company, provisions must be made for division or assignment of the sales commission.

Commissions

The amount of the commissions should be specified on either a linear or non-linear scale. For example, a representative may be paid a certain percentage of sales up to a certain amount and a larger or smaller percentage for sales over that amount. There may also be distinctions between the particular accounts. For example, the company may have been selling to regular customers in the territory for a period prior to the advent of the representative. These may be designated as “house accounts” in the agreement and be subject to a lower rate.

The agreement may also provide for a “draw” by which the sales representative can receive advances against future commissions.

Usually the commission is expressed as a percentage of sales, but the calculation of the applicable sales price must be specified. It is usual for the commission to exclude items on which the selling company has no mark-up, such as duties, sales or use taxes, license fees and shipping expenses. The sales price may be expressed as net of trade discounts, returns and allowances. It must be specified when and under what conditions the commissions are paid to the representative. For example, commissions may be paid when the orders are received, when the merchandise is shipped, or when the monies are received from the customer. The agreement may provide for advances against commissions to the representative.

Sales Expenses

Provision must be made for the traveling, entertainment and other expenses of the representative. These may be paid in whole by the salesperson and compensated by a higher commission rate. Alternatively, the sales representative may be given a fixed monthly allowance for expenses, or may submit expense reports from time to time for reimbursement. The company may wish to limit expenses to those approved in advance by the company.

Authority of the Sales Representative

This is an important provision. To just what extent is the sales representative permitted to bind the company? Is he permitted to issue a quote on specifications, price or delivery? Does he have the power to accept a purchase order that binds the company to the terms of the order? Is the sales representative to be given any latitude in the pricing of the goods? Most often, the sales representative is barred from making any price, delivery or performance commitments not previously approved by the company or making other binding commitment on the company. Ordinarily, all purchase orders taken by the representative are subject to acceptance by the company. It is usual to prohibit the representative from removing or altering trademarks or from creating or distributing any literature not previously approved by the company.

Employment of Others

The representative may be limited to his own personal activities or he may be permitted to have employees or other independent representatives to assist in the sales efforts. The agreement should be specific on these points and, if employees or representatives are permitted, the primary representative should be required to enter into agreements with each associate to abide by and carry out the terms of the primary agreement.

Confidentiality

It is usually important that a sales representative be prohibited from using the information gained while representing the company to the detriment of the company during or after the period of the sales representation agreement. This can include a non-disclosure or confidentiality agreement and the same considerations apply as were discussed in Chapter 5. However, such agreements do not usually limit confidential information to written materials.

In the case of a sales representative, it is usually wise to place more emphasis on customer lists and sales information. These are covered in the sample agreement set forth below.

Term and Termination

The term and the conditions of termination must be specified. The agreement may have an initial specified term after which either party may terminate the agreement after some specified period of notice. Sometimes a shorter period of notice is specified for the initial period of the agreement. The conditions following termination may be different depending upon which party terminates.

Subsequent to termination of the agreement, it is important that the sales representative does not immediately become the sales representative for a competing product. The sales agreement will usually require the salesperson to refrain, during and for a time subsequent to termination of the sales relationship, from competitive activities that would be harmful to the company. Such provisions are more likely to be enforceable if the representative is an independent contractor than they would be if he were an employee. It is, nevertheless, important to include: specific geographical areas from which competitive activities are barred; a time limit for the restrictions; and a clear definition of the prohibited activities. Philosophically, the agreement should be tempered to permit the widest possible latitude in the activities of the representative short of actual damage to the company.

It is also customary to continue to pay commissions to the representative for sales made in his territory for some period after the termination. This provides some compensation to the representative for sales efforts made prior to the termination and for refraining from competitive activities for some period of time. Another provision that can serve as an aid in keeping current on sales prospects is one that limits post-termination commissions to sales made to prospects that were previously reported to the company.

Reporting of Activities

It is important the company be at all times fully informed of activities carried on by the representative, including copies of all correspondence and current lists of all sales prospects. It is also advisable, in most cases, to have a periodic report from the representative including a forecast of activities for the ensuing period and a forecast of sales. The details of such a report will vary widely depending upon the industry and the particular sales arrangements.

The following is one example of a more or less typical sales representative agreement. However, the arrangements vary widely from company to company, so the agreement must be tailored to best fit the needs of your particular situation.

SALES REPRESENTATIVE AGREEMENT *(Example 1)*

This Agreement, effective as of July 1, 1989, between Sharleen Corporation, a Delaware corporation, ("Sharleen") and George A. Smith, whose address is 2256 Myland Avenue, Sylvan Lake, Michigan 48053 ("Smith").

Background

Sharleen is in the business of manufacturing non-woven products and desires to sell such products in the automotive field. Peters is experienced in selling to the automotive industry and desires to act as sales representative for Sharleen in that industry.

1) "Vehicles" means automobiles, trucks, vans, and other power driven vehicles, including component parts therefor, intended for use on the public highways.

2) "Net Sales" means the net invoice price, less discounts, shipping charges, returns and allowances, of goods sold by Sharleen for use in the manufacture of Vehicles.

3) "Annual Period" means the period from January 1 through the next succeeding December 31. The first Annual Period shall be deemed to begin on the effective date of this Agreement and end on December 31, 1990.

4) Smith will act as sales representative for Sharleen in the area of Vehicle supplies and agrees to exert his best efforts in the promotion and sales of products manufactured by Sharleen. It is acknowledged that Smith will be the sole representative of Sharleen in the United States and Canada with respect to goods used in the manufacture of Vehicles. Smith may act as sales representative for other manufacturers or distributors whose products may or may not be complimentary to those sold by Sharleen, but Smith shall not act as sales representative for, or

continued on page 8-5

continued from page 8-4

in any way promote, any product in direct competition with products handled by Smith for Sharleen.

5) Sharleen agrees to pay Smith a commission of seven percent (7%) on the first One Million Dollars ($1,000,000.00) of Net Sales and five percent (5%) of the Net Sales in excess of One Million Dollars ($1,000,000.00) in each Annual Period.

6) If the total commissions accruing to Smith under Paragraph (5) for the first Annual Period shall amount to less than Twenty-eight Thousand Dollars ($28,000.00), then Sharleen agrees to pay to Smith the difference between such accrued commissions and Twenty-eight Thousand Dollars ($28,000.00).

7) Sharleen shall pay commissions accruing hereunder to Smith on the Fifteenth day of each month for all payments on Net Sales received by Sharleen during the previous calendar month.

8) This Agreement may be terminated at any time by either party upon thirty (30) days written notice. If such notice of termination is given by Sharleen, commissions shall be payable on all Net Sales from orders received by Sharleen within one year from the date of such notice, provided, however, if such notice of termination is given by Sharleen within the first Annual Period of this Agreement, such payments shall be limited to commissions on Net Sales initiated by and resulting directly from the efforts of Smith. Nothing herein shall affect the minimum commission payment guaranteed under Paragraph (6) hereof.

9) Notices under this Agreement shall be effective four days after the date of mailing by certified mail, return receipt requested:

if to Sharleen, to:

Office of the President
Sharleen Corporation
2727 Market Street
Wilmington, Delaware
19801

if to Smith, to:

George A. Smith
2256 Myland Avenue
Sylvan Lake, Michigan
48053

continued on page 8-6

continued from page 8-5

10) This Agreement is the only agreement between the parties and is in lieu of any and all previous understandings, representations, and agreements, whether oral or written.

11) This Agreement may not be assigned by Smith other than to a corporation in which Smith is the beneficial owner of a majority of the outstanding shares of voting stock.

Sharleen Corporation

By_________________________
President

____
George A. Smith

The above agreement was prepared for the specific situation. It does not include any terms relating to expenses of the representative, reporting of sales activities to the company, confidentiality, or non-competition.

The following example is somewhat more typical, but the terms must always be tailored to the particular situation at hand.

SALES REPRESENTATION AGREEMENT *(Example 2)*

This is an Agreement, effective July 1, 1983, between First Science Corporation, a Delaware corporation, ("FSC") and John Francis Associates, a California corporation, (the "Representative").

Background

The Representative has an established business in which it sells products in fields related to those of interest to FSC. The Representative desires to act as manufacturers representative for products of FSC in the territory and on the terms as set forth herein. It is not contemplated the Representative will establish any new quarters or incur any unusual expenses in preparing itself to perform the tasks contemplated by this Agreement and will not be required to forego any income-producing present efforts or enterprises.*

*This sentence is more important in agreements with overseas representatives, where the laws concerning the termination of a representative are somewhat different from those in the United States.

1. Definitions

"Territory" means California, Nevada, Arizona, Oregon, Washington, and Hawaii.

continued on page 8-7

continued from page 8-6

"Products" means integrated solid state circuits, intermodal conversion devices, and memory enhancement boards manufactured by FSC.

"Net Sales" means the invoiced price of Products excluding duties, tariffs, insurance, sales and other taxes, and shipping expenses, net of returns and allowances to the extent such returns and allowances are customary in the trade.

2. Appointment of Representative

FSC appoints the Representative as its exclusive [non-exclusive] representative in the Territory. FSC agrees to forward to the Representative, for action, copies of all inquiries, quotations and correspondence to and from customers or potential customers in the Territory concerning the Products.

3. Acceptance and Duties of the Representative

The Representative accepts the appointment as exclusive [non-exclusive] manufacturer's representative for FSC in the Territory and agrees to:

a) use its best efforts to promote and sell the Products within the Territory and to support FSC in every reasonable way with the objective of enhancing the profitability of FSC;

b) attend and represent FSC at all trade shows in which FSC has arranged for an exhibit;

c) issue quotations to prospective customers only in accordance with the published then current terms and prices of FSC;

d) furnish FSC promptly with copies of each quotation submitted by the Representative including the date and the name of the prospect;

e) provide for FSC each month copies of all documents and correspondence in the possession of the Representative relating in any way to the business of FSC, whether generated or received by the Representative;

f) provide to FSC, within thirty days after the end of each calendar quarter, a summary of all visits to customers or potential customers, and its best forecast of orders expected to be received in the ensuing quarter; and

continued on page 8-8

continued from page 8-7

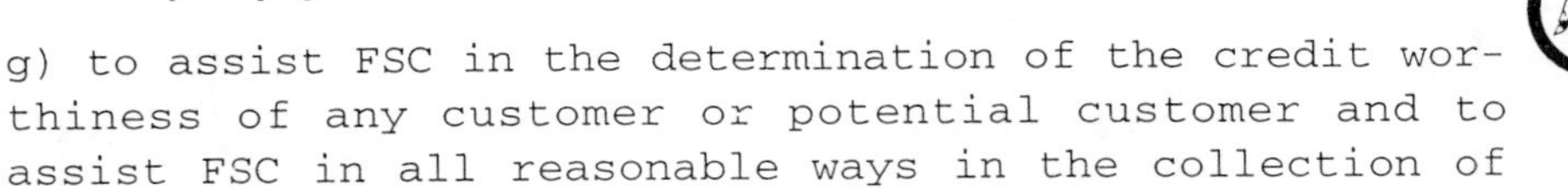

g) to assist FSC in the determination of the credit worthiness of any customer or potential customer and to assist FSC in all reasonable ways in the collection of overdue amounts resulting from sales within the Territory.

4. Prices and Terms of Payment

FSC shall have the sole right to establish and, from time to time, revise, the prices and terms and conditions of sale of the Products. All prices and payments shall be in United States Dollars.* FSC shall make reasonable efforts to give the Representative reasonable advance notice of changes in prices or terms of sale, but reserves the right to make such changes at any time. The Representative shall have no authority to bind FSC to any contract or order and no such contract or order shall be binding on FSC until accepted in writing by FSC.

*This sentence is appropriate for representatives in foreign countries. It may be omitted from domestic agreements.

5. Commission Payments

FSC agrees to pay to the Representative a commission of Ten Percent (10%) of the Net Sales made within the Territory, subject to the limitations of Section 5 "Split Commissions". All commission payments will be made before the fifteenth day of the month following receipt of payment by FSC. Each commission payment will be accompanied by an accounting report of each invoice on which the commissions are computed. All shipments and invoices are to be made directly from FSC to the customer.

6. Split Commissions

The Representative will receive full commissions on each sale which is obtained by the Representative without material assistance of any other representative of FSC and which is shipped into the Territory. If FSC deems a sale to have been made through material efforts of one or more other representative along with the Representative, it shall have authority to divide the commission among the representatives, and its decision in this matter shall be final, provided, the total commission paid to all representatives shall not be less than the commission rate provided for herein. The following shall serve as non-binding guideposts for FSC in making its determination:

a) One-half of the commission to be paid to the representative of the territory in which the major selling effort was performed;

b) One-fourth of the commission to be paid to the repre-

continued on page 8-9

continued from page 8-8

sentative for the territory from which a formal order is received;

c) One fourth of the commission to be paid to the representative of the territory into which the Product is first shipped.

7. Returns and Allowances

Charges against commissions based on returns or allowances shall be made against the Representative's next payable commission until charged in full.

8. Sales and Promotional Expenses

FSC shall supply the Representative with sales promotion literature, without charge, that in its judgment is deemed adequate and desirable. The Representative shall bear all expenses incidental to selling, whether direct or indirect, provided, FSC may, in its sole discretion, arrange for trade shows in the Territory and shall pay all expenses of such trade shows other than the direct expenses of the Representative. The Representative shall have the right to arrange for trade shows on its own behalf, but shall not be entitled to reimbursement for any expense in connection therewith. FSC shall not be responsible for any expenses incurred by the Representative unless approved in writing by FSC.

9. Demonstration Equipment

FSC may from time to time, at its own discretion, consign equipment to the Representative for demonstration purposes. FSC shall pay the shipping charges of such equipment to the Representative, but the Representative shall be responsible for all return shipping charges. The Representative agrees to carry, at its own expense, broad coverage insurance on all equipment so consigned to the extent necessary to fully protect the interests of FSC. The Representative agrees to return all consigned equipment at any time upon the request of FSC.

10. Competitive Products

The Representative shall not promote, offer for sale, or demonstrate any product or service that FSC reasonably deems to be competitive with the Products. The Representative agrees to keep FSC fully informed of the name and product line of each company it represents. The Representative agrees that all information of FSC related to the Products,

continued on page 8-10

continued from page 8-9

customer lists, sales techniques, operating plans, and technical information are confidential information of FSC and agrees to maintain all such information in confidence and not to release such information to others without the written authorization of FSC. This obligation of confidentiality shall survive any termination or expiration of this Agreement for a period of three years thereafter.

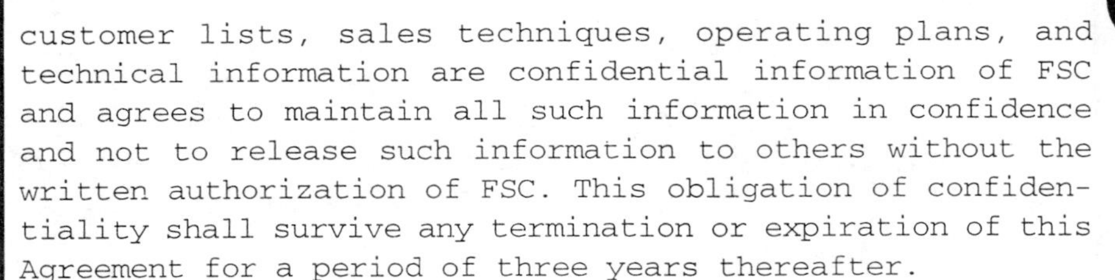

Each party agrees it will not employ or offer employment to, or make any other sales, service or consulting arrangement with any individual employed by the other during the term of this Agreement. This restriction shall survive any termination of this Agreement for a period of one year after such termination.

11. Term and Termination

This Agreement shall continue in force until terminated by one of the parties hereto. Either party shall have the right to terminate this Agreement at any time by ninety (90) days advance notice, provided, if either party shall reasonably conclude that this Agreement is being breached by the other, and such violation is not cured within ten days after notice thereof, the party not in breach shall have the right to terminate this Agreement by twenty (20) days advance notice.

Upon termination by either party, all conditions of this Agreement shall terminate as of the effective date of such notice except for the following:

a) The Representative shall promptly deliver to FSC, not later than the effective date of such termination, all equipment, parts, manuals, sales literature, prospect lists, customer correspondence and all other property belonging to FSC or which is generated by the Representative during this Agreement and which relates to the Products or to FSC.

b) FSC agrees to credit the Representative with all commissions based on orders received and accepted by FSC prior to the date of termination. Further, if this Agreement is terminated by FSC, for any reason other than breach of this Agreement, the Representative shall be credited with commissions on orders received and accepted by FSC within six months after the date of termination, provided, such orders were documented and forecasted by the Representative prior to the notice of termination. All commission payments provided for in this Section 11 shall be subject to the conditions set forth in Sections

continued on page 8-11

continued from page 8-10

5 and 6 hereof. Renewals or extensions of existing orders or contracts beyond their original fixed terms shall be considered to be new orders.

c) Upon termination by either party for any cause, the Representative agrees that it will not, for a period of one year after the effective date of termination, promote, offer for sale or demonstrate any product or service that is directly competitive with the Products, provided, this restriction shall not apply to any geographical area in which FSC is not active in sales promotion at the time of termination of this Agreement.

d) The confidentiality obligations and the restrictions on employment of employees of the other party as set forth in Section 10 hereof shall survive termination of this Agreement.

12. Complete Agreement and Assignment Rights

This Agreement represents the full understanding between the parties, and all prior agreements, understandings, and representation, whether written or oral, are of no further force or effect. This Agreement is for personal sales and promotional services and is not assignable by the Representative.

13. Notices

All notices hereunder shall be effective on the date received and shall be sent by certified mail, return receipt requested,

if to the Representative, to:	and if to FSC, to:
John Francis Associates 14570 Ventura Boulevard North Hollywood, CA 91604	First Science Corporation 1414 Young Street Lincolnshire, IL 60197

John Francis Associates	First Science Corporation
By____________________	By____________________
Title:	Title:

Here is another form of representative agreement in which the representative is permitted to sell other non-competing products and which contemplates overseas representatives. The representative is the exclusive representative for certain defined products, but is permitted to sell and collect commissions for other products of the company.

MARKETING AGREEMENT *(Example 3)*

CANFIELD MANUFACTURING CORPORATION

This is an agreement, effective July 15, 1986, between Canfield Manufacturing Corporation, a Delaware corporation, ("Canfield") and John Garson, an individual residing at 432 Mindell Street, Brookeville, Maryland ("Garson").

1. Background

Garson has had extensive experience in the marketing and sales analysis of microwave analysis systems. Canfield is in the business of developing and manufacturing such microwave analysis systems. It is the desire of both parties that Garson serve, under the conditions set forth below, as sales specialist and representative for microwave analysis systems to be designed and manufactured by Canfield.

2. Definitions

"Products" means microwave analysis systems sold by Canfield, but does not include recording systems or media. Products shall be deemed to include service contracts on Products and to exclude peripheral equipment used in connection with such Products, including but not limited to computer systems, custom interfaces, software packages purchased from others for resale, and photographic and other materials and supplies.

"Territory" means the entire world.

"Net Sales" means monies received by Canfield, less trade discounts and allowances, shipping costs, duties, tariffs, and costs of returns, from sales of Products.

3. Appointment of Garson

Canfield appoints Garson as its exclusive world-wide sales representative for Products. Garson accepts the appointment and agrees to use his best efforts to promote and support the business of Canfield, provided, however, Garson shall have the right to simultaneously engage in other non-competitive business efforts. Garson shall

continued on page 8-13

continued from page 8-12

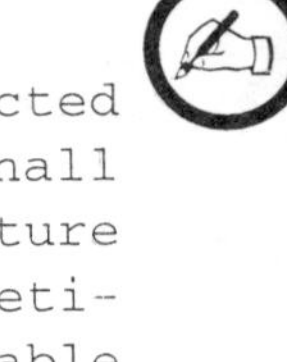

provide assistance in preparing specifications directed to the requirements of the market place. Garson shall assist Canfield with the content of product literature and shall be involved in discussions regarding competitive pricing of Products. Garson shall make reasonable efforts to locate potential customers, prepare specifications, and work in conjunction with Canfield in the preparation of proposals for special systems. The terms of sale and commissions shall be negotiated by the parties for such special equipment in each instance.

Canfield will provide reasonable support for Garson and shall provide Garson, on a regular basis, with literature, price information, demonstrations at Canfield's facility, Product output samples and the like. All quotations issued by Garson shall be in accordance with Canfield's standard terms and conditions, as set forth from time to time by Canfield, subject to special exceptions as may be agreed upon in advance by Canfield.

Garson will furnish Canfield promptly with copies of all letters and quotations submitted to or received from customers or prospective customers and copies of every other document, either generated or received by Garson, which relate in any way to the subjects matter of this Agreement.

At the end of each calendar quarter, or oftener at the option of Garson, Garson shall deliver to Canfield a written forecast of sales of Products by Garson for the ensuing three, six and nine month periods. Such forecasts shall include the names of prospective customers and the associated Product designations.

Garson represents and warrants that no requirement of or provision in this Agreement in any way violates or is in conflict with any other agreement or legal obligation of Garson.

Canfield understands the competitive value and possible overlap of prospects from one principal to another and agrees for a period of one year after termination of this Agreement to hold the proprietary information of Garson in confidence and not to disclose such information to any third party, but Canfield shall have the unrestricted right to use such information in the conduct of its own business affairs.

4. Prices and Terms of Payment

Canfield shall, from time to time, fix prices and terms of sale of the Products and shall notify Garson of any

continued on page 8-14

continued from page 8-13

change in such prices or terms of sale. Canfield shall have sole authority with respect to the extension of credit to any customer of Canfield, provided, Garson shall assist Canfield in determining the credit worthiness of customers or prospective customers, and shall provide Canfield with any information known to Garson relating to such credit decisions. Garson shall have no power to bind Canfield to any agreement without the advance written approval of Canfield.

5. Commission Payments

Canfield shall pay to Garson commissions on the Net Sales as follows:

Products sold and delivered in North America:	17.5%
Service contracts on Products:	17.5%
Products ordered from and shipped to destinations outside North America (in addition to commissions paid by Canfield to foreign representatives):	7.5%
Sales of other Canfield products initiated and negotiated by Garson:	17.5%

All commissions shall be paid to Garson on the fifteenth day of the month following the month in which the monies for the corresponding sales are received by Canfield. Each commission payment to Garson will be accompanied by a statement listing each invoice on which the commission was computed. Canfield will invoice each customer directly for all shipments and shall forward a copy of each invoice to Garson. In the event any customer is delinquent in its payment obligations to Canfield, Garson agrees to assist Canfield in all reasonable ways to collect such overdue payments. Charges against commissions based on returns, claims and allowances, as determined by Canfield, shall be made against Garson's next payable commissions until fully adjusted.

6. Sales and Promotional Expenses

Garson shall be an independent contractor and shall have no authority to make any binding commitments upon Canfield other than those expressly provided for in writing by Canfield. Garson shall bear all expenses in connection with sales, whether direct or indirect, other than for sales literature, technical data, price sheets, demonstrations at Canfield's facility, etc. as provided

continued on page 8-15

continued from page 8-14

by Canfield. Canfield shall not be responsible for and shall not reimburse Garson for any expenses incurred without the prior written approval of Canfield.

7. Competitive Activities

Garson shall not promote, offer for sale, or demonstrate any product or service that Canfield reasonably deems to be competitive with the Products. Garson agrees that all sales techniques developed pursuant to this Agreement and all trade secrets and proprietary information are the exclusive property of Canfield. Garson agrees to keep all such information confidential, during and subsequent to the term of this Agreement, and shall not disclose such information to anyone, except as authorized in writing by Canfield.

8. Patent, Trademark and Copyright Warranty

Canfield agrees to defend at its own expense any suit or legal action brought against Garson based on alleged infringement of any patent, trademark or copyright resulting from the sale or use of any Product, any trademark applied to any Product by Canfield, or any written material provided by Canfield, provided such suit or action is in no way based on or the result of any act by Garson not authorized in writing by Canfield. Canfield agrees to defend at its own expense any action against Garson based on a warranty by Canfield of any Product or liability from the use of any Product sold by Garson, provided such action is not in any way the result of any modification of the Product by or upon the advice of Garson or on any warranty, express or implied, made by Garson without the express written authorization of Canfield. No provision of this Section shall be binding upon Canfield unless Garson shall have given prompt written notice to Canfield of any legal action or threatened action.

9. Employment

Canfield and Garson each agree they will not negotiate in connection with the employment of, or employ, anyone employed by the other at any time during the term of this Agreement and will not do so for a period of two (2) years after the termination of this Agreement.

10. Trademarks

Garson agrees to use due care in the protection of any trademark adopted by Canfield and not to cover, modify or

continued on page 8-16

continued from page 8-15

remove any Canfield trademark applied to any Product. Garson agrees not to make use of any Canfield trademark in connection with any other product or service and not to use any other trademark or trade designation in connection with any Product.

11. Term of Agreement

This Agreement shall continue in force until terminated by ninety (90) days notice by either party to the other, provided, however, if Canfield shall reasonably judge that Garson is in breach of this Agreement or is not making his best efforts to promote and sell the Products, Canfield shall have the right to terminate this Agreement by thirty (30) days notice to Garson. Upon notice of termination, Garson shall promptly deliver to Canfield, not later than the effective date of such termination, all equipment, software, parts, manuals, sales literature, customer lists, prospect lists and all other property generated pursuant to this Agreement or otherwise belonging to Canfield. Upon such notice of termination, all conditions of this Agreement shall terminate on the effective date of such notice, except for the following:

(a) the provisions specifically stated herein to apply subsequent to termination of this Agreement; and

(b) Canfield shall credit Garson with commissions in accordance with the terms, conditions and limitations of this Agreement, (a) for all sales of Products (including sales of other products of Canfield that were initiated and negotiated by Garson) resulting from orders received by Canfield prior to the effective date of termination of this Agreement and accepted by Canfield; and (b) If this Agreement is terminated by notice given by Canfield, Garson shall, in addition, be credited with the stated commissions for all sales of Products (including sales of other products of Canfield that were initiated and negotiated by Garson) resulting from orders received by Canfield within thirteen (13) months after the date of such termination that are accepted by Canfield and were documented and forecasted by Garson prior to notice of termination.

12. Notices

All notices under this Agreement shall be in writing and sent by Certified Mail Return Receipt Requested and shall be effective as of the date of mailing.

continued on page 8-17

continued from page 8-16

Such notices if to Canfield

shall be sent to:

Canfield Manufacturing
Corporation
Post Office Box 275
Nashua, New Hampshire
03061

and if to Garson, to:

John Garson
P.O. Box 6541
Olney, MD 20832

13. Entire Agreement

This Agreement represents the full understanding between the parties and all prior agreements, understandings, promises and the like, whether oral or written, are hereby cancelled and of no further effect.

14. Assignment of Agreement

This Agreement is for professional services to be rendered by Garson and is not assignable by him to any other entity, whether voluntarily or involuntarily, except with the written advance approval of Canfield, and upon any attempted assignment in violation of this Agreement, Canfield shall have the right to terminate this Agreement immediately.

____
John Garson

Canfield Manufacturing
Corporation

By________________________
Title:

Distributor Agreements

Distributors are more than sales representatives. Usually, the distributor carries an inventory and resells product he buys from the manufacturing company. Most often, the distributor sells many different products, usually into related markets. Distributor agreements are more diverse with respect to terms even than representative agreements. Each one must be crafted carefully to fit the needs of the situation. Some of the terms to be considered include the following.

Provisions of a Distributor Agreement

- Conduct of the Business
- The inventory requirements to be placed on the distributor.
- The terms of payment by the distributor, prices and volume discounts.
- Minimum Purchases
- Restrictions on the distributor with respect to trademarks, warranties, and representations.
- Insurance requirements on the distributor—for inventory and product liability.
- Promotion and advertising responsibilities of the distributor.
- Exclusivity with respect to competitive products.
- Pricing structure and guarantees. Delivery obligations.
- Term and Termination.
- Post Termination Conditions.

DISTRIBUTION AGREEMENT

LASER CORPORATION OF ATLANTA

This is an Agreement, effective January 1, 1989, between Laser Corporation of Atlanta, a Georgia corporation ("Laser") and Oriel Johnson Company, a Delaware corporation, (the "Distributor").

1. Background

Laser is engaged in the design, manufacture and sale of lasers and laser products. The Distributor is experienced in the merchandising of technical devices and instruments in fields related to lasers and laser products. The Distributor desires to add the products of Laser to its inventory and to actively promote the sale of Laser products.

continued on page 8-19

continued from page 8-18

2. Appointment and Acceptance

Laser appoints the Distributor its exclusive distributor of certain laser and laser products, defined specifically in Appendix A, (the "Products") directly sold to and installed in the territory described in Appendix B (the "Territory") and the Distributor accepts that appointment. Laser agrees it will not, during the term of this Agreement, offer Products for direct sale or delivery in the Territory except through the Distributor and agrees to refer to the Distributor all inquiries and orders for Products received from any entity in the Territory. Irrespective of the foregoing, Laser may make direct sales to entities having a place of business or a subsidiary or associated company within the Territory provided such entity has a principal place of business outside the Territory and such Products are not shipped by Laser into the Territory.

3. Partial Obligations of the Distributor and Laser

The Distributor agrees to purchase from Laser an initial inventory as set forth in Appendix C and further agrees that it will subsequently maintain an inventory of Products at least equal to the initial inventory. The Distributor agrees to vigorously promote the sale of Products within the Territory and to support the business of Laser in every reasonable way with the objective of increasing the profits of Laser. All quotations made by the Distributor shall be made in accordance with Laser's standard prices and terms of sale as set forth from time to time by Laser. The Distributor shall not deviate from such terms or prices without advance written authorization by Laser. The Distributor will furnish Laser promptly with copies of all letters and quotations submitted to or received from customers or prospective customers and copies of every other document, either generated or received by the Distributor, that relates in any way to the subjects matter of this Agreement. Laser agrees to supply the Distributor, without charge, with such sales promotion materials, literature, specifications, and price lists that in its reasonable judgment are adequate and desirable. Laser agrees to forward to the Distributor for follow-up, copies of all inquiries it receives from the Territory.

4. Prices and Terms of Payment

Laser reserves the right to fix, and from time to time to revise, the prices and terms of sale of the Products, but shall give the Distributor at least thirty (30) days

continued on page 8-20

continued from page 8-19

advance notice of any such change. The Distributor shall be responsible for any extension of credit to its customers and collections of such accounts shall be the sole responsibility of the Distributor. Laser shall retain a security interest in all Products shipped to or on behalf of the Distributor until Laser has been paid in full for such Products, and the Distributor agrees to execute all proper documents for filings under the Uniform Commercial Code. The Distributor shall receive discounts from Laser's then current list prices in accordance with the schedule set forth in Appendix D. All shipping costs, duties and other charges relating to transport or transfer of the Products to the Distributor or its customer shall be the responsibility of the Distributor.

5. Relationship of the Parties

Each party hereto is an independent contractor. Neither party shall act as the representative or legal agent of the other and neither party shall assume or create any obligation, express or implied, in the name of or on behalf of the other.

6. Conduct of the Business

a) The Distributor represents that it has the personnel, facilities and skill required to act as distributor for the Products and agrees to maintain appropriate sales and service offices in the Territory. The Distributor agrees to use its best efforts and devote such time and expend such funds as may reasonably be necessary to sell, service and promote the Products throughout the Territory.

b) The Distributor will conduct all of its business in its own name, except as otherwise provided herein or authorized in writing by Laser, in such manner as it sees fit. The Distributor will pay all expenses related to its office, sales efforts, travel and other activities. Laser shall be responsible for the expenses and acts of its employees and agents.

c) Laser shall be solely responsible for the design, development, supply, production and performance of the Products. The Distributor shall assist Laser in the promotion and preservation of its trademarks and shall not remove or alter any trademark in literature or on Products supplied by Laser. The Distributor agrees to cooperate fully with Laser in the prosecution or defense of any action of trademark or patent infringement related to the Products.

continued on page 8-21

continued from page 8-20

7. Limited Warranty

The Products shall be warranted by Laser as set forth in Appendix E and the Distributor shall pass this warranty through to its customers. Laser makes no other warranty of any kind and any warranty of suitability for any particular purpose is specifically disclaimed. Under no circumstances shall Laser be responsible for consequential damages. The Distributor shall be responsible for informing the customer of all disclaimers and limitations of liability by Laser. The warranty terms of Appendix E, and no others, shall apply to all customers of the Distributor, but Laser's direct responsibility shall be to the Distributor and no Products shall be returned to Laser except by the Distributor after written permission is provided by Laser.

8. Forecasts of Expected Orders

The Distributor agrees to furnish to Laser, quarterly reports of calls on or to customers and prospective customers on behalf of Laser together with its best forecast of expected orders, including the names and addresses of the associated customers, for the subsequent three and six month periods.

9. Minimum Purchases

It is an express condition of the continuation of this Agreement that the Distributor makes minimum purchase of the Products in each calendar quarter as set forth in Appendix A. Laser shall have the right to change the minimum levels of purchase as set forth in Appendix A by twelve (12) months advance notice to the Distributor.

10. Competitive Products

The Distributor shall not promote, offer for sale, or demonstrate any product or service that Laser reasonably deems to be competitive with the Products. The Distributor agrees that Laser shall be privy to all customer and prospect lists developed pursuant to this Agreement and all confidential information and trade secrets shall remain the exclusive property of Laser. The Distributor agrees to retain in confidence all such confidential information, during and subsequent to the term of this Agreement, and shall not use or disclose such information to anyone unless authorized in writing by Laser. Confidential information shall be limited to information that Laser notifies the Distributor is proprietary or of a confidential nature.

continued on page 8-22

continued from page 8-21

11. Shipments

Laser shall quote to the Distributor available shipping dates and agrees to make shipment as promptly as circumstances reasonably permit. Title to and responsibility for Products shipped to the Distributor shall pass to the Distributor upon delivery by Laser to a common carrier or such other agency as the Distributor may request.

12. Responsibility for Unforeseeable Circumstances

Neither party shall be responsible for failure to conform to this Agreement, except for payment by the Distributor for Products, if such failure results from causes beyond its control including strikes, riots, labor disputes, storms, fires, embargoes, acts of war, and the like.

13. Insurance

The Distributor agrees to carry broad coverage accident and liability insurance in an amount not less than two million dollars ($2,000,000.00) per occurrence, to make copies of such policies available to Laser on request, and upon request by Laser to make Laser a named insured under such policies as its interests may appear.

14. Acceptance of Orders

a) No order shall be deemed to be accepted by Laser unless a final formal purchase order has been received by Laser and has been acknowledged in writing.

b) Laser shall reasonably promptly, but in no event later than thirty (30) days after receipt thereof, notify the Distributor of its acceptance or refusal to accept each order received by Laser. Laser shall have the right to refuse any order it deems not in the best interests of Laser to accept and shall notify the Distributor promptly of its reasons for any such refusal.

15. Term and Termination

This Agreement shall continue in force for a period of one year from the effective date hereof and may be terminated on the first anniversary of such date by either party by sixty (60) days advance notice. In the event this Agreement is not so terminated, it shall remain in force until terminated at the end of any calendar year by either party by ninety (90) days advance notice, provided, however, (a) if the Distributor fails to make payments for

continued on page 8-23

continued from page 8-22

any Products as provided herein, Laser shall have the right to terminate this Agreement by ten (10) days advance notice, provided, if the Distributor brings the account to current status within such ten-day period such notice shall be of no effect; or (b) if the Distributor fails in any calendar quarter to purchase the minimum quantity of Products as provided herein, Laser shall have the right to terminate this Agreement by thirty (30) days advance notice, provided, if the Distributor places sufficient orders for immediate delivery to bring the purchases for that quarter to the requisite total, such notice shall be of no effect; or (c) if either party shall in any other way breach this Agreement, the other party shall have the right to terminate this Agreement by sixty (60) days advance notice, including the details of the alleged breach, provided, if such party cures the breach within the sixty-day notice period, such notice shall be of no effect.

16. No Assignment of this Agreement

This Agreement is not assignable by either party without the written consent of the other party.

17. Notices

Notices under this Agreement shall be effective only if in writing and mailed by certified mail, return receipt requested,

if to the Distributor to:

Oriel Johnson Company
21 Commerce Drive
Cranford, NJ 07016

if to Laser to:

Laser Corporation of
Atlanta
2345 Peach Tree Road
Atlanta, Georgia 30304

18. Complete Agreement

This Agreement represents the full understanding between the parties and all prior agreements, understandings and promises, whether oral or written, are hereby cancelled and of no further effect.

continued on page 8-24

continued from page 8-23

19. Execution

Each party executing this Agreement on behalf of a corporation personally warrants he has full authority to execute this Agreement on behalf of such corporation and that this Agreement is binding on that corporation.

Laser Corporation of
Atlanta

By_______________
Title:

Oriel Johnson Company

By_________________
Title:

Chapter Nine

Patent License Agreements and Assignments

The preparation, filing, and prosecution of patent applications are beyond the reach of most individuals and, indeed, are beyond the capabilities of most attorneys. A special breed of attorney trained in this particular discipline is required. You can, of course, make use of the information provided here to gain the most from such an attorney. The same general rules apply: There is no requirement that patent applications be written in obtuse, nonsensical, legalistic language. After the application is prepared by the attorney, be sure you read it carefully and be sure you understand everything in it. You will have a better patent for exercising this care. However, the same limitations do not apply to license agreements. You can perfectly well write your own license agreements.

Protection of Conception Dates

Even though you don't write your own patent applications, a procedure should be established for protecting the conception dates of any inventions. The procedure is simple if it is carried out methodically. The first step is a full written disclosure, that is, a written description of the idea and the best known structures or steps for implementing it. This disclosure should not wait until a model has been built or it is confirmed that the idea has merit. The disclosure cost is little and a written description, accompanied by drawings as necessary, should be prepared. When the disclosure is completed, make a copy on a conventional copy machine. Then have each page of the copy of the disclosure signed and dated by the inventor or inventors and by at least one other party who would make a reliable witness if necessary. The mother of the inventor might not be considered an unbiased witness. The original disclosure should be followed by updated disclosures as the development proceeds. The more important the development is likely to be, the more care should be taken to document every event.

Basic Elements of a Patent License Agreement

A patent license usually has these basic elements:

- The nature of the license—exclusive, non-exclusive, or sole.
- The license grant: specific designation of just what is being licensed.
- Geographical limitations.
- Future inventions.
- Term and termination of the license agreement.
- Royalty payments.
- Right to audit.

- Infringement by others.
- Right to sublicense.
- Patent assignment.

Nature of License

A grant under a patent or a patent application may be non-exclusive, sole, or exclusive. A non-exclusive license is one in which the licensee is permitted to operate under the patent coverage, but the licensor is free to grant licenses to others. A sole license is one in which the licensee is the only licensee, but the licensor is permitted to operate under the licensed patent coverage. An exclusive license is one in which the licensor agrees to license no one else and to refrain from operating under the patent coverage.

The License Grant

A license may be granted to an invention for which no patent application has been filed, or to an invention for which a patent is pending in the Patent Office, or to one for which a patent has been issued. The terms will vary somewhat for each of these situations and are represented by the alternative provisions in the sample license agreement below.

In most cases, the licensor grants just the rights that he has received, or expects to receive, from the Patent Office. A United States patent on a mechanical device or method grants to the inventor the exclusive right to make, use and sell the claimed invention within the United States for a period of 17 years from the date of issue of the patent. The licensor cannot grant more in a license agreement, for those rights are all the patentee has. Sometimes attorneys become confused about just what a license is and adopt the age old practice of trying to cover everything by the use of endless redundant words and phrases and expressions that go far beyond the rights available to the licensor.

One mistake, found in even standard form books, is the granting of exclusive rights to unpatented technology. Unpatented technology is not the property of the licensor and it cannot be the subject of an exclusive license. The most the licensor can do is to agree to disclose the technology fully to the licensee and retain the technology in confidence, or agree to grant an exclusive license when and if a patent issues.

The following "grant" provision is from a license agreement proposed by a multiple-name San Francisco law firm representing Cipher Data Company, Inc., a San Diego manufacturer, to an individual inventor:

he licensed vention had thing to do with y software

1. Grant of License.

Licensor hereby grants to Cipher a worldwide, irrevocable assignable, exclusive license (the "License") to use, make, have made, copy, manufacture, modify, improve, enhance, revise, translate, abridge, condense, expand, recast, transform, adapt, and sell, lease distribute, license, sublicense, advertise, promote and otherwise commercially exploit the Licensed Products during the term of this Agreement. "Licensed Products" shall be deemed to include all patents, copyrights, trade secrets,

continued on page 9-3

continued from page 9-2

trademarks, inventions, ideas, know-how, technology, data and all other information relating to the Licensed Products, all versions of the source code and object code of all software* which is included in Licensed Products, all manuals and other documentation relating to the Licensed Products, all versions of the Licensed Products for different equipment, operating systems and applications, and all improvements and revisions to, and all modifications, translations, abridgments, condensations, expansions, recastings, transformations, adaptations and enhancements of, any of the foregoing which may hereafter be developed by Licensor or by Cipher. The License shall be exclusive to Cipher during the term of this Agreement and the rights granted to Cipher pursuant to the License may not be exercised by any other person, including (without limitation) Licensor.

Somehow, I have the feeling the above provision was drafted by the same person who wrote the speech given by airline staff explaining how to buckle a seat belt. Well, as Professor Fred Rodell, a Yale University law professor, wrote in 1936: "There are two things wrong with almost all legal writing. One is form. The other is content."

The only prizes the proposed language might win would be for redundancy and irrelevancy. There is no purpose in analyzing any of the multitude of things wrong with the quoted passage; your own reading of it should convince you that attorneys can do irreparable damage to corporate affairs.

My draft, which the Cipher attorney refused to consider, said simply:

LICENSE GRANT

The Licensor grants to Cipher a worldwide exclusive license to make, use and sell Licensed products under any patents or patent rights now or hereafter owned by the Licensor.

The deal died in the arms of the attorneys.

Geographical Limitation

A license may be limited to a particular geographical area, or it may be worldwide. A licensee may have an exclusive license to sell in certain states or countries and be prohibited from selling in other areas. Most often, the license is worldwide.

Term and Termination

The term of patent licenses is most often for the life of the latest patent licensed under the agreement. In special situations, a shorter period may be specified. If improvement inventions are included in the license, as they are most often, the life of the latest improvement patent is included in determining the life of the agreement.

Usually, the licensee has a right to terminate the agreement, but there may be a requirement for a minimum period, or a minimum royalty payment, before the license can be terminated. It is often provided that the license can be terminated only at the end of a calendar year or some annual period of the agreement. A requirement for six months' advance written notice is not unusual. As a general rule, you should not accept a patent license without a right to terminate at some reasonable time. A typical termination provision might be like this:

> Licensee shall have the right to terminate this Agreement at the end of any annual period of this Agreement by six months advance notice, which notice may not be given prior to the end of the third annual period. Such termination shall not prejudice the payment of royalties accruing prior to the date of termination.

Or:

> Licensee shall have the right to terminate this Agreement at the end of any annual period of this Agreement by six months advance notice to the Licensor, provided the Licensee shall have no right to terminate until the total royalties paid hereunder shall have amounted to at least Four Million Dollars ($4,000,000.00). Such termination shall not prejudice the payment of royalties accruing prior to the date of termination.

In each case, the term "annual period" will have been defined elsewhere in the agreement. For example, if an agreement is signed on March 22, 1988, the definition might be: "The first annual period of this Agreement shall be deemed to end on March 31, 1989."

Usually the Licensor has no right to terminate except for breach of the agreement. The following provision is more or less typical:

> If the Licensee fails to make any payment hereunder when due, or otherwise breaches this Agreement, the Licensor shall have the right to terminate this Agreement by thirty days notice to the Licensor, provided, if the Licensee cures such breach within that thirty day period, such notice shall be of no effect.

Royalty Payments

A payment is usually made upon execution of a license agreement. This payment may, in some cases, be considered an advance payment of royalties, but that is not necessarily so. The important thing is to specify clearly whether the payment is an advance on royalties or a payment independent of subsequent royalties.

Usually license agreements provide for some minimum annual royalty payment. The Licensor does not benefit by granting a license to someone who does not use the license and pays no royalties. The minimum payment should be large enough to insure the licensee is making a sincere effort to promote the licensed product or method. A rather usual provision is for the minimum annual royalty to be adjusted for inflation. If this author's guess about the future of a currency steadily debased by concerted government action is anywhere near the mark, a yearly adjustment for changes in the CPI (Consumer Price Index) will be a requirement of the licensor.

The payments are most often expressed as a percentage of the sales price of the licensed product, although a fixed royalty per unit is not too unusual. If the royalty is a percentage, it is important to specify just what is to be considered as the sales price of the licensed article. For example, suppose a manufacturer of gasoline engines takes a license on an invention embodied in a carburetor. The licensee obviously does not want to pay royalties on the entire price of the engine. However, if the carburetor is not sold separately, it may be difficult to determine a fair sales price for the carburetor portion of the engine. One way is to agree in advance on the likely price of a carburetor, determine the royalty from an agreed percentage, and designate a fixed royalty for each carburetor delivered by the licensee.

The sales price or "net" sales price may be defined as the price for which the licensed article is sold by the licensee less the usual trade discounts, returns and allowances, and transportation costs.

A typical definition of net sales might be:

> The term "Net Sales" means the total net sales of all reclining chairs sold by the Licensee that are covered by any claim of any patent licensed hereunder, less discounts, returns and allowances customary in the trade.

A sample royalty provision follows:

> The Licensee agrees to pay to the Licensor Fifty-thousand Dollars ($50,000.00) upon execution of this Agreement. In addition, the Licensee agrees to pay to the Licensor a royalty equal to Two Percent (2.0%) of the Net Sales, which payments shall be made within sixty days after the close of each calendar quarter accompanied by an accounting of all sales of licensed products made by the Licensee during such quarter.

The initial payment is not an advance royalty payment: The percentage royalty is paid in addition to the initial payment.

Patent Expenses

License agreements, particularly exclusive agreements, sometimes require the licensee to pay the costs of filing, prosecuting and maintaining patent applications and patents. This is more usual in connection with foreign patents. One rather common arrangement is for the licensee to specify those countries in which it wants patent protection and to pay all of the costs in those countries. The license agreement is limited to those particular countries. The licensee usually has the right, by reasonable notice, to terminate the payment of costs in any particular countries in return for giving up the license rights in those countries.

Right to Audit

Usually, the Licensor has a right to audit, or to have an independent CPA audit, the books and records of the Licensee to determine the accuracy of the royalty payments. One such provision:

The Licensor shall have the right to inspect the books and records of the Licensee at any time for the purpose of determining the accuracy of the royalty payments made hereunder.

Or a somewhat more restricted right:

The Licensor shall have the right to have an independent CPA examine the books and records of the Licensee for the sole purpose of verifying the accuracy of royalty payments hereunder. Such examination shall be made during regular business hours and upon five days advance notice. No more than two such examinations shall be made within any twelve month period.

Arbitration

Arbitration provisions are frequently included in patent licenses and other agreements. They are no panacea. The arbitration procedure suffers from the same bureaucratic idiocies as our court system. Nevertheless, arbitration is frequently the lesser of two evils. The following is a typical arbitration provision suitable for use in a license agreement:

(a) Except as to issues relating to validity, construction or effect of any patent licensed hereunder, all claims or disputes between the parties

continued on page 9-7

continued from page 9-6

arising in connection with this Agreement, which have not been resolved by good faith negotiations between the parties, shall be resolved by arbitration in ________________ [city and state where arbitration is to take place] under the rules of the American Arbitration Association then in effect. The arbitrators shall have no power to modify any of the terms of this Agreement. Any award rendered in such arbitration may be enforced by either party in either the courts of _______ [state where arbitration is to take place] or in a United States District Court of the same state, to whose jurisdiction each party irrevocably agrees to submit.

(b) Disputes concerning the validity, construction or coverage of any patent licensed hereunder may be resolved in any court having jurisdiction thereof.

(c) If, in any arbitration proceeding, any issue shall arise concerning the validity, construction or effect of any patent licensed hereunder, the arbitrators shall assume the validity of all claims set forth in such patent and shall not delay the arbitration proceeding for the purpose of obtaining, or permitting either party to obtain, a judicial resolution of such issue, unless an order staying such arbitration proceeding is entered by a court of competent jurisdiction. Neither party shall raise any issue concerning the validity, construction or effect of any patent licensed hereunder in any proceeding to enforce any arbitration award unless an action between the parties concerning such issue is then before a court of competent jurisdiction or a judicial finding has been entered in such court relating to such issue.

Infringement by Others

In the case of an exclusive license, provisions may be included dealing with possible infringement of the licensed patents by another party. This is a complex subject and is omitted from many agreements and left to be dealt with at the time of any infringement. This is not an unreasonable course when the licensee has a right to cancel the license agreement. One possible provision is:

1. If during the term of this Agreement, either party shall notify the other in writing of an infringement of any patent licensed hereunder, which in its opinion constitutes a substantial infringement thereof, the

continued on page 9-8

continued from page 9-7

parties thereupon shall in good faith attempt to reach agreement as to which or both of them shall institute suit against the alleged infringer and as to a fair and equitable apportioning of litigation expenses and any recoveries or damages.

2. If the parties are unable to agree on all terms in connection with the infringement within sixty (60) days after such notice of infringement, the matter shall be submitted to arbitration in accordance with Section XXX hereof [see above example] for the purpose only of setting forth an equitable arrangement of all matters relating to such infringement, provided, if such arbitration decision requires either or both parties to assume any expense of litigation, any party required to assume such expenses may reject the arbitration decision by notice to the other party within thirty (30) days after the arbitration decision. If the arbitration decision is so rejected, the matter shall again be submitted to arbitration for the purpose of again setting forth an equitable arrangement in relation to such infringement with due consideration being given to the refusal of the rejecting party to assume any litigation expense.

Right to Sublicense

The licensee may have or not have the right to sublicense others under the licensed patents. Or the licensee may have the right to sublicense with the consent of the licensor and such provision may be accompanied by a statement that the consent will not be unreasonably withheld. Usually provisions are included making the licensee responsible for performance by the sublicensees. A more or less typical provision is:

The Licensee shall have the right to sublicense others under this Agreement with the consent of the Licensor, which consent shall not be unreasonably withheld. In the event of any such sublicense, the Licensor shall be provided with a copy of each sublicense agreement. The sublicensee shall adopt and agree to be bound by all of the terms of this Agreement, except the right to sublicense, and the Licensee hereunder shall be responsible for payment of all royalties to the Licensor.

Before considering a practical license agreement, let's consider an impractical agreement. The following agreement also demonstrates that legal gobbledygook is not limited to United States attorneys: This one was offered to a United States company by a Canadian firm of barristers and solicitors. We'll consider just some of the choice provisions. The names of the participants have been changed, as has the description of the licensed products.

```
LICENSE AGREEMENT

THIS LICENSE AGREEMENT made as of this 14th day of May
1989.
```

No need to bother with complete sentences when writing legal.

```
BETWEEN:

James Madison of the City of Manchester, Massachusetts,
United States of America (hereinafter called the
"Licensor") OF THE FIRST PART;

and

MISTU INC., a corporation incorporated pursuant to the
laws of the Province of Ontario (hereinafter called the
"Licensee") OF THE SECOND PART.

WHEREAS the Licensor is the owner of all right, title
and interest, including all patents, trademarks,
copyright and design in and to a certain technology and
related improvements for an automatic sound disc
duplication process;

AND WHEREAS the Licensee is desirous of securing a
license for the manufacture, promotion, use, leasing,
distribution, sale and sublicense worldwide of products
and processes involving the said technology.
```

That is an outstanding example of goop intended by the legal profession to impress the businessman with the impossibility of writing his own business contracts. It would, too, if all that nonsense were necessary. But it isn't. Even in Canada. In addition to the fruity language, there are dangers. For example, it states the Licensor is the "owner of all... patents...relating to a certain technology and related improvements for an automatic sound disc duplication process." Of course, that is not true. The Licensor has developed a particular system of duplicating sound discs. He does not own all of the patents in the world related to his technology. He doesn't even have a list of those patents. In this situation, copyright and trademarks are superfluous. The Licensor has only developed a machine. He doesn't have any trademarks or copyrights. But what is the attorney to do? It is on the word processor hard disk. All of the above can be replaced by a simple introductory paragraph such as we have already discussed. A Background provision would be helpful by way of explaining just how the parties got to this point and what they expect to accomplish by this agreement.

NOW THEREFORE THIS AGREEMENT WITNESSETH that in consideration of the premises and mutual covenants and agreements herein contained (the sufficiency of which consideration is hereby acknowledged by the parties), THE PARTIES COVENANT AND AGREE WITH EACH OTHER AS FOLLOWS:

Balderdash! The entire paragraph should be interred. As we have discussed, when there is obvious consideration, as there is in this agreement, no recitation of the consideration is required.

ARTICLE I

RECITALS CORRECT

1.01 The parties hereto respectively acknowledge and declare that the foregoing recitals, insofar as they relate to such party, are true and correct both in substance and in fact.

The licensor is not only asked to make obviously false statements, he is now asked to certify their truth. One could comment on the construction: Could the statements be true and not correct? Could the statements be true in substance, but not in fact? Or vice versa? But it would be rude to ask. Redundancy does not stop at international borders.

ARTICLE II

DEFINITIONS AND INTERPRETATIONS

2.01 Definitions

As used in this Agreement or any amendment hereof, the following terms shall have the following meanings:

That adds two more lines to the agreement. Not much, but fees are fees. If an agreement states that "'black' means anything darker than...," it can be assumed the term as used in the agreement will have that definition. It is not necessary to define the definition. As for the amendment, maybe there won't be one and the sentence isn't required. If there is one, the subject can be dealt with better in that amendment.

(a) "Business" means the business of automatic sound disc duplication process in connection with the manufacture and sale of the Products, the leasing of the Products, the distribution of the Products, the

continued on page 9-11

continued from page 9-10

sublicensing of the Know-How, Licensed Patents and Technical Data to third parties, the use of Products for the purpose of automatic sound disc duplication process;

Once again, it is of primary importance that an agreement state the terms clearly with as little ambiguity as possible. For one thing, clarity makes it advisable to introduce a character before one starts vilifying him. The above paragraph uses the terms "Products," "Know-how," "Licensed Patents," and "Technical Data." Each of these terms is specially defined by this agreement, but the definition is later in the agreement. It would have been easier for the likes of us to understand the agreement if the definitions had preceded their use. Aside from the use of the defined terms prior to the definitions, the paragraph is confusing as to its precise meaning. As we shall see later, this paragraph is not only unnecessary, it makes the agreement more difficult to understand. This paragraph could have been omitted to the benefit of the agreement.

(b) "Business Day" means any day except Saturdays, Sundays and holidays as defined under the Interpretation Act (Canada);

Now that is a nice definition which we assume, not knowing a damned thing about the "Interpretation Act," means that Thanksgiving Day in the United States does not count as a holiday, but the Canadian Thanksgiving Day does. Certainly well to have that clarified, except for one thing: The expression "Business Day" does not appear again in the entire agreement. No matter, the word processor managed to add a few lines, a bit of confusion, and maybe a couple of bucks to the fee.

(c) "Sound Design Division" means the operating division of Licensee which shall carry on the Business;

(d) "Know-How" shall mean the accumulated knowledge, experience and information acquired by the Licensor as evidenced in some form of physical matter such as, without limitation, drawings, designs, blueprints, drafts, plans, specifications, material lists, catalogues, processed descriptions, research and production reports, formulae, production manuals, quality controls, and manuals relating to disk duplication and shall include in addition any modifications and improvements to such Know-How made during the period of this Agreement;

All clear? Understand just what is meant? I don't. "Know-how" means the faculty of knowing how. The general usage of know-how means the information and understanding of a particular subject, field, or thing. In a more homely way, the agreement might have said: "'Know-How' means everything the Licensor knows about automatic sound disk duplication." And there is no need to limit the know how to that which is "evidenced by some form of physical matter…" In a practical sense, there is little reason to clutter an agreement with a definition of know-how, except in special circumstances when the intended meaning is different from that of general usage.

(e) "Licensed Patents" shall mean patents and patent applications listed in Schedule "A" attached hereto as may be modified from time to time, covering inventions in the field of automatic sound disc duplication and shall include, without limitation, any patents applied for after the date of this Agreement by the Licensor pertaining to said application and shall include inventions made during the period of this Agreement for which the Licensor shall obtain patent [sic] or file applications therefore;

More unnecessary legal goop. There is no need to define Licensed Patents. The license usually is a right to make, use and sell a specified product or process under all patents of the licensor. Sometimes the patents are listed, sometimes not. Later we shall see examples of patent licenses where the confusion of the above clause is eliminated by omitting the clause.

(f) "Products" shall mean any units of equipment for use in automatic sound disc duplication industry which embody, or the manufacture, use or sale of which employ any inventions claimed under the Licensed Patents, Know-How or Technical Data including computer hardware, and peripherals and software;

Later, we shall see how this confusing language contributes to the redundancy of the license grant.

(g) "Technical Data" shall mean knowledge, experience and information whether or not incorporated in some form of physical matter such as drawings, blueprints, tools, plans, etc. related to automatic sound disc duplication;

Clear? Understand just how Technical Data differs from Know-How? I do not. It is clear that Know-How is embodied in a physical form, while Technical Data need not be. The Technical Data definition serves only to lengthen and further confuse an already confusing situation.

(h) "Territory" shall mean the world;

Just another example of a useless definition. The word "Territory" is used only once in the remainder of the Agreement. It would have saved words to state in the grant that the license is "worldwide."

```
2.02 Interpretation

All words and personal pronouns relating thereto shall
be read and construed as to number, gender and tense as
the context in each case requires, and the verb shall
be read and construed as agreeing with the required
word and pronoun.
```

Legal graffito. If the writing of an agreement is so obtuse that it cannot be understood, this paragraph is unlikely to save it. Write clearly and leave out the nonsense.

```
2.03 Headings

Division of this Agreement into Articles and Sections
and the use of headings is for convenience of reference
only and shall not modify or affect the interpretation
or construction of this Agreement, or any provision
hereof.
```

We can't add anything to what we said about this clause in Chapter 2. If the other party insists on this paragraph, let him trade you something for it.

```
2.04 Time Periods

When calculating the period of time within which or
following which any act is to be done or step taken
pursuant to this Agreement, the date which is the
reference date in calculating such period shall be
excluded.
```

Big deal. The license period may be interpreted to be 15 years and one day instead of a mere 15 years. The 30-day notices remain 30-day notices.

```
2.05 Severability

If any Article, Section or portion of any Section of
this Agreement is determined to be unenforceable or
invalid by any Court of competent jurisdiction and that
decision is not appealed or appealable, for any reason
whatsoever, that unenforceability or invalidity shall
not affect the enforceability or validity of the
```

continued on page 9-14

continued from page 9-13

```
remaining portions of this Agreement and such
unenforceable or invalid Article, Section or portion
thereof shall be severed from the remainder of this
Agreement.
```

See the comments about clauses of this kind in Chapter 2. It is not apparent how this clause benefits or harms either party. Its possible consequences are wrapped in mystery. But the longest odds (and I do mean long) are that it will have no effect. It serves only to make the agreement longer. The unnecessarily wordy construction makes it even longer.

```
2.06 Entire Agreement

This Agreement constitutes the entire agreement between
the parties hereto with respect to all matters herein
and its execution has not been induced by, nor do any
of the parties hereto rely upon or regard as material,
any representation or writing not incorporated herein
or made a part hereof.
```

We discussed "Entire Agreement" clauses in Chapter 2, but this is a different wolf. And if your client is not the con man, it should raise a red flag. This clause says that no matter what you were told, or what was given to you in written form, to induce you to enter this agreement, it doesn't count now. If this is to be a fair and equitable agreement, this clause isn't needed—if the deal isn't equitable and fair the sucker should object to it!

```
2.07 Jurisdiction                 (Omitted)

2.08 Schedules                    (Omitted)

ARTICLE I I I

GRANT OF LICENSE

3.01 The Licensor hereby grants to the Licensee the
exclusive right and license in the Territory to
manufacture, promote, use, lease, distribute and sell the
Products and all past and future modifications,
revisions, and improvements thereof, together with the
right to use the Licensed Patents, Know-How and Technical
Data in conjunction therewith and with the prior written
consent of the Licensor (not to be unreasonably withheld)
to sublicense others to manufacture, promote, use, lease,
distribute and sell the Products in the Territory or part
thereof and to use the Licensed patents, Know-How and
Technical Data in conjunction therewith on the terms and
conditions hereinafter set forth.
```

This is an example of just about everything that can be wrong with a grant clause: It grants the wrong things; it is redundant; and it is a jumble of words. First, the exclusive grant includes things the licensor has no exclusive rights in, such as "Know-How" and "Technical Data." The most that can be asked of the licensor is a full disclosure of Know-How and Technical Data to the licensee and a promise not to disclose the information to others. If that information is not covered by a patent, the licensor has no exclusive rights to it and he cannot grant any exclusive rights. The redundancy, for example, as incorporated in the definitions of "Know-How" and "Technical Data" makes it even more difficult to understand just what is being granted. The patent grant is simple: It grants to the inventor an exclusive right to "make, use and sell" the invention for a limited period of time. This is all the licensor can grant. The talk about the right to "promote,...lease, distribute..." is nonsense, as is the recitation of "...all future modifications, revisions, and improvements..." In the provision for sublicensing, these terms are repeated—needlessly. This long convoluted paragraph could better be stated:

> The Licensor grants to the Licensee an exclusive world-wide license to make, use and sell the Products under all patents now or hereafter owned by the Licensor. The Licensee shall have the right to grant sublicenses hereunder, with the consent of the Licensor, which consent shall not be unreasonably withheld, so long as the sublicensee assumes the obligation to pay royalties to the Licensor as set forth herein and the Licensee assumes responsibility for such payments.

The agreement continues for 14 additional pages. The businessman receiving this proposed agreement faces something of a negotiating dilemma. If he completely rewrites the agreement, he will likely jar the nerves of the attorney who composed the original masterpiece and make it more difficult to negotiate favorable terms. If he tries to merely amend the agreement, the amendments will be longer than the original document and probably even more confusing. The best approach would seem to be to exercise your most skillful diplomatic tactics and rewrite the agreement.

Examples of License Agreements

Here is a sample license agreement of the more practical type:

> LICENSE AGREEMENT
>
> This is an Agreement, effective as of August 14, 1980, between William G. Kirkman, an individual residing at 97 Precint Street, Lowell, Massachusetts 01852 (the "Licensor") and Quick Manufacturing Corporation, a Massachusetts corporation, (the "Licensee").
>
> Background
>
> The Licensor is the owner and inventor of certain inventions relating to bandages and processes for

continued on page 9-16

continued from page 9-15

making such bandages including those covered by an application for United States Letters Patent entitled Shirred Laminate and Method of Producing Same, Serial No. 075,038 filed September 14, 1979. The Licensee desires to obtain an exclusive license for the manufacture, use and sale of bandages for veterinary and human use under all of the patents and rights of the Licensor. The Licensor has agreed, for consideration separate from this Agreement, to construct and place in operation a machine to manufacture such bandages. The parties agree as follows:

1. Definitions

(a) "Patent Rights" means the United States Patent Application identified above, including all related: (i) applications for patents filed in the future; (ii) continuations; (iii) continuations-in-part; (iv) divisions; (v) reissue patents; (vi) all patents issuing therefrom; and (vii) present and future applications, patents and utility model registrations in foreign countries.

(b) "Licensed Products" means bandages for use on humans or animals and comprising a laminate of non-elastic scrim and one or more layers of non-woven foam or the process by which such a bandage is made and which

(a) during the first five annual periods of this Agreement are within the scope of any claim of a pending application or issued patent licensed hereunder, or (b) subsequent to such fifth annual period, are covered by a claim of an issued patent licensed hereunder.

(c) The first "annual period" of this Agreement shall be deemed to end on September 30, 1981.

(d) "Net Sales" means Licensee's invoiced selling price of Licensed Products to a Customer, less trade discounts, credits for returned merchandise, sales and excise taxes, transportation, and customs and duties actually paid by the Licensee. A sale to a "Customer" means a bona fide sale resulting from an arms length transaction to an unaffiliated entity beyond the control of the Licensee. No sale or transfer of Licensed Products shall be made to any entity that is not a Customer without the express written consent of the Licensor.

continued on page 9-17

continued from page 9-16

2. Grant

The Licensor grants to the Licensee the exclusive right and license in the entire world to make, use and sell Licensed Products under all patent rights now or hereafter owned by the Licensor.

3. Royalty Payments

(a) Upon the execution of this Agreement, the Licensee shall pay to the Licensor an advance royalty of Forty Thousand Dollars ($40,000.00), which royalty shall be deductible from future royalties accruing to the Licensor.

(b) The Licensee agrees to pay to the Licensor a royalty based on a percentage of the Net Sales during each annual period of this Agreement as follows: one and one-half percent (1.5%) of the first Five Hundred Thousand Dollars ($500,000.00); two percent (2%) of the next One Million Dollars ($1,000,000.00); and three percent (3%) of all over One Million Five Hundred Thousand Dollars ($1,500,000.00).

(c) The Licensor shall promptly disclose to the Licensee any future improvements or developments of Licensed Products conceived or acquired by the Licensor.

4. Reports and Royalty Payments

(a) Within sixty (60) days after the end of each of its fiscal quarters, the Licensee shall report to the Licensor, in such detail as may reasonably be required by the Licensor, the Net Sales anywhere in the world during such fiscal quarter together with an accounting of accrued royalties payable thereon and an explanation of any offset credit allowances.

(b) Simultaneously with each such report, the Licensee shall remit all royalty payments due thereon.

(c) All records of the Licensee pertaining to the manufacture and sale of Licensed Products shall be maintained by the Licensee for a minimum period of five (5) years after the payment of royalties thereon. The Licensor shall have the right to have a Certified Public Accountant inspect, during regular business hours, the books and records of the Licensee for the purpose of ascertaining the accuracy of the royalty

continued on page 9-18

continued from page 9-17

payments by the Licensee, provided, Licensor shall notify the Licensee five days in advance of any such inspection and no more than one inspection shall occur within any twelve (12) month period.

5. Term and Termination

(a) Unless sooner terminated as provided, this Agreement shall terminate upon the latest expiration of any patent under which the Licensee is licensed hereunder.

(b) This Agreement may be terminated by the Licensee at the end of any annual period hereof by thirty (30) days advance notice to the Licensor.

(c) If the royalties accruing and payable hereunder shall amount to less than Ten Thousand Dollars ($10,000.00) for any annual period hereof, the Licensor shall have the right, at any time within six months after the end of such annual period, by thirty (30) days advance notice to the Licensee, to terminate this Agreement, provided, if the Licensee shall, prior to the expiration of such thirty (30) day period of notice, make sufficient payments to bring the total royalties for that annual period to the amount specified herein, then such notice shall be of no effect.

(d) Upon termination, the license granted herein shall cease, all rights granted hereunder shall revert to the Licensor, and all obligations for payments by the Licensee to the Licensor shall cease, without prejudice to the payment of royalties accruing prior to such termination. Licensee shall have the right, subsequent to termination, to dispose of existing inventory, paying any royalties due thereon in accordance with the percentages set forth herein.

6. Enforcement Rights

(a) If during the term of this Agreement, any patent licensed hereunder shall appear to be infringed by a third party, then the party hereto first becoming aware of such infringement shall promptly notify the other. The Licensee shall have the right, but not the obligation, to notify the infringer and to initiate and control litigation or legal proceedings to abate the infringement, without the prior consent of the Licensor. The Licensor may elect to join in any such legal proceedings against the alleged infringer, and if

continued on page 9-19

continued from page 9-18

not so electing, agrees to be joined as an involuntary party plaintiff. If the Licensee has not initiated such legal proceedings within one (1) year after becoming aware of the infringement, then the Licensor may initiate legal proceedings on his own behalf, and the Licensee may elect to join in those proceedings.

(b) If either party elects to join in legal proceedings commenced by the other party, then the control of such proceedings shall remain in the hands of the initiating party and all fees and costs incurred by the initiating party, along with all damages and awards recovered thereby, shall be shared equally between the parties. If one party elects not to join in legal proceedings initiated by the other party, then such other party shall be responsible for all fees and costs incurred therein, and shall receive all damages and awards recovered thereby.

(c) Each party shall cooperate fully with the other in all aspects of any such litigation whether or not joining in the proceedings.

7. Sublicense and Assignment

The Licensee shall have no right to grant sublicenses hereunder without the consent of the Licensor. Neither party shall have the right to assign this Agreement without the consent of the other, which consent shall not be unreasonably withheld.

8. Warranties

(a) The Licensor makes no warranty as to the validity of Patent Rights, but does warrant that the patent application identified above is on file in the United States Patent and Trademark Office and has not been abandoned.

(b) The Licensor warrants he has the sole right to enter into this Agreement, that he is the sole owner of Patent Rights, and that he has not entered into and will not enter into any other agreement in conflict herewith.

9. Breach of the Agreement

In the event of a breach of this Agreement by either party, the other party shall have the right to terminate this Agreement by notice setting forth the details and the date of the purported breach. If the

continued on page 9-20

continued from page 9-19

breach is not cured within thirty (30) days after such notice, the party alleging the breach shall have the right to terminate this Agreement by further notice to such other party and this Agreement shall terminate as of the date of such further notice and shall be null and void without further effect, provided, such termination shall not relieve the Licensee of previously accrued royalty obligations.

10. Patent Marking

The Licensee shall mark all Licensed Products with appropriate patent references, complying in all respects with the governing laws.

11. Unavoidable Events

Neither party hereto shall be considered in breach of its obligations if it shall fail to fulfill its obligations hereunder wholly or principally because of acts of God, war, riot, civil commotion, tempest, flood, fire, strike, or any other circumstance beyond the control of the party which would otherwise be in default of its obligations, provided that such obligation is fulfilled within a reasonable period after such cause shall have been removed.

12. Notices

Any notice given hereunder shall be in writing and shall be effective on the date mailed by certified mail, return receipt requested:

if to the Licensor, to:

William G. Kirkman
97 Precint Street
Lowell, Massachusetts
01852

if to the Licensee, to:

Legal Department
Quick Manufacturing
Corporation
1278 Burton Street
Haverhill, Massachusetts
01830

continued on page 9-21

continued from page 9-20

13. Execution

Each individual executing this Agreement on behalf of a corporation warrants that he is authorized to enter into this Agreement on behalf of such corporation and that this Agreement is binding on that corporation.

____
William G. Kirkman,
Licensor

Quick Manufacturing
Corporation

By______________________________
Title:

Another sample of a simple patent license agreement follows. However, in this case, the inventor has assigned his inventions to a whollyowned corporation. Provisions are made for reduced payments during an initial period to allow time for a new corporation to get started. In this example, the exclusive license can be converted to a non-exclusive license, at a reduced royalty rate, if the royalty payments do not meet the specified minimum. This example includes a percentage royalty. In "what-iffing" the agreement, the Licensor became concerned that the Licensee might sell the media to an affiliated organization at an unrealistically low price and thus reduce the royalty payments. For that reason, the agreement also specifies a minimum fixed royalty per recording unit. An alternative arrangement is to provide that the royalty shall not be less than the stated percentage of the fair market value of the licensed product that is sold, transferred or donated to any entity.

LICENSE AGREEMENT

This is an Agreement, effective as of ____________ 1988, among Magnetic Recording Co. Inc., a California corporation, (the "Licensee"), Holding Company, Inc., a Delaware corporation (the "Licensor), and John Smith, an individual, ("Smith").

1. Background

Smith has made certain inventions related to magnetic recording of digital data and has assigned his rights in those inventions to the Licensor, a corporation wholly owned by Smith. The Licensee desires to have a license under such inventions and the parties have agreed as follows.

continued on page 9-22

continued from page 9-21

2. Definitions

"Media" means media for magnetic recording of digital information in a readable format making use of storage elements within laminated plastic and processes for recording on and reading from such media.

"Net Sales" means Licensee's invoiced sales of Media, less discounts and allowances in accordance with accepted industry norms.

3. License Grant

The Licensor grants to the Licensee a worldwide exclusive license to make, use and sell Media under any patents or patent rights now or hereafter owned by the Licensor. Smith agrees to assign, and hereby does assign, to the Licensor all patent rights to any future inventions made by him relating to optical recording.

4. Royalty Payments

The Licensee agrees to pay to the Licensor a royalty of six percent (6.0%) of the Net Sales, but in no event less than eight cents ($0.08) per Media unit sold by the Licensee. The Licensee shall make monthly advance royalty payments of Ten Thousand Dollars ($10,000.00) beginning July 1, 1988, which payments shall be credited against royalties accruing in the same annual period of this Agreement, provided, for a period of six months beginning July 1, 1988, such advance monthly royalty payments shall be Four Thousand Dollars ($4,000.00). Within forty-five (45) days after the end of each calendar quarter the licensee shall report to the Licensor: (a) the total number of units of Media sold during the preceding quarter; (b) the unit selling prices of the Media; and (c) the total Net Sales. The Licensee shall with such report pay to the Licensor all accrued royalties.

5. Minimum Royalty Payments

The minimum annual royalty payment hereunder shall be One Hundred Thousand Dollars ($100,000.00), which minimum shall be adjusted on July 1 of each year, beginning in 1989, in accordance with the percentage change in the Consumer Price Index for the preceding calendar year as published by the United States Department of Labor, or if no such index is published, in accordance with an equivalent index. The first annual period of this Agreement shall be deemed to end on June 30, 1989. If the

continued on page 9-23

continued from page 9-22

royalties paid hereunder for any annual period after the fourth shall total less than Three Hundred Thousand Dollars ($300,000.00), the Licensor shall have the right, by thirty (30) days notice, to convert the license granted hereunder into a non-exclusive license, provided, if the Licensee shall during such thirty day period pay sufficient additional amount as is required to bring the total to Three Hundred Thousand Dollars ($300,000.00), such notice shall be of no effect.

In the event the license granted hereunder is converted into a non-exclusive license in accordance with the foregoing, the minimum annual royalty and the percentage royalty on Net Sales shall each be reduced by thirty-five percent (35%). The provisions of Section 6, Patent Expenses, shall no longer apply and the Licensor shall pay its own patent expenses.

6. Patent Expenses

The Licensor will continue to prosecute and maintain pending United States and foreign patent applications and will file new applications on inventions relating to Media as appropriate. During the term of this Agreement, the Licensee shall pay the expenses of filing, prosecuting and maintaining the patents and applications licensed hereunder. Licensee shall have the right, by sixty (60) days advance notice, to refuse to make further payments in connection with any such patent or patent application, and such application or patent, and all divisions and continuations thereof, shall thereafter be excluded from the license herein granted.

7. Examination of Records

All records of the Licensee pertaining to the manufacture and sale of Media shall be maintained by the Licensee for a minimum period of five (5) years after the payment of royalties thereon. The Licensor shall have the right, at reasonable times, to have a Certified Public Accountant inspect the books and records of the Licensee for the purpose of ascertaining the accuracy of the royalty payments by the Licensee.

8. Term and Termination

(a) Unless sooner terminated as provided, this Agreement shall terminate upon the latest expiration of any patent under which the Licensee is licensed hereunder.

continued on page 9-24

continued from page 9-23

(b) This Agreement may be terminated by the Licensee at the end of any annual period hereof, after the third, by six (6) months advance notice to the Licensor.

(c) (i) If the royalties accruing and payable hereunder for any annual period shall amount to less than One Hundred Thousand Dollars ($100,000.00), the Licensor shall have the right, at any time within six months after the end of such annual period, by thirty (30) days advance notice to the Licensee, to terminate this Agreement, or (ii) if the Licensee shall fail to make any payment hereunder when due, the Licensor shall have the right to terminate this Agreement by thirty (30) days notice, provided, if the Licensee shall, prior to the expiration of any such thirty (30) day period of notice, make sufficient payments to bring the total royalties for that fiscal year to the amount specified herein, or to bring current any overdue amounts, as the case may be, then such notice shall be of no effect.

9. Sublicense and Assignment

The Licensee shall have no right to grant sublicenses hereunder without the consent of the Licensor. Neither party shall have the right to assign this Agreement without the consent of the other.

10. Notices

Any notice given hereunder shall be in writing and shall be effective on the date mailed by certified mail, return receipt requested:

if to the Licensor or Smith, to:

John Smith
Holding Company, Inc.
972 Morreno Blvd.
Encinata, CA 92024

if to the Licensee, to:

Magnetic Recording
Company, Inc.
905 Washington Avenue
Towson, Maryland 21204

or to such other address as any party may designate by notice hereunder.

continued on page 9-25

continued from page 9-24

```
11. Execution

Each individual executing this Agreement on behalf of a
corporation warrants that he is authorized to enter
into this Agreement on behalf of such corporation and
that this Agreement is binding on that corporation.


                                   Holding Company, Inc.
                                   Licensee,

                                   By______________________
                                   Title:

                                   Magnetic Recording Co.
                                   Inc.

                                   By_________________________
                                   Title:

                                   ___________________________
                                   John Smith
```

Basic Elements of a Patent Assignment

When the entire rights under a patent are to be assigned, the basic elements are:

- date of the assignment;
- identification of the parties;
- accurate identification of the patent or a pending application;
- a recitation of the consideration or an acknowledgment of receipt of adequate consideration;
- the assignment;
- a statement regarding the assignment of patents deriving from the assigned patent or application, foreign and domestic; and
- a recitation of any special conditions such as payments to be made in the future or any reversionary rights of the assignor.

Patent Assignment—Examples

This is a typical assignment form:

ASSIGNMENT

The undersigned, Robert E. Lee, an individual residing at 22 Brewster Avenue, San Diego, California, (the "Assignor") for valuable consideration, the receipt and adequacy of which are acknowledged:

(1) represents that he is the sole owner of United States Patent 5,012,567 entitled "Machine for Making Carbizdos" issued April 24, 1991 (the "Patent");

(2) represents that no license rights under said patent are presently held by any other party, and

(3) assigns to Ulysses S. Grant Inc., a Delaware corporation, his ownership of the Patent, together with all rights owned by the Assignor in patents and applications deriving from the Patent or its previous patent application together with all foreign patent rights corresponding to the disclosures in the Patent.

____
Robert E. Lee

Date ______________________

That simple assignment is adequate for many situations, but an attorney couldn't charge much for such a simple document. The following will be more to the liking of some attorneys:

ASSIGNMENT

This Agreement, effective December 13, 1992, by and between Robert E. Lee, an individual residing at 22 Brewster Avenue, San Diego, California, (hereinafter termed the "Assignor") and Ulysses S. Grant, Inc., a Delaware corporation, (hereinafter termed the "Assignee")

WITNESSETH THAT:

WHEREAS, the Assignor has made a certain invention described and claimed in United States Patent No. 5,012,567 entitled "Machine for Making Carbizdos"

continued on page 9-27

continued from page 9-26

issued April 24, 1991 (hereinafter termed the "Patent"); and

WHEREAS, the Assignor desires to sell, and the Assignee desires to buy, the entire right, title and interest of the Assignor in and to the Patent;

NOW, THEREFORE, for good and valuable consideration the parties have agreed as follows:

(1) The Assignor represents, warrants and certifies that he is the sole owner of all right, title and interest in and to the Patent; that no interest has been transferred to any other entity; and that the Patent is free from all liens and encumbrances.

(2) The Assignor hereby assigns to the Assignee all right, title, and interest in and to the Patent together with all right, title and interest in and to any continuations, continuations-in-part, divisions and any other patent rights deriving from the Patent or its previous application in the United States Patent Office and including all foreign patents and applications related in any way to the Patent or any application or patent deriving therefrom.

(3) The Assignee agrees to pay to the Assignor upon execution of this Assignment the sum of Fifty Thousand Dollars ($50,000.00).

IN WITNESS WHEREOF the parties hereto have set their respective hands and seals this Thirteenth day of December 1992.

____

Robert E. Lee, (Assignor)

Ulysses S. Grant, Inc.

By__________________________

Title:

This is a more legalistic document that doesn't accomplish anything worthwhile over the previous simple example.

Recording of Patent Assignments

A special statute permits recording the assignment of patents in the Patent and Trademark Office in much the same manner that real estate deeds are recorded in the various states. The procedure is simple: First, determine the recording fee by writing to the Patent and Trademark Office.

As of this writing the fee is $8.00 for one patent plus $8.00 for each additional patent mentioned in the assignment. Send the specified amount with the original of the assignment together with a letter requesting the recording to The Commissioner of Patents and Trademarks, Washington, D.C. 20231. The Patent Office will record the assignment, note the book and page where it is recorded and return the assignment to you. No attorney is necessary for this simple procedure.

Chapter Ten

Leases

There are many kinds of business leases: leases for equipment, automobiles, real estate, and many other items. Most of these can be handled satisfactorily under the guidelines set forth here, but some are in specialized categories that require other expertise. For example, real estate leases can be complicated, not only because of the nature of the subject but because of the varied statutes in the different states. In general, you will be able to find printed forms for real estate leases that will serve as a useful basis for devising your own lease agreement. An alternative is to consult an experienced real estate broker who may know more about the subject than your local lawyer. Such leases can become quite complicated, with provisions relating to: fire or other destruction of part or all of the leased property; options for extension with rates adjusted for inflation; allocation of taxes and other expenses; provisions for subordination to banks or other financiers; restrictions on alterations or modifications by the lessee; etc. Two sample lease agreements for commercial property are included here. One is a simplified form and the other is a longer more detailed agreement. The form and specific provisions can vary widely depending upon the particular circumstances. A problem with a lease can sometimes threaten the very existence of a business. In such a situation, the lease obviously deserves the full attention of the principals.

Provisions for Equipment Leases

Leases for commercial equipment will usually contain the expected provisions:

- identification of the parties;
- an accurate description of the equipment to be leased;
- the term of the lease;
- the rights of the lessor for breach of the agreement;
- conditions under which lessee may terminate;
- option for the lessee to purchase the equipment during or at the end of the lease period;
- maintenance and care of the equipment;
- restrictions on location of the equipment.

The terms of an equipment lease, like all leases, will depend to a considerable extent upon the particular circumstances. Sometimes the lessor is a purely financial concern whose only interest is in the return on the capital invested. The selection, cost and maintenance of the equipment is the responsibility of the lessee.

Sample Equipment Lease

The following is a more or less typical lease for a piece of commercial equipment.

LEASE AGREEMENT

This is an agreement, effective November 23, 1988, between Lease Financing of America, Inc. a Delaware corporation, (the "Lessor") and Joseph Green dba Joe's Garage, of 16 Elm Street, Towanda, Kansas (the "Lessee").

Background

The Lessee operates an automobile garage and desires to install equipment for measuring automobile emissions at a total cost of Sixteen Thousand Dollars ($16,000.00). The Lessor has agreed to purchase an Automotive Emission Tester, Model 127B, from Macon Laboratories of Plainsville, Texas, (the "Equipment") and to lease the Equipment to the Lessee under the following terms:

Terms

(1) The Lessee will order the Equipment and the Lessor will make payment therefore directly to the manufacturer and receive title to the Equipment. The Lessee agrees to install and maintain the Equipment at 16 Elm Street, Towanda, Kansas, and not to move the Equipment to any other location without the advance written consent of the Lessor. The Lessee agrees, at his own expense, to maintain the Equipment in proper operating condition and to abide by all operating and maintenance instructions issued by the manufacturer.

(2) The Lessee agrees to provide at all times broad coverage fire and theft insurance on the Equipment in a minimum amount of Sixteen Thousand Dollars ($16,000.00) and liability insurance in an amount of at least Three Hundred Thousand Dollars ($300,000.00) per occurrence. Each policy shall list the Lessor as a named insured.

(3) The Lessee agrees to pay to the Lessor on the first day of each month beginning on January 1, 1989 the amount of Four Hundred Eighty-eight Dollars ($488.00) per month continuing for a period of forty-eight months.

(4) Title to the Equipment shall remain at all times in the Lessor, provided, Lessee shall have the option, for thirty (30) days after making total payments to the Lessor of Twenty-three Thousand Four Hundred Twenty-four Dollars ($23,424.00), to purchase the Equipment for One Dollar

continued on page 10-3

continued from page 10-2

($1.00). The Lessee agrees that if he does not elect to purchase the Equipment, the Lessor has the right to enter the premises of the Lessee and remove the Equipment.

(5) The Lessor shall have the right at all reasonable times during usual business hours, and without any advance notice, to enter the premises of the Lessee and to inspect the Equipment.

(6) In the event of breach of this Agreement by the Lessee for any reason, including failure to properly insure or maintain the Equipment or failure to make payments as provided herein, and the failure of Lessee to cure such breach within thirty days after written notice by the Lessor, the Lessor shall have the absolute right, without further notice, to enter upon the premises of the Lessee and remove the Equipment. The Lessee shall thereupon have no further right to use or purchase the Equipment, but shall be liable for all damages to or losses of the Lessor resulting from such breach of the Agreement.

Accepted and Agreed to by:

____
Joseph Green,
dba Joe's Garage

Lease Financing of
America, Inc.

By____________________________
Title:

Commercial Real Estate Leases

For most businesses, large and small, a real estate lease represents a major commitment. It is a commitment that goes beyond the financial outlay: it circumscribes the location of the business, the expansion opportunities, the operating environment, and other matters. Accordingly, the preparation of a real estate lease is not a matter to be entrusted to, and—God forbid—negotiated by, a mere lawyer. The business manager or owner should make the relevant decisions about the lease. Once those decisions have been made, then a lawyer can serve as a mechanic to put them on paper. Or the competent business man can do it himself and then have the lawyer check it over for the fine details of real estate law. *The most important thing about a lease is to make sure that all relevant conditions are spelled out in plain unambiguous language.*

Usually the landlord will propose a form of lease that provides the prospective lessee with a starting point. But before entering into the lease, there are a number of matters that should be considered.

The Term of the Lease

This represents a dilemma for both the landlord and the lessee. If the lease is for a short period, the lessee may soon be faced with a decision on the desirability of moving—or that decision may be forced upon him. If the period is inflationary, the lessee will want as long a term as possible without an increase in rent. Vice versa for the lessor. The term desired by the business manager will depend upon a great many factors, including whether and under what circumstances the lease can be renewed or extended. Usually, commercial leases are for terms of three to ten years, but provisions for renewal options may extend for longer periods.

The term of the lease is defined by stating precisely when the lease starts and when it ends. However, the starting time is not always so simple. Suppose the premises under consideration are already occupied and the current tenant is scheduled to vacate before the starting date of the lease. If the tenant refuses to move, what then? The lease should state clearly what happens if the premises are not ready for occupancy by the starting date. This matter can be critical if you are under a deadline to move from your present premises. If premises are to be completed or remodeled prior to the starting date, delays in construction, even those beyond the control of the owner, can cause major difficulties. These contingencies should be considered in advance and the lease worded accordingly. If there is any doubt about the actual starting date of the lease, provide some leeway in your own schedule: it may be difficult to operate your business from a moving van.

The Right to Renew

If a term lease carries no option to renew or extend the lease, the tenant has no rights over any other prospective tenant and will certainly have to pay the going rate for a renewal. Options of renewal are usually at an increased rate. If the renewal price proves to be significantly above the market, negotiations with the landlord are in order.

The lease may provide for the exercise of the option in different ways. For example, the lease may provide that the tenant must give notice six months or a year in advance in order to exercise the option. If the tenant "forgets" to give such notice, the lease expires. Or the lease may be extended automatically in the absence of advance notice by the tenant. This may be the better arrangement if your docketing system is not reliable.

The Rented Space and its Cost—Kinds of Leases

Commercial leases are most often priced by the square foot of leased space. That may seem like a simple and straightforward procedure: just measure the space and that is it. Not necessarily. There are a number of different ways that leased space is measured, so be sure your lease specifies exactly how the square footage is to be computed. It is usual to measure commercial space on the basis of the outside measurements of the building. This may result in including a number of square feet in the rent computation that in fact will be unavailable to you. Moreover, in multiple-tenant buildings, the "public" areas of the building are usually apportioned among the tenants. The space that is provided for use by all tenants or by customers or clients of the tenants may includc lobbies, hallways, elevator shafts, janitor rooms, rooms for heating and air-conditioning equipment, stairways, etc. Be sure you know just how much space you are getting for your own use. Don't be surprised if 20% to 30% of the space you are being charged for is apportioned as public space.

There are a number of so-called "standard" methods of allocating the public space in multi-floor buildings. The "Boston Method" apportions charges for the lobbies and hallways on each floor, but not the bathrooms, elevator shafts, and mechanical rooms. The "New York Multiple Tenancy Floor Method" apportions the space taken by bathrooms and lobbies among the tenants on each floor, but excludes elevator shafts and stairways. The "BOMA International Method" apportions all of the public areas on multiple-tenant floors to the building as a whole and then apportions the space among the tenants. In order to compare rents among different buildings, it is necessary to know precisely how the square footage is to be computed.

The cost of a commercial lease can be deceptive because of hidden costs and escalation formulas. Before you can compare the relative costs of different premises, it is necessary to understand fully just how the rent is to be calculated. The first step is to determine what charges are to be added to the base rent.

There are a number of widely used kinds of leases. A *Gross* lease requires only that the tenant pay a fixed charge and the landlord is responsible for building maintenance, taxes, insurance, and operating expenses. You are unlikely to find commercial space with such a lease. Even under a Gross lease, there may be an add-on charge for electricity and heat depending upon the tenant's usage or requirements.

Net leases require the tenant to pay all or a portion of the real estate taxes. If the building is a single-tenant building, the tenant usually pays all of the real estate taxes. In multi-tenant buildings, the taxes are usually prorated on the basis of square feet.

A *Net Net* lease includes all of the charges of a Net lease plus a charge for insurance on the building. This cost can vary considerably depending upon the breadth of coverage of the insurance. Before agreeing to such a provision, the particular insurance coverage should be specified.

A *Net Net Net* lease is most common when an entire building is occupied by a single tenant. Under such a triple-net lease, the tenant pays all of the costs of the building including maintenance, repairs, grounds upkeep, snow removal, and the like. An annual rental of $10 per square foot may cost $10 per square foot — or it may cost $15, or more, per square foot.

Retail outlets in shopping malls usually pay a base rent plus a percentage of gross revenues. This surcharge takes care of the mall upkeep, parking facilities, security protection, etc.

Escalation Clauses

Some leases provide for a fixed incremental increase in the rent at selected times during the term of the lease. This may not be the best way, but it is certainly the most predictable and the easiest to understand. The lease may provide for an escalation of the rent in the event of any increase in the real estate taxes.

There may also be escalations based on increased costs of maintenance, utilities, and other building expenses. Most escalations are dc*—they only act to increase the rent, never to decrease it.

**Like direct current, the flow is in only one direction.*

Adjustment for Inflation

A usual provision is for the rent to be adjusted annually on the basis of inflation as measured, for example, by the Consumer Price Index published by the United States Labor Department. If the rent is to be adjusted by the same percentage as the percentage change in the CPI, it usually overstates the actual costs. The building itself is already built—inflation does not increase the cost of the building, only its dollar value. Some smaller adjustment should be called for.

Escalation clauses are most often determined from a *base year*. This may be the preceding year, the current year, or even the next full year. The selection of the base year can make an appreciable difference in the rent.

The Right to Sublease

The longer the term of the lease, the more important it is to have some right to sublease. The inherent uncertainties of business make it impossible to accurately forecast the needs of a business some years into the future. The right to sublease offers some comfort in the event of an unforeseen turn of events—either good or bad. A right to sublease is usually restricted at least to the extent of requiring the consent of the landlord. This restriction is not objectionable if it includes the caveat that the permission will not be unreasonably withheld. Even then, there can be disputes over what is "reasonable." The subtenant must meet the same standards as the other tenants in the building and must accept all the restrictions included in the original lease. If you occupy high-tech space in a research-oriented building, the landlord would be within his rights to object to a sublease to a heavy machinery fabrication company.

If the property is subleased, the original tenant usually remains responsible for the lease payments. If the new tenant defaults, the original tenant will be liable for the rents. The landlord is not likely to negotiate this position away. However, that raises the question of who keeps the gain if the new tenant pays a higher price than called for in the original lease. In recent years, that has been a frequent occurrence in many non-Texas areas.

If your lease contains no right to sublease, you will need to be sure that the corporate entity holding the lease is not changed. For example, what if the tenant corporation merges with another corporation? If the surviving corporation is the tenant, there is not likely to be a problem. But if the other corporation is the survivor, it may have no right to the leased premises.

Environmental Protection

The tenant is entitled to have some negative control over other tenants in the building. For example, if the leased property is a retail outlet, the tenant would not like to have a direct competitor in the same area. The tenant also needs the right to object to any other tenant that interferes with its peaceful use of the property—excessive noise, odors, elevator usage, interference with parking, etc.

Remodeling and Improvements

Commercial space usually requires finishing or remodeling before the tenant occupies the space. Sometimes, the landlord allows a fixed sum for such improvements which may include partitions, lighting, carpets, painting, etc. Before executing the lease, the tenant should be satisfied that the allowance will in fact cover the cost, or be within limits tolerable to the tenant. Either the tenant or the landlord is carrying the cost of the space during the remodeling—and this cost can be appreciable, particularly when one recalls how seldom a construction job is completed on time. The landlord will be more cooperative in sharing or paying for improvement costs if the improvements add to the value of the building. If the improvements merely adapt the premises for the special or unique use of the tenant, the landlord will be reluctant to participate. Moreover, the landlord usually has the right to require the tenant to remove such improvements at the end of the lease and return the premises to its original condition.

Agreements about renovations should be put into writing and be accompanied by detailed floor plans and cost estimates from a reliable builder. This agreement, which may be separate from the lease, should specify who owns particular improvements. The general rule is that, in the absence of a contrary agreement, everything that is fastened to the real estate is the property of the building owner. If a tenant installs, at its own expense, partitions, air conditioners, light fixtures, and even manufacturing machinery that is secured to the building, all belong to the landlord.

Services

The landlord may agree to provide such services as electricity, heating, ventilation, air conditioning and cleaning services. It is not enough to merely enumerate these services in the lease. To protect the landlord, there should be a limit on usage so that if the tenant installs equipment requiring greater amounts of power, the tenant pays an additional charge.

Heating, ventilation, and air conditioning in a commercial building is usually provided only during normal business hours. The hours should be specified and if insufficient for a particular tenant, arrangements for added services should be made before the lease is executed.

Cleaning of the public areas is usually the responsibility of the landlord, but they are of importance to every tenant. The lease should specify the extent and schedule of the cleaning services.

Insurance

There are a number of different kinds of insurance carried by the landlord and by the tenants. These policies may overlap, causing needless expense, or they may leave uninsured "holes." It is in the interest of both the landlord and the tenants to have a coordinated insurance program and it should be a subject of agreement before the lease is entered into. In this area, it is advisable to seek the help of an expert, not a lawyer and not an insurance broker, but a firm of insurance experts whose only business is advising business clients about insurance coverage. Often, such experts represent a savings, not an expense.

The landlord will likely carry a comprehensive insurance policy on the building that covers liability for the public areas such as lobbies, stairways, elevators, and parking lots, as well as casualty protection for the building itself. The landlord will usually insist that the tenant carry insurance to protect the landlord against the claims arising from the conduct of the tenant's business. The landlord will also request insurance coverage on contents and improvements to protect the investment in the property whether made by the landlord or by the tenant.

Prior Rights

A lease gives the tenant a very real interest in the building including all of the privileges set forth in the lease. However, all of this is subject to any party having a prior and conflicting interest in the property. For example, if the building carries a mortgage, the landlord defaults and the bank forecloses, the lease may be void and the bank may have the right to evict the tenant. To protect the tenant, the bank should enter into a recognition agreement by which the bank, in the event of foreclosure, agrees to honor the terms of the lease.

The landlord will want to be free to place future mortgages on the building without being restricted by existing leases. The tenant is usually asked to grant this right in return for a recognition agreement as part of any future mortgages.

There is sometimes a three-tier hierarchy: the mortgagee or a ground lessor, the landlord and the tenant. The assumption of risk is usually least for the mortgagee or ground lessor, greater for the landlord, and greatest for the tenant. The typical commercial lease reflects this graduation of risk.

Loss or Damage to Leased Property

During the term of the lease there may be some event, such as fire, flood, eminent domain, etc., that makes the property of no use, or of lessened utility, to the tenant. Provisions to cover such contingencies can be complicated. The extent to which each possible situation is resolved, and the detail with which it is described, will depend, at least in part, upon the dollar importance of the lease and upon the difficulties the particular event would cause the tenant or the landlord. The first example below has a simple provision that is adequate for many leases. The second example has a more complicated provision of the kind that may be desirable in some leases.

Examples of Lease Terms

Commercial property leases, because of the importance and number of items that must be covered, are generally long. Thirty to sixty pages is usual. We'll consider two lease forms, a short version and another longer version. The shorter version first:

LEASE

This is a Lease Agreement, effective June 25, 1989, between Perimet Associates, Inc., a New Hampshire Corporation, ("Lessor") and City Development Corporation, a Delaware corporation, ("Lessee").

Background: The Lessor owns a building at 45 Pexter Road, Nashua, New Hampshire (the "Building"). The Lessee desires to lease space in that building and the parties have agreed to the following terms.

1. Leased Premises: The premises to be leased comprise an area of Ten Thousand square feet, identified as Unit #5 (the "Leased Property") in the building located at 45 Pexter Road, Nashua, New Hampshire, (together with the land on which the building is situated, the "Premises"). The area of the Leased Property, as shown on the ground plan in Exhibit A, is measured from the outside of the exterior walls and from the center of partition to the center of partition of interior walls. It is agreed that the area of the Leased Property

continued on page 10-9

continued from page 10-8

represents Twenty-two percent of the total rentable space of the Building (the "Percentage").

2. Term: The lease shall be for five years commencing on September 1, 1989 (the "Beginning Date") and ending on September 1, 1994 (the "Ending Date")

3. Rent: The annual rent to be paid to the Lessor shall be computed at the rate of Ten Dollars ($10.00) per square foot (Exhibit A), payable in advance in monthly installments commencing on October 1, 1989.

4. Security Deposit: The Lessee herewith deposits Ten Thousand Dollars ($10,000.00) to be held by the Lessor to be returned to the Lessee at the termination of this Lease, provided the Lessee has complied with all terms of this Lease Agreement.

5. Utilities and Services: The Lessee shall pay for the following services for the Leased Property: heat; electricity for air conditioning, lighting and other purposes; replacement of electric lamps; water and sewage charges; replacement of broken glass; janitorial and cleaning services; window washing; and all maintenance and repairs. The Lessor shall be responsible for the care and maintenance of all common areas, but the expenses associated with common areas, including snow removal, sanding, utility room; and grounds maintenance, shall be pro-rated among the tenants or rentable space and Lessee shall pay the Percentage of such expenses.

The Lessor shall provide and maintain heating and air conditioning equipment and ducts, and water, gas, and electrical installations. Utility payments to be made by the Lessee shall be made to the Lessor at the same rate as those charged by the utility company.

6. Real Estate Taxes: (a) Lessee shall pay, as additional rent, the Percentage of all real estate taxes and other assessments levied against the Premises before any penalty for non-payment, for the period of this Lease. Payments shall be pro-rated for portions of tax-years not within the lease term.

(b) Lessee shall deposit with the Lessor on the first day of each month during the term hereof, a sum equal to one-twelfth of the annual real estate taxes and other assessments against the Premises (estimated on the basis of current taxes and assessments). The Lessor shall deposit such money in an interest bearing account

continued on page 10-10

continued from page 10-9

at a bank, selected by the Lessor, and will use such money only for the purpose of paying taxes and assessments on the Premises. Accrued interest on such deposit shall be credited to the Lessee. Upon the receipt of each semi-annual tax bill, or any assessment, the Lessor will make an accounting to the Lessee. The Lessee shall promptly make any payment required in excess of the money on deposit.

7. Insurance: The Lessor will maintain all-risk property insurance on the Premises in the amount of at least Six Hundred Thousand Dollars, which insurance shall include a loss-of-rents rider that, when in effect, and while said rents are being received by the Lessor, will relieve the Lessee from its obligation to pay rent. The Lessor will also maintain combined bodily injury and property damage insurance on the Premises in an amount of at least One Million Dollars.

The Lessee shall be responsible for maintaining its own liability insurance on its business and operation in the amount of at least Five Hundred Thousand Dollars and, in addition, appropriate coverage of its own personal property and equipment.

8. Quiet Possession: So long as the Lessee performs its obligations, Lessor warrants that the Lessee shall have quiet and peaceful possession of the Leased Property and the right to use it free of interference from noise, noxious or unpleasant fumes or odors, or other disturbances from other tenants in the same building.

9. Lessee's Obligations: The Lessee agrees as follows:

(a) to pay rent and other charges when due and to deliver possession of the Leased Property to the Lessor upon termination of this lease in the same condition as when first occupied by the Lessee, ordinary wear and tear and damage by fire, the elements or other casualty excepted; and

(b) to use the Premises in a quiet and orderly manner without disturbing other tenants; and

(c) not to assign or sublet the Leased Property, or any part of it, without the prior written consent of the Lessor; and

(d) to follow all reasonable regulations concerning such matters as parking and trash collections.

continued on page 10-11

continued from page 10-10

10. Lessor's Remedies: The Lessor may terminate this lease and enter and take possession of the Lease Property, without waiving any legal rights and without further notice or demand, except as specifically set forth herein, following any of these events:

(a) the Lessee fails to pay rent or other charges within ten days after written notice of such default; or

(b) the Lessee fails to commence curing any other violation of its obligations hereunder within ten days after written notice thereof or, having commenced to cure such violation, fails to complete such cure with due diligence; or

(c) the Lessee is adjudicated to be a bankrupt or a receiver is appointed for its property.

11. Damage to the Premises: If the Leased Property or any part of it, is made untenantable by fire, the elements or other casualty, rent for the Leased Property, or the affected portion thereof, shall stop from the date of such casualty to the restoration of tenantability. The Lessor shall restore the property with all reasonable speed and, if the Lessor fails to restore the Leased Property, or the affected part of it, to tenantability within sixty (60) days, the Lessee may then terminate this Lease. If more than fifty percent of the Leased Property is rendered untenantable by such casualty, either the Lessor or the Lessee may terminate this lease, unless the Lessor can restore the Leased Property within ninety (90) days of such casualty. No rent shall accrue for the period of untenantability.

12. Inspection: The Lessor shall have the right to enter the Leased Property during usual business hours for reasonable inspections and shall have the right to show the Leased Property to prospective tenants during the last four months of the lease term.

13. Signs: All signs, plaques or other identification to be erected by the Lessee shall be subject to advance approval by the Lessor. All signs or other identification affixed to the Leased Property shall remain the property of the Lessee and shall be removed by the Lessee at the end of the lease and the Lessee shall be responsible for restoring the Leased Property to its original condition. All signs shall conform with local zoning ordinances and regulations.

continued on page 10-12

continued from page 10-11

14. The Lessee's Alterations and Improvements: The Lessee is granted permission to make those alterations and improvements described in Exhibit B. The Lessee agrees to pay for all such alterations and improvements and to indemnify the Lessor for any costs arising therefrom. The Lessor shall not unreasonably withhold consent to the Lessee to make further alterations and improvements to the Leased Property.

15. Lessee's Improvements: Any installations or modifications that are affixed to the real estate by the Lessee, including without limitation ceilings, flooring, carpeting, shelving, partitions, walls and wall coverings, shall become the property of the Lessor. Upon termination of this Lease, the Lessee may remove all of its personal property not considered part of the real estate, provided, the Lessee shall at the request of the Lessor, and at the expense of the Lessee, remove any or all of the modifications or installations affixed to the real estate by the Lessee and restore the appropriate part of the Leased Property to its original condition.

16. Condemnation: If the Premises, or any substantial part of it, are taken by eminent domain, or condemned for public use, this lease may be terminated by either the Lessee or the Lessor, and all awards from such taking shall be the exclusive property of the Lessor, provided, the Lessee shall not be precluded from prosecuting any claim directly against the condemning authority for any loss caused by such condemnation so long as such claim shall not adversely affect Lessor's award or that of any mortgagee.

17. Subordination: This Lease shall, at the election of the holder of any mortgage or ground lease on the Premises, be subordinate to all mortgages and ground leases on the Premises, so that the lien imposed by any such mortgage or ground lease shall be superior to all rights vested in the Lessee, provided the holder of any such mortgage or ground lease shall execute and deliver to the Lessee a binding and recordable agreement by which if such mortgage or ground lease is foreclosed by entry or sale, the Lessee, so long as it meets its obligations hereunder, shall peaceably enjoy the Leased Property for the remainder of this Lease or any extension thereof upon the same terms as are contained in this Lease and without hindrance or interruption from such holder.

continued on page 10-13

continued from page 10-12

18. Parking Facilities: The Lessee shall have the right to use such parking facilities as are designated on the Plan shown in Exhibit C. The Lessee agrees not to encroach on parking facilities designated for other tenants.

19. Legal Fees: If the Lessor brings legal action against the Lessee for the collection of rent or other charges under this Lease, or because of any default by the Lessee, then, if the Lessor prevails in such action, the Lessee shall reimburse the Lessor for all reasonable attorney's fees incidental to such action.

20. Liens: The Lessee shall keep the Premises free from liens arising from any work performed, materials furnished, or obligations incurred by the Lessee. If the Lessee fails within ten days following the imposition of any such lien, to cause the same to be released, all sums paid by the Lessor in connection therewith, including without limitation attorneys' fees, court costs, and other expenses of litigation, shall be payable by the Lessee to the Lessor on demand. Nothing herein shall be construed as constituting the consent of the Lessor to any contractor, or any other party, for the performance of any services or the furnishing of any materials that would give rise to the filing of any mechanic's lien against the Premises.

21. Entire Agreement: This Lease Agreement embodies the entire agreement between the parties with respect to the subject matter hereof. This Agreement may only be modified in writing executed by both parties.

22. Authorization to Execute this Agreement: Each individual executing this Lease Agreement on behalf of a corporation or other entity warrants that he or she is authorized to execute this Lease Agreement on behalf of such corporation or other entity and that this Lease Agreement is binding upon such corporation or other entity.

City Development
Corporation,Lessee

By________________________
Title:

Perimet Associates, Inc.,
Lessor

By________________________

That is not an unreasonable lease, but like most leases it tends to favor the landlord. The extent to which the lease can be modified depends upon the negotiating positions of the parties. Whether the above lease form, or any other simplified lease, is adequate for the purposes depends upon the relative importance of the lease in the life of the business. If the lease, for example, is vital to the very existence of the business, then a somewhat more sophisticated lease may be in order. However, if the lease is for extra space and the loss of the leased premises would have no major impact on the business, then a lease even more simple than the above may be in order.

Arbitration Clauses

In any lease, but more particularly in a simplified lease that may not cover all the bases, an arbitration provision is desirable. In a simplified lease, it is of little advantage to have a lease provision that follows the rules of the American Arbitration Association. It is better to spend the additional time and expense in preparing a more complete lease document. But a provision along these lines is helpful:

Arbitration: If a dispute arises between the parties in connection with this Lease Agreement, either party may, by ten days written notice to the other, request settlement by arbitration under the following terms: The date of giving such notice is the "Notice Date". Within twenty days after the Notice Date, each party shall appoint an arbiter to represent it in the dispute. The two arbiters, within thirty days after the Notice Date, shall by mutual agreement appoint a third arbiter. The three arbiters shall consider all of the facts relative to the dispute and consider the arguments and reasons presented by each party. Each party shall cooperate fully with the arbiters and make any relevant documents available to the arbiters. The arbiters shall, by majority agreement, render a decision within sixty days after the Notice Date, which decision shall be binding on the parties and enforceable in any court having jurisdiction of the parties. The arbiters shall give first consideration to the intent of this Lease Agreement. If the intent is unclear or not expressed with respect to any element of this Lease Agreement, the arbiters shall take into account the usual and customary provisions and customs relative to commercial leases of similar properties in the area.

A More Complex Lease

The following example is a more or less typical lease agreement suitable, with appropriate modifications to suit it to the particular circumstances, for larger lease commitments. Like most commercial leases, this one was prepared by the attorneys for the landlord and accordingly favors the landlord in many important respects. Whether a tenant would accept this lease depends upon the relative bargaining strength of the parties. If the prospective tenant is a small business renting a relatively small amount of space in a large building, the lease would be presented as "our standard lease" and the tenant would have little room to negotiate more favorable terms. If, however, the prospective tenant is a large organization renting all or a substantial portion of the building, it would be unlikely to accept these terms. Discussion of alternate terms, and the objectionable parts of this lease, are reserved for Chapter 13 where the lease is considered again in connection with "What-iffing" the contract.

COMMERCIAL BUILDING

Lease to Science Renters Club, Inc.

Table of Contents

continued on page 10-16

continued from page 10-15

7.3 Personal Property at Risk
7.4 Landlord's Insurance
7.5 Waiver of Subrogation
8. Casualty and Eminent Domain
8.1 Restoration Following Casualty
8.2 Landlord's Termination Election
8.3 Tenant's Termination Election
8.4 Casualty at Expiration of Lease
8.5 Eminent Domain
8.6 Rent After Casualty or Taking
8.7 Temporary Taking
8.8 Taking Award
9. Default
9.1 Tenant's Default
9.2 Damages
9.3 Cumulative Rights
9.4 Landlord's Self-help
9.5 Enforcement Expense
9.6 Late Charges and Interest on Overdue Payments
9.7 Landlord's Right to Notice and Cure
10. Mortgagees' and Ground Lessors' Rights
10.1 Subordination
10.2 Prepayment of Rent Not to Bind Mortgagee
10.3 Tenant's Duty to Notify Mortgagee; Mortgagee's Ability to Cure
10.4 Estoppel Certificates
11. Miscellaneous
11.1 Notice of Lease
11.2 Notices
11.3 Successors and Limitation on Liability of the Landlord
11.4 Waivers by the Landlord
11.5 Acceptance of Partial Payments of Rent
11.6 Interpretation and Partial Invalidity
11.7 Quiet Enjoyment
11.8 Brokerage
11.9 Surrender of Premises and Holding Over
11.10 Security Deposit
11.11 Financial Reporting

Exhibit A - Land Description
Exhibit B - Parking Map
Exhibit C - Floor Area of the Building
Exhibit D - Standard Services

continued on page 10-17

continued from page 10-16

LEASE

This is a Lease Agreement (the "Lease") effective June 3, 1986, between Landmark Development Corporation, a Delaware corporation, (the "Landlord") and Science Renters Club, Inc., a Massachusetts corporation (the "Tenant").

1. Background and Definitions

The Landlord is the owner of a certain building and the parties mutually desire that part of the building be leased to the Tenant. The parties agree on the following terms.

1.1 Definitions

"Building" means the Carmont Building located at 56 Earnest Street, Boston, Massachusetts in which the Premises are located.

"Premises" means the portion of the Building leased by Tenant at any given time during the Term.

"Land" means the parcel of land on which the Building is situated as described in Exhibit A.

"Property" means the Land and the Building.

"Common Building Areas" means those portions of the Building which are not part of the Premises and to which the tenant has appurtenant rights.

"External Causes" means events caused by (i) Acts of God, war, civil commotion, fire, flood or other casualty, strikes or other extraordinary labor difficulty, unforeseeable shortages of labor or materials in the ordinary course of trade, government order or regulations or other cause not reasonably within the control of the party who would otherwise be in default under this lease and not caused primarily by the negligence of such party; and (ii) any act, failure to act or neglect of the other party, its employees or agents or any party claiming through such party, which delays either the Landlord or the Tenant in the performance of any act required under this Lease.

"Term" means the period of this Lease from January 1, 1988 (the "Commencement Date") through December 31, 1994 (the "Ending Date") together with any extensions of this Lease as provided for herein.

continued on page 10-18

continued from page 10-17

"Annual Fixed Rent" means the annual rent payable in each annual period and is subject to change in accordance with schedules set forth herein.

"Additional Rent" means all charges payable by the Tenant other than Annual Fixed Rent, including such items as parking charges; Tenant's Tax Expense, as defined in Subsection 3.2(b); Tenant's Operating Expenses as defined in Subsection 3.3(a); and amounts payable for special services.

"Prime Rate" means the prime rate as published in the Wall Street Journal as representative of the base rate charged by the major banks or, if such index is no longer published, an equivalent index from another source.

"HVAC" means the heating, ventilating and air conditioning Systems.

2. Premises and Term

2.1 Premises. The Landlord leases to the Tenant and the Tenant leases from the Landlord the Premises for the Term. The Premises shall exclude the entry and main lobby of the Building, first floor elevator lobby, first floor mail room, the common stairways and stairwells, elevators and elevator wells, boiler room, sprinklers, sprinkler rooms, elevator rooms, mechanical rooms, loading and receiving areas, electric and telephone closets, janitor closets, Building shower room, and pipes, ducts, conduits, wires and appurtenant fixtures and equipment serving exclusively or in common other parts of the Building. If the Premises at any time includes less than the entire rentable floor area of any floor of the Building, the Premises shall also exclude the common corridors, vestibules, walkways and bridges, elevator lobby and toilets located on such floor.

The Tenant acknowledges, except as expressly set forth in this Lease, there have been no representations or warranties by the Landlord with respect to the Premises, the Building or the Property or with respect to the suitability of any of them for the conduct of the Tenant's business. The taking of possession of the Premises by the Tenant shall conclusively establish that the Premises and the Building were at such time in satisfactory condition.

continued on page 10-19

continued from page 10-18

2.2 Appurtenant Rights. The Tenant shall have, as appurtenant to the Premises, the nonexclusive right to use in common with others, subject to reasonable rules of general applicability to occupants of the Building from time to time made by the Landlord of which the Tenant is given notice: (i) the entry, vestibules and main lobby of the Building, first floor mailroom, atrium bridges and walkways, the common stairways, Building shower room, elevators, elevator wells, boiler room, elevator rooms, sprinkler rooms, mechanical rooms, electric and telephone closets, janitor closets and the pipes, sprinklers, ducts, conduits, wires and appurtenant fixtures and equipment serving the Premises in common with others; (ii) common walkways and driveways necessary or reasonably convenient for access to the Building, (iii) access to the loading area and freight elevator subject to Rules and Regulations then in effect, and (iv) if the Premises at any time include less than the entire rentable floor area of any floor, the common toilets, corridors, vestibules, bridges and walkways, and elevator lobby of such floor.

2.3 Landlord's Reservations. The Landlord reserves the right from time to time, without unreasonable interference with the Tenant's use: (i) to install, maintain, repair, replace and reallocate for service to the Premises and other parts of the Building, pipes, ducts, conduits, wires and appurtenant fixtures and equipment, wherever located in the Premises or the Building, and (ii) to alter or reallocate any other common facility, provided that substitutions are at least substantially equivalent.

2.4 Parking. The Landlord shall provide and the Tenant shall pay for parking privileges for use by the Tenant's employees and business invitees and visitors in accordance with Exhibit B. The Landlord shall have the right to designate, and change, from time to time, the location within the Property that shall be used for the Tenant's parking. The Tenant's parking privileges may be on a non-exclusive basis. The Tenant agrees that it and all persons claiming under it shall abide by the reasonable regulations promulgated by the Landlord with respect to the use of the parking facilities provided by the Landlord.

The Tenant shall pay to the Landlord for Tenant's parking privileges the monthly rent at which the Landlord from time to time offers to make parking facilities available to tenants and other users who

continued on page 10-20

continued from page 10-19

make use of such parking facilities and which pay rent therefore. Monthly parking charges shall constitute Additional Rent and shall be payable at the time and in the manner in which the Annual Fixed Rent is payable hereunder.

2.5 Extension Options. If there has been no Event of Default, as defined in Subsection 9.1, on the part of the Tenant, other than any which have been waived by the Landlord, the Tenant shall have the right to extend the term hereof for one period of five (5) years (the "Extension Term"), such option to be exercised by notice to the Landlord at least twelve (12) months prior to the expiration of the then current term. No additional documents need be exercised for such extension of the term. Time is of the essence in the giving of such notice. The Extension Term shall be upon the terms of this Lease except the Annual Fixed Rent during such extension term shall be the fair market rental value (the "Fair Rental Value") of the Premises for such Extension Term, as determined below, but in no event less than the Annual Fixed Rent in effect immediately prior to the commencement of the Extension Term. If not agreed upon prior to three months before the date on which the Extension Term is to commence, such Fair Rental Value shall be determined by three appraisers, one selected by the Tenant, one selected by the Landlord, and the third by the two appraisers so selected. Each appraiser shall have had at least ten years experience in appraising commercial real estate in the Greater Boston area, and be a member of (i) the American Institute of Real Estate Appraisers, or (ii) the Massachusetts Board of Real Estate Appraisers. Each appraiser shall independently determine the Fair Rental Value of the Premises, taking into account all of the terms and conditions of this Lease and the condition of the Premises. The Fair Rental Value shall be deemed to be the average of the two appraisals arithmetically closest in amount. The cost of the third appraiser shall be borne equally by the Landlord and the Tenant. The cost of the other two appraisers shall be borne by the party selecting them.

3. Rent and Other Payments

3.1 Annual Fixed Rent. The Annual Fixed Rent for the first two (2) years of the Term shall be $10.25 per square foot, and for the remaining three (3) years shall be 12.25 per square foot. The area of the Premises shall be deemed, for purposes of rent

continued on page 10-21

continued from page 10-20

computation, to have an area of 9,230 square feet. Beginning on the Commencement Date, the Tenant shall pay to the Landlord, in advance on the first day of each calendar month of the Term, a monthly rental installment equal to one-twelfth of the Annual Fixed Rental then applicable to the Premises. The total rentable floor area of the Building shall be as shown in Exhibit C.

3.2 Real Estate Taxes. The following terms are defined as used in this Section 3.2:

(a) "Tax Year" means the 12-month period beginning July 1 each year, or if the appropriate governmental tax fiscal period shall begin on any date other than July 1, such other date.

(b) The "Tenant's Tax Expense" means (i) that portion of the Landlord's Tax Expenses for a Tax Year that bears the same proportion thereto as the Rentable Floor Area of the Building and (ii) in the event the Premises are improved to a standard that is significantly higher than other portions of the Property, and such improvement results in an increase in Real Estate Taxes on the Property, such portion of the Real Estate Taxes on the Premises with respect to any Tax Year shall be adjusted as is appropriate and equitable so that the Tenant bears the portion of the Real Estate Taxes that are properly allocable to the Premises, as reasonably determined by the Landlord based on information made available by assessing authorities.

(c) The "Landlord's Tax Expenses" with respect to any Tax Year means the aggregate Real Estate Taxes on the Property with respect to that Tax Year, reduced by any abatement receipts with respect to that Tax Year.

(d) "Real Estate Taxes" means all taxes and special assessments of every kind assessed by any governmental authority on the Property and reasonable expenses of any abatement proceedings and appeals. The amount of special taxes or special assessments to be included shall be limited to the amount of the installment (plus any interest thereon) required to be paid during the Tax Year for which tax charges are computed. All income, estate, succession, inheritance, excess profit, franchise and transfer taxes shall be excluded, provided if at any time during the term the present system of ad valorem taxation of real property shall be changed so that in lieu of the whole or any part of the

continued on page 10-22

continued from page 10-21

ad valorem tax on real property, there shall be assessed on the Landlord a capital levy or other tax on gross rents received from the Property, or if a tax, levy, assessment, or other charge by any governmental agency (distinct from any now in effect) based in whole or in part upon any such gross rents, then such charges, to the extent so based, shall be included in Real Estate Taxes.

Payments by the Tenant for the Tenant's Tax Expense shall be made monthly in an amount of one-twelfth of the Tenant's Tax Expense for the current Tax Year as reasonably estimated by the Landlord.

Within ninety (90) days after the Landlord's Tax Expenses are determinable for each Tax Year during the Term, the Landlord shall provide the Tenant with a statement showing in reasonable detail the applicable real estate taxes and assessments, expenses and abatements or refunds related to the computations and the details of the calculation of the distribution of such taxes and assessments. If the Tenant for such Tax Year has paid either more or less than the Tenant's Tax Expenses, then the difference shall be adjusted by payment to the appropriate party within 15 days.

3.3 Operating Expenses. Definitions for this Section:

(a) The "Tenant's Operating Expenses" means that portion of the Operating Expenses for the Property which bears the same proportion thereto as the Rentable Floor Area of the Premises bears to the Total Rentable Floor Area of the Building.

(b) "Operating Expenses for the Property" means Landlord's cost of operating, cleaning, maintaining and repairing the Property, the parking lots and garages for tenants in the Building and the roads, driveways and walkways for providing access to the Building and such parking facilities and shall include all insurance costs, the deductible amounts from any insurance recovery by the Landlord, compensation and all fringe benefits, worker's compensation insurance premiums, and payroll taxes in connection with persons engaged in the operation, maintenance, or cleaning of the Property and such parking facilities; interior plant supply and maintenance, steam, water, sewer, gas, oil, electricity, telephone and other utility charges (excluding charges separately chargeable directly to tenants); cost of providing conditioned water for HVAC

continued on page 10-23

continued from page 10-22

services; cost of building and cleaning supplies; rental costs for equipment used in the operating, cleaning, maintaining or repairing of the Property, or the applicable fair market rental charges in the case of equipment owned by the Landlord; cost of cleaning; cost of maintenance, repairs and replacements; cost of snow removal; cost of landscape maintenance; security services; the cost of capital improvements made for the purpose of reducing operating expenses or to comply with applicable law, which cost shall be amortized over such reasonable period as the Landlord shall determine, together with interest on the unamortized balance at the Prime Rate or such higher rate as may have been paid by the Landlord on funds borrowed for the purpose of constructing such capital improvements; and all other reasonable and necessary expenses paid in connection with the operation, cleaning, maintenance and repair of the Property. If for any reason portions of the Premises were not occupied by tenants or the Landlord was not supplying all tenants with the services being supplied under the Lease or a lesser level of standard services than those supplied to the Tenant under this Lease, Landlord's Operating Expenses for the Property shall include the amounts reasonably determined by the Landlord which would have been incurred if all of the rentable area in the Building were occupied and were supplied with the same level of standard services as supplied to the Tenant under the Lease.

Operating Expenses for the Property shall not include: the Landlord's Tax Expense; cost of repairs or replacements (i) resulting from eminent domain takings, (ii) to the extent reimbursed by insurance, or (iii) required, above and beyond ordinary periodic maintenance, to maintain in serviceable condition the major structural elements of the Building, including the roof, exterior walls and floor slabs; replacement or contingency reserves; the cost of capital reserves; the cost of capital improvements (other than as specifically provided above); ground lease rents or payment of debt obligations; legal and other professional fees for matters not relating to the normal administration and operation of the Property; promotional, advertising, public relations or brokerage fees and commissions paid in connection with services rendered for securing or renewing leases, the Landlord's Operating Expenses shall be reduced by the amount of any proceeds, payments, credits or reimbursements that the Landlord receives from sources

continued on page 10-24

continued from page 10-23

other than tenants and which are applicable to such Operating Expenses for the Property.

Payments by the Tenant on account of the Tenant's Operating Expenses shall be made monthly at the time and in the fashion herein provided for the payment of Annual Fixed Rent. The amount so paid to the Landlord shall be an amount from time to time reasonably estimated by the Landlord to be sufficient to aggregate a sum equal to the Tenant's Operating Expenses for each calendar year.

Not later than ninety (90) days after the end of each calendar year or fraction thereof during the Term or fraction thereof at the end of the Term, the Landlord shall provide a detailed statement, according to usual accounting practices, certified by a representative of the Landlord, showing for the preceding calendar year or fraction thereof, as the case may be, the Operating Expenses for the Property and the Tenant's Operating Expenses, such statement to show the calculations and all relevant information used in arriving at the final figures. If the Tenant has paid more or less, for the applicable period, than the Tenant's Operating Expenses, then within thirty (30) days after such statement is provided, an appropriate adjustment shall be made either by Additional Rent payment by the Tenant or by a cash refund by the Landlord.

3.4 Other Utility Charges. During the Term, the Tenant shall pay directly to the provider, all separately metered charges for steam, heat, gas, electricity, fuel and other services and utilities furnished to the Premises.

3.5 Above-standard Services. If the Tenant requests and the Landlord elects to provide any service to the Tenant in addition to those described in Exhibit D, the Tenant shall pay to the Landlord as Additional Rent, the amount billed to the Landlord for such services at Landlord's standard rates as from time to time in effect. If the Tenant has requested that such services be provided on a regular basis, the Tenant shall, if requested by the Landlord, pay for such services at the time and in the manner in which Annual Fixed Rent under this Lease is payable, otherwise, the Tenant shall pay for such additional services within fifteen (15) days after receipt of an invoice from the Landlord. The Landlord shall have the right from time to time to inspect Tenant's utility meters and to install timers

continued on page 10-25

continued from page 10-24

thereon at Tenant's expense for monitoring above-standard service usage. Tenant shall pay for such work within fifteen (15) days after receipt of an invoice from the Landlord.

3.6 No Offsets. Annual Fixed Rent and Additional Rent shall be paid by the Tenant without offset, abatement or deduction.

3.7 Net Lease. It is agreed that this Lease is a net lease and that the Annual Fixed Rent is absolutely net to the Landlord excepting only the Landlord's obligations to pay any debt service or ground rent on the Premises, to provide the Landlord's services, and to pay the real estate taxes and operating expenses which the Tenant is not required to pay under this Lease.

4.0 Alterations

4.1 Consent Required for Tenant's Alterations. The Tenant shall make no alterations or additions to the Premises except in accordance with the building standards from time to time in effect, with construction rules and regulations from time to time in effect, and with reasonable construction rules and regulations promulgated from time to time by the Landlord and applicable to all tenants in the Building, and with plans and specifications therefor first approved by the Landlord, which approval shall not be unreasonably withheld. The withholding by the Landlord of approval of any alterations or additions that (i) involve or might affect any structural or exterior element of the Building, any area or element outside the Premises, or any facility serving any area of the Building outside of the Premises, (ii) will require unusual expense to readapt the Premises to normal use unless the Tenant first gives assurance acceptable to the Landlord that such readaptation will be made prior to termination of this Lease without expense to the Landlord, or (iii) would not be compatible with existing mechanical or electrical, plumbing, HVAC or other systems in the Building, in each case, as reasonably determined by the Landlord.

4.2 Ownership of Alterations. All alterations and additions shall be part of the Building and owned by the Landlord unless prior to their installation, the Landlord shall specify the same for removal at the end of the Term.

continued on page 10-26

continued from page 10-25

4.3 Construction Requirements for Alterations. All construction work by the Tenant shall be done in a good and workmanlike manner employing only first-class materials and in compliance with all applicable laws and all lawful ordinances, regulations and orders of Governmental authority and insurers of the Building. The Landlord, or its representative, may, without any implied obligation to do so, inspect the work of the Tenant at reasonable times and shall give notice of observed defects. All of the Tenant's alterations and additions and installation of furnishings shall be (a) coordinated with any work being performed by the Landlord and in such manner as to maintain harmonious labor relations and not to damage the Building or interfere with Building construction or operation and, except for installation of furnishings; and (b) performed by the Landlord's general contractor or by contractors or workmen first approved by the Landlord, which approval shall not be unreasonably withheld or delayed. The Tenant before starting any work, shall receive and comply with the Landlord's construction rules and regulations and (a) shall cause Tenant's contractors to comply therewith; (b) shall secure all licenses and permits necessary therefor and shall deliver to the Landlord a statement of the names of all of its contractors and subcontractors and the estimated cost of all labor and material to be furnished by them together with security satisfactory to the Landlord protecting the Landlord against liens arising out of furnishing of such labor and material; and (c) cause each contractor to carry workmen's compensation insurance in statutory amounts covering all of the contractors' and subcontractors' employees and comprehensive general public liability insurance with such reasonable limits as the Landlord may require, but in no event less than $1,000,000 (individual) and $3,000,000 (occurrence), to be written by companies approved by the Landlord. All such policies shall name the Landlord, and individuals and entities associated with the Landlord, as named insureds, and shall provide that the Landlord shall receive thirty (30) days written notice prior to any cancellation, non-renewal or material modification thereof. The Tenant shall provide Landlord with a copy of each such policy.

4.4 Payment for Tenant Alterations. The Tenant agrees to pay promptly when due the entire cost of any work on the Premises by the Tenant, its agents, employees or independent contractors, and not to permit any liens for labor or materials performed or furnished in

continued on page 10-27

continued from page 10-26

connection therewith to be attached to the Premises or the Property and promptly to discharge any such liens which may so attach. If any such lien shall be filed against the Premises or the Property and the Tenant shall fail to cause such lien to be discharged within ten (10) days after the filing thereof, the Landlord may cause such lien to be discharged by payment, bond or otherwise, without investigation as to the validity thereof or as to any offsets or defenses which the Tenant may have with respect to the amount claimed. The Tenant shall reimburse the Landlord, as Additional Rent, for any costs so incurred and shall indemnify the Landlord for any costs, including reasonable attorneys' fees, incurred by reason of such lien or its discharge.

5. Responsibility for Condition of Building and Premises

5.1 Maintenance of Building and Common Areas by the Landlord. Except as otherwise provided in Section 8, the Landlord shall make such repairs of the major structural elements of the Building, including the roof, exterior walls and floor slabs as may be necessary to keep and maintain the same in serviceable condition and maintain and make such repairs to the Common Building Areas as may be necessary to keep them in good order, condition and repair, including without limitation the glass in the exterior walls of the Building, and all mechanical systems and equipment serving the Building and not exclusively serving the Premises. The Landlord shall further perform the services set forth in Exhibit D, provided the Landlord may from time to time amend in Landlord's sole discretion the level and content of such services. Landlord shall from time to time upon request by the Tenant replace all lighting tubes, bulbs and ballasts at Tenant's expense, to be paid by Tenant within ten (10) days after receipt of Landlord's invoice therefor. The Landlord shall in no event be responsible to the Tenant for any condition of the Premises or the Building caused by an act or neglect of the Tenant, or any employee, invitee, or contractor of the Tenant. Landlord's costs in performing such services shall be reimbursed by the Tenant to the extent provided in Section 3.3.

5.2 Maintenance of Premises by Tenant. The Tenant shall keep neat and clean and maintain in good order, condition and repair the Premises and every part thereof and all Building and mechanical equipment

continued on page 10-28

continued from page 10-27

exclusively serving the Premises, reasonable wear and tear excepted, and further excepting those repairs for which the Landlord is responsible under Section 5.1 and damage by fire or other casualty and as a consequence of the exercise of the power of eminent domain and shall surrender the Premises and all alterations and additions thereto, at the end of the Term, in such condition, first removing all goods and effects of the Tenant, all alterations and additions made by the Tenant and repairing any damage caused by such removal and restoring the Premises and leaving them clean and neat. The Tenant shall be responsible for the cost of repairs made necessary by damages to common areas in the Building by the Tenant, or any of the invitees or contractors of the Tenant.

5.3 Delays in Landlords Services. The Landlord shall not be liable to the Tenant for any compensation or reduction of rent by reason of inconvenience or annoyance or for loss of business arising from the necessity of the Landlord or its agents entering the Premises for any purposes authorized in this Lease, or for repairing the Premises or any portion of the Building. If the Landlord is prevented or delayed from making any repairs, alterations or improvements, or furnishing any services or performing any other covenant or duty to be performed on the part of the Landlord, by reason of any External Cause, the Landlord shall not be liable to the Tenant therefor, or, except as otherwise expressly provided herein, shall the Tenant be entitled to any abatement or reduction of rent by reason thereof, or shall the same give rise to a claim in the Tenant's favor that such failure constitutes actual or constructive, total or partial, eviction from the Premises.

The Landlord reserves the right to stop any service or utility system when necessary by reason of accident or emergency, until necessary repairs have been completed; provided, in each instance of stoppage, the Landlord shall exercise reasonable diligence to eliminate the cause thereof. Except for emergency repairs, the Landlord will give the Tenant reasonable advance notice of any contemplated stoppage and will use reasonable efforts to avoid unnecessary inconvenience to the Tenant by reason thereof. In no event shall the Landlord have any liability to the Tenant for the unavailability of heat, light or any utility or service to be provided by the Landlord to the extent that such unavailability is caused by External Causes.

continued on page 10-29

continued from page 10-28

6. Tenant's Covenants

The Tenant covenants during the time when the Tenant occupies any part of the Premises:

6.1 Permitted Uses. The Tenant shall occupy the Premises only for the Permitted Uses, and shall not injure or deface the Premises or the Property, or permit any auction sale on the Premises. The Tenant shall give written notice to the Landlord of any materials on OSHA's right to know list or which are subject to regulation by any other federal, state, municipal or other governmental authority and which the Tenant intends to have present on the Premises. The Tenant shall comply with all requirements of public authorities and of the Board of Fire Underwriters in connection with methods of storage, use and disposal of such materials. The Tenant shall not permit in the Premises any nuisance, or the emission from the Premises of any objectionable noise, odor or vibration, or use or devote the Premises or any part thereof for any purpose that is contrary to law or ordinance or that may invalidate or increase premiums for any insurance on the Building or its contents or may make necessary any alteration or addition to the Building, or permit any waste with respect to the Premises, or generate, store or dispose of any oil, hazardous wastes, or hazardous material, or permit the same within the Premises.

6.2 Laws and Regulations. The Tenant shall comply with all federal, state and local laws, regulations, ordinances, executive orders and similar requirements in effect from time to time, including without limitation, local ordinances with respect to hazardous waste and any such requirements pertaining to employment opportunity, anti-discrimination and affirmative action and permit access to the Tenant's facilities and any related books, accounts or other sources of information by the Landlord or its designees which may be determined by the Landlord to affect the Tenant's obligations with respect thereto.

6.3 Rules and Regulations. The Tenant shall not obstruct in any manner any portion of the Property not hereby leased; shall not permit the placing of any signs, curtains, blinds, shades, awnings, aerials or flagpoles, or the like, visible from outside the Premises; and shall comply with all reasonable rules and regulations of uniform application to all occupants

continued on page 10-30

continued from page 10-29

of the Building now or hereafter made by the Landlord, of which the Tenant has been given notice, for the care and use of the Property and its parking facilities. The Landlord shall not be liable to the Tenant for failure of other tenants to conform to any such rules and regulations. The Landlord shall provide, at the Tenant's expense, a Building Standard name sign at the entryway to the Premises.

6.4 Safety Compliance. The Tenant shall keep the Premises equipped with all safety appliances required by law or ordinance or any other regulations of any public authority because of any non-office use made by the Tenant and to procure all licenses and permits so required because of such use and, if requested by the Landlord, do any work so required because of such use, it being understood that the foregoing provisions shall not be construed to broaden in any way the Tenant's Permitted Uses.

6.5 Landlord's Entry. The Tenant shall permit the Landlord and its agents, after reasonable notice except for emergencies, to enter the Premises at all reasonable times for the purpose of inspecting, making repairs, or showing the Premises to prospective tenants and mortgagees at all reasonable times.

6.6 Floor Load. The Tenant shall not place a load upon any floor in the Premises exceeding the floor load per square foot of area which such floor was designed to carry and which is allowed by law; and not move any safe, vault or other heavy equipment in, about or out of the Premises except in such manner and at such time as the Landlord shall in each instance authorize. The Tenant's machines and mechanical equipment shall be placed and maintained by the Tenant at the Tenant's expense in settings sufficient to absorb or prevent vibration or noise that may be transmitted to the Building structure or to any other space in the Building.

6.7 Personal Property Tax. The Tenant shall pay promptly when due all taxes that may be imposed upon personal property, including without limitation, fixtures and equipment in the Premises irrespective of to whom assessed.

6.8 Assignment and Subleases. The Tenant shall not assign, mortgage, pledge, hypothecate, or otherwise transfer this Lease, or sublet (which term, without limitation, shall include granting of concessions,

continued on page 10-31

continued from page 10-30

licenses and the like) the whole or any part of the Premises without, in each instance, having first received the consent of the Landlord, which consent may, in the sole discretion of the Landlord, be withheld or conditioned on the payment of such consideration as the Landlord may deem appropriate. Any assignment or sublease made without such consent shall be void. Whether or not the Landlord consents to any assignment or subletting, the Tenant shall remain fully and primarily liable for the obligations of the tenant hereunder, including without limitation the obligation to pay the Annual Fixed Rent and Additional Rent under this Lease.

The Tenant shall give the Landlord notice of any proposed sublease or assignment, specifying the provisions of the proposed subletting or assignment, including (i) the name and address of the proposed subtenant or assignee, (ii) a copy of the proposed subtenant's or assignee's most recent annual financial statement, (iii) all of the terms and provisions upon which the proposed subletting or assignment is to be made and such other information concerning the proposed subtenant or assignee as the Tenant has obtained in connection with the proposed subletting or assignment. The Tenant shall reimburse the Landlord promptly for reasonable legal and other expense incurred by the Landlord in connection with any request by the Tenant for consent to any assignment or subletting. If this Lease is assigned, or if the Premises or any part thereof is sublet or occupied by any one other than the Tenant, the Landlord may at any time and from time to time, collect rent and other charges from the assignee, sublessee or occupant and apply the net amount collected to the rent and other charges herein reserved, but no such assignment, subletting, occupancy or collection shall be deemed a waiver of the prohibitions contained in this Section 6.8 or the acceptance of the assignee, sublessee or occupant as a tenant, or a release of the Tenant from the further performance by the Tenant of covenants on the part of the Tenant herein contained. The consent by the Landlord to an assignment or subletting shall not be construed to relieve the Tenant from obtaining the express consent in writing of the Landlord to any further subletting or assignment.

7. Indemnity and Insurance

7.1 Indemnity. To the maximum extent this Lease may be made effective according to law, the Tenant agrees to

continued on page 10-32

continued from page 10-31

indemnify the Landlord from all expenses, including defense costs and reasonable attorneys' fees, for claims of whatever kind arising from, or claimed to have arisen from, any act, omission or negligence of the Tenant, or the Tenant's contractors, licensees, invitees, agents, servants or employees, or arising from any accident, injury or damage whatsoever caused to any person or property, occurring during the Term or during any period Tenant occupies any part of the Premises, in or about the Property.

7.2 Liability Insurance. The Tenant agrees to maintain in full force, so long as the Tenant occupies any portion of the Premises, a policy of comprehensive general liability insurance under which the Landlord (and any individuals or entities affiliated with the Landlord, and ground lessor and any holder of a mortgage on the Property of whom Tenant is notified by the Landlord) and the Tenant are named as insureds, and under which the insurer provides a contractual liability endorsement insuring against all cost, expense and liability arising out of or based upon any and all claims, accidents, injuries and damages described in Section 7.1 in the broadest form of such coverage from time to time available. Each such policy shall be noncancellable and nonamendable (to the extent that any proposed amendment reduces the limits or the scope of the insurance required by this Lease) with respect to the Landlord and such ground lessors and mortgagees without thirty (30) days prior notice to the Landlord and such ground lessors and mortgagees and at the election of the Landlord, either a certificate of insurance or a duplicate original policy shall be delivered to the Landlord. The minimum limits of liability of such insurance as of the Commencement Date shall be Five Million Dollars ($5,000,000.00) for combined bodily injury or death and damage to property (per occurrence) and from time to time during the Term such limits of liability shall be increased to reflect such higher limits as are customarily required pursuant to new leases of space in the adjacent area with respect to similar properties.

7.3 Personal Property at Risk. The Tenant agrees that all of the personal property of every kind of the Tenant and of all persons claiming through the Tenant which, during any occupancy under this Lease, may be anywhere on the Property shall be at the sole risk of the Tenant, and if the whole or any part thereof shall be destroyed or damaged by fire, water or otherwise or

continued on page 10-33

continued from page 10-32

lost by reason of theft or other cause, no part of such loss or damage is to be borne by the Landlord, except that the Landlord shall not be exonerated from any liability for any injury, loss, damage or liability to the extent such exoneration is prohibited by law.

7.4 Landlord's Insurance. The Landlord shall carry such casualty and liability insurance upon and with respect to operations in the Building , as may from time to time be deemed reasonably prudent by the Landlord or required by any mortgagee holding a mortgage thereon or any ground lessor of the Land, and in any event, insurance against loss by fire and the risks customarily covered by extended coverage endorsements in an amount at least equal to eighty percent of the replacement value of the Building.

7.5 Waiver of Subrogation, Any insurance carried by either party with respect to the Property or any property therein or occurrences thereon shall, without further request by either party, if it can be so written without additional premium, or with an additional premium which the other party elects to pay, include an endorsement denying to the insurer rights of subrogation against the other party to the extent rights have been waived by the insured party prior to occurrence of injury or loss. Each party, notwithstanding any provisions of this Lease to the contrary, waives any rights of recovery against the other for injury or loss, including, without limitation, injury or loss caused by negligence of such other party, due to hazards covered by insurance containing such clause or endorsement to the extent of the indemnification received thereunder.

8. Casualty and Eminent Domain

8.1 Restoration Following Casualty. If, during the Term, the Building or the Premises shall be damaged by fire or casualty, subject to the exceptions and limitations provided below, the Landlord shall proceed promptly to exercise reasonable efforts to restore the Building or Premises to substantially the condition at the time of such damage, but the Landlord shall not be responsible for delay in such restoration resulting from any cause beyond its reasonable control. The Landlord shall have no obligation to expend in the reconstruction of the building more than the actual amount of the insurance proceeds made available to the Landlord by its insurer and not retained by the Landlord's mortgagee or ground

continued on page 10-34

continued from page 10-33

lessor. Any restoration of the Building or Premises shall be altered to the extent necessary to comply with then current laws and codes.

8.2 Landlord's Termination Election. If the Landlord reasonably determines the amount of insurance proceeds available to the Landlord is insufficient to cover the cost of restoring the Building or if in the reasonable opinion of the Landlord the Building has been so damaged that it is appropriate for the Landlord to raze or to substantially alter the Building, then the Landlord may terminate this Lease by giving notice to the Tenant within sixty (60) days after the date of the casualty or such later date as is required to allow the Landlord a reasonable time to make either such determination. Any such termination shall be effective on the date designated in such notice from the Landlord, but not later than sixty (60) days after such notice, and if no date is specified, effective upon delivery of such notice.

8.3 Tenant's Termination Election. Unless the Landlord has earlier advised the Tenant of the Landlord's election to terminate this Lease pursuant to Section 8.2, or to restore the Premises and maintain this Lease in effect, the Tenant shall have the right after the expiration of ninety days after any casualty which materially impairs a material portion of the Premises to give a written notice to the Landlord requiring the Landlord within ten days thereafter to exercise or waive any right of the Landlord to terminate this Lease pursuant to Section 8.2 as a result of such casualty and if the Landlord fails to give timely notice to the Tenant waiving any right under Section 8.2 to terminate this Lease based on such casualty, the Tenant shall be entitled, at any time until the Landlord has given notice to the Tenant waiving such termination right, to give notice to the Landlord terminating this Lease. Where the Landlord is obligated to exercise reasonable efforts to restore the Premises, unless such restoration is completed within one (1) year from the date of the casualty or taking, such period, however, being subject to extension where the delay in the completion of such work is the result of External Causes, but not longer than 18 months from the date of the casualty or taking, the Tenant shall have the right to terminate this Lease at any time after the expiration of such one-year (as extended) period until the restoration is substantially completed, such termination to take effect as of the date of the Tenant's notice.

continued on page 10-35

continued from page 10-34

8.4 Casualty at Expiration of Lease. If the Premises shall be damaged by fire or casualty in such manner that the Premises cannot, in the ordinary course, reasonably be expected to be repaired within four (4) months from the commencement of repair work and such damage occurs within the last eighteen (18) months of the Term (as the same may have been extended prior to such fire or casualty) either party shall have the right by giving notice to the other not later than sixty (60) days after such damage, to terminate this Lease, whereupon this Lease shall terminate as of the date of such notice.

8.5 Eminent Domain. Except as hereinafter provided, if the Premises, or such portion thereof as to render the remainder (if reconstructed to the maximum extent practicable in the circumstances) unsuitable for the Tenant's purposes, shall be taken by condemnation or right of eminent domain, the Landlord or the Tenant shall have the right to terminate this Lease by notice to the other of its election to do so, provided that such notice is given not later than thirty (30) days after the effective date of such taking. If so much of the Building shall be taken that the Landlord determines it would be appropriate to raze or substantially alter the Building, the Landlord shall have the right to terminate this Lease by giving notice to the Tenant of the Landlord's election to do so not later than thirty (30) days after the effective date of such taking.

Should any part of the Premises so taken or condemned during the Term, and should this Lease be not terminated in accordance with the foregoing provisions, the Landlord agrees to use reasonable efforts to put what may remain of the Premises into proper use and occupation as nearly like the condition of the Premises prior to such taking as shall be practicable, subject to applicable laws and codes then in existence and to the availability of sufficient proceeds from the eminent domain taking not retained by any mortgagee or ground lessor.

8.6 Rent After Casualty or Taking. If the Premises shall be damaged by fire or other casualty, except as provided below, the Annual Fixed Rent and Additional rent shall be justly and equitably abated according to the nature and extent of the loss of use thereof. If the casualty was caused by the Tenant, such abatement shall be only to the extent the Landlord is fully compensated

continued on page 10-36

continued from page 10-35

therefore by any lost rent insurance. In the event of a taking which permanently reduces the area of the Premises, a just proportion of the Annual Fixed Rent shall be abated for the remainder of the Term.

8.7 Temporary Taking. If any taking of the Premises or any part thereof is for a temporary use not in excess of six (6) months, (i) this Lease shall be and remain unaffected thereby and Annual Fixed Rent and Additional Rent shall not abate, and (ii) the Tenant shall be entitled to receive for itself such portion of any award made for such use with respect to the period of the taking that is within the Term.

8.8 Taking Award. Except as otherwise provided in Section 8.7, the Landlord shall have and hereby reserves and excepts, and the Tenant grants and assigns to the Landlord, all rights to recover for damages to the Building and the Land, and the leasehold interest created by this Lease, and to compensation accrued or to accrue by reason of such taking, damage or destruction, as aforesaid, and by way of confirming the foregoing, the Tenant grants and assigns to the Landlord, all rights to such damages or compensation. Nothing contained herein shall be construed to prevent the Tenant from prosecuting in any condemnation proceedings a claim for relocation expenses, provided such action shall not affect the amount of compensation otherwise recoverable by the Landlord from the taking authority pursuant to the preceding sentence.

9. Default

9.1 Tenant's Default. Each of the following shall be an Event of Default:

(a) Failure on the part of the Tenant to pay all Annual Fixed Rent and all Additional Rent for which provision is made herein on or before the date on which the same become due, if such condition continues for ten (10) days after the same are due.

(b) Failure on the part of the Tenant to perform or observe any other term or condition in this Lease if the Tenant shall not cure such failure within thirty (30) days after notice from the Landlord, provided, in the case of a breach of an obligation under this Lease that is susceptible to cure but cannot be cured within thirty days through the exercise of reasonable efforts, so long as Tenant commences such cure within thirty

continued on page 10-37

continued from page 10-36

(30) days, such breach remains susceptible to cure, and the Tenant diligently pursues such cure, such breach shall not be deemed to create an Event of Default.

(c) The taking of the estate created by this Lease on execution or by other process of law; or a judicial declaration that the Tenant is bankrupt or insolvent according to law; or any assignment for the benefit of creditors; or the appointment of a receiver, guardian, conservator, trustee in bankruptcy or other similar officer to take charge of any substantial part of the Tenant's property by a court of competent jurisdiction; or the filing of an involuntary petition against the Tenant under any provisions of any present or future bankruptcy law if the same is not dismissed within ninety (90) days; the filing by the Tenant of any voluntary petition for relief under the provisions of any present or future bankruptcy law.

If an Event of Default shall occur, then the Landlord may at any time thereafter give notice to the Tenant specifying the Event of Default and this Lease shall come to an end on the date specified therein as fully and completely as if such date were the date of expiration of the Term, and the Tenant shall surrender the Premises to the Landlord, but the Tenant shall remain liable as provided herein.

9.2 Damages. If this Lease is terminated, the Tenant covenants to pay the Landlord on demand, as compensation, an amount (the "Lump Sum Payment") equal to the excess, if any, of the discounted present value of the total rent reserved for the remainder of the Term in excess of the then discounted present fair rental value of the Premises for the remainder of the Term. In calculating the rent reserved, there shall be included, in addition to the Fixed Annual Rent and all Additional Rent, the value of all other considerations agreed to be paid or performed by the Tenant during the remainder of the Term. In addition, the Tenant shall pay punctually to the Landlord all the sums (the "Periodic Payments") and perform all obligations that the Tenant covenants in this Lease to pay and to perform in the same manner and to the same extent and at the same time as if this Lease had not been terminated. In calculating the amounts to be paid by the Tenant under the foregoing covenant, the Tenant shall be credited with the net proceeds of any rent obtained by reletting the Premises, after deducting all of the Landlord's costs in connection with such reletting, including without limitation, all repossession costs, brokerage commissions,

continued on page 10-38

continued from page 10-37

fees for legal services, and cost of preparing the Premises for such reletting. The Tenant shall also be entitled to credit against the last Periodic Payment which would otherwise become due for the amount, if any, paid to the Landlord as a Lump Sum Payment. The Landlord may (i) relet the Premises, or any part thereof, for a longer or shorter period than the period that would otherwise have constituted the remainder of the Term, and may grant concessions and free rent as the Landlord may reasonably consider advisable or necessary to relet the same. No action of the Landlord in accordance with the foregoing or failure to relet or collect rent from a reletting shall release or reduce Tenant's liability. The Landlord shall be entitled to seek or rent other properties of the Landlord prior to reletting the Premises.

9.3 Cumulative Rights. The specific remedies to which the Landlord may resort under the terms of this Lease are cumulative and are not intended to be exclusive of any other remedies or means of redress to which it may be lawfully entitled in case of any breach or threatened breach by the Tenant of any provisions of this Lease. In addition to other remedies provided in this Lease, the Landlord shall be entitled to restraint by injunction of the violation or attempted or threatened violation of any of the covenants, conditions or provisions. Nothing contained in this Lease shall limit or prejudice the right of the Landlord to prove for and obtain in proceeding for bankruptcy, insolvency or like proceedings by reason of the termination of this Lease, an amount equal to the maximum allowed by any statute or rule of law in effect at the time when, and governing the proceeding in which, the damages are to be proved, whether or not the amount be greater, equal to or less than the amount of the loss or damages referred to above.

9.4 Landlord's Self-help. If the Tenant shall at any time default in the performance of any obligation under this Lease, the Landlord shall have the right, but no obligation, upon reasonable, but not more than ten (10) days, notice to the Tenant (except in case of emergency, in which case no notice need be given) to perform such obligation. The Landlord may exercise its rights under this Section without waiving any other rights or releasing the Tenant from any of its obligations under this Lease.

9.5 Enforcement Expenses. The Tenant shall promptly reimburse the Landlord for all costs, including without

continued on page 10-39

continued from page 10-38

limitation, legal fees incurred by the Landlord in exercising and enforcing its rights under this Lease following the Tenant's failure to comply with its obligations hereunder, whether or not such failure constitutes an Event of Default by the Tenant, together with interest at the applicable rate specified in Section 9.6 from the date paid by the Landlord.

9.6 Late Charges and Interest on Overdue Payments. In the event payment of any Annual Fixed Rent or Additional Rent shall remain unpaid for a period of five (5) business days after notice by the Landlord that such payment is overdue, there shall become due as Additional Rent and as compensation for the Landlord's extra administrative costs in investigating the circumstances of late rent, a late charge of three percent (3%) on the overdue amount. In addition, any Annual Fixed Rent and Additional Rent not paid when due shall bear interest from the date due to the Landlord until paid at a rate equal to the higher of (i) the rate at which interest accrues on amounts not paid when due under the terms of Landlord's financing for the Building, as from time to time in effect and (ii) one hundred twenty-five percent (125%) of the Prime Rate.

9.7 Landlord's Right to Notice and Cure. The Landlord shall in no event be in default in the performance of any obligation hereunder until the Landlord shall have failed to carry out such obligation within thirty (30) days, or such additional time as is reasonably required to correct the default, after notice by the Tenant to the Landlord expressly specifying wherein the Landlord has failed to carry out such obligation.

10. Mortgagees' and Ground Lessors' Rights

10.1 Subordination. This Lease shall, at the election of the holder of any mortgage or ground lease on the Property, be subordinate to all mortgages and ground leases on the Property, so that the lien of any mortgage or ground lease shall be superior to all rights vested in the Tenant.

10.2 Prepayment of Rent Not to Bind Mortgagee. No Annual Fixed Rent, Additional Rent, or other charge payable to the Landlord shall be paid more than thirty (30) days prior to the due date thereof under the terms of this Lease and payments made in violation of this provision shall (except to the extent such payments are received by a mortgagee or ground lessor) be a nullity

continued on page 10-40

continued from page 10-39

as against such mortgagee or ground lessor and the Tenant shall be liable for the amount of such payments to such mortgagee or ground lessor.

10.3 Tenant's Duty to Notify Mortgagee; Mortgagee's Ability to Cure. No act or failure to act on the part of the Landlord which would entitle the Tenant under the terms of this Lease, or by law, to be relieved of the Tenant's obligations to pay Annual Fixed Rent or Additional Rent or to terminate this Lease, shall result in a release or termination of such obligations of the Tenant or a termination of this Lease unless (i) the Tenant shall have first given written notice of the Landlord's act or failure to act to the Landlord's mortgagees and ground lessors of record, of whose identity and address the Tenant shall have been given notice, specifying the act or failure to act on the part of the Landlord that would give rise to the Tenant's rights; and (ii) such mortgagees and ground lessors, after receipt of such notice, have failed or refused to correct or cure the condition complained of within a reasonable time, which shall include a reasonable time for such mortgagee or ground lessor to obtain possession of the Property if possession is necessary for the mortgagee or ground lessor to correct or cure the condition and if the mortgagee or ground lessor notifies the Tenant of its intention to take possession of the Property and correct and cure the condition.

10.4 Estoppel Certificates. The Tenant shall from time to time, upon not less than fifteen (15) days prior written request by the Landlord, execute, acknowledge and deliver to the Landlord a statement in writing certifying to the Landlord or an independent third party, with a true and current copy of this Lease attached thereto, (i) that this lease is unmodified and in full force and effect (or, if there have been any modifications, that the same is in full force and effect as modified and stating the modifications); (ii) that the Tenant has no knowledge of any defenses, offsets or counterclaims against its obligations to pay the Annual Fixed Rent and Additional Rent and to perform its other covenants under this Lease (or if there are defenses or counterclaims, setting them forth in reasonable detail); (iii) that there are no known uncured defaults of the Landlord or the Tenant under this Lease (or if there are known defaults, setting them forth in reasonable detail); (iv) the dates to which the Annual Fixed Rent, Additional Rent and other charges have been paid; (v) that the Tenant has

continued on page 10-41

continued from page 10-40

accepted, is satisfied with, and is in full possession of the Premises, including all improvements, additions, and alterations thereto required to be made by the Landlord under this Lease; (vi) that the Landlord has satisfactorily complied with all of the requirements and conditions precedent to the commencement of the Term of the Lease as specified therein; (vii) the Term, the Commencement Date, and any other relevant dates, and that the Tenant has been in occupancy since the Commencement Date and paying rent since the specified dates; (viii) that no monetary or other consideration, including but not limited to, rental concessions by the Landlord, special tenant improvements or Landlord's assumption of prior lease obligations of the Tenant have been granted to the Tenant by the Landlord for entering into this Lease, except as specified; (ix) that the tenant has no notice of a prior assignment, hypothecation or pledge of rents or of the Lease; (x) that the Lease represents the entire agreement between the Landlord and the Tenant; (xi) that no prepayment or reduction of rent and no modification, termination or acceptance of this Lease will be valid as to the party to whom such certificate is addressed without the consent of such party; (xii) that any notice to the Tenant may be given by certified mail, return receipt requested, or delivered at the Premises , or to another address specified; (xiii) the extent to which Tenant has exercised its option set forth in Section 2.5; and (xiv) such other matters with respect to the Tenant and this Lease as the Landlord may reasonably request. On the Commencement Date, the Tenant shall, at the request of the Landlord, promptly execute and deliver to the Landlord a statement in writing that the Commencement Date has occurred, that the Annual Fixed Rent has begun to accrue and that the Tenant has taken occupancy of the Premises. Any statement delivered pursuant to this Section may be relied upon by any prospective purchaser, mortgagee or ground lessor of the Premises and shall be binding on the Tenant.

11. Miscellaneous

11.1 Notice of Lease. The Tenant agrees not to record this Lease, but upon request of either party, both parties shall execute and deliver a memorandum of Lease in a form appropriate for recording, an instrument acknowledging the Commencement Date of the term, and if this Lease is terminated before the term expires, an instrument in such form acknowledging the date of termination.

continued on page 10-42

continued from page 10-41

11.2 Notices. Whenever any notice, approval, consent, request, election, offer or acceptance is given or made under this Lease, it shall be in writing and hand delivered, or forwarded by certified mail, return receipt requested,

if to the Landlord, to:

Landmark Development
Corporation
One Financial Center
Boston, MA 02111

if to the Tenant, to:

Science Renters Club, Inc.
24 Holyhock Road
Lowell, MA 01852

or to such other address as may from time to time be requested by either party by notice hereunder. Any communication or notice so addressed and transmitted shall be deemed to have been received on the earlier of (i) the date received, or (ii) the third business day following the day of mailing.

11.3 Successors and Limitation on Liability of the Landlord. The obligations of this Lease shall run with the land, and this Lease shall be binding upon and inure to the benefit of the parties hereto and their respective successors and assigns, except that the Landlord named herein and each successor landlord shall be liable only for obligations accruing during the period of its ownership. The obligations of the Landlord shall be binding upon the assets of the Landlord consisting of an equity ownership of the Property but not upon other assets of the Landlord and neither the Tenant, nor anyone claiming under it, shall be entitled to obtain any judgment creating personal liability on the part of the Landlord or enforcing any obligations of the Landlord against any assets of the Landlord other than an equity ownership in the Property.

11.4 Waivers by the Landlord. The failure of the Landlord or the Tenant to seek redress for violation of, or to insist upon strict performance of, any covenant or condition of this Lease, shall not be deemed to be a waiver of such violation or prevent a subsequent act, which would have originally constituted

continued on page 10-43

continued from page 10-42

a violation, from having all the force and effect of an original violation. The receipt by the Landlord of Annual Fixed Rent or Additional Rent with knowledge of the breach of any covenant of this Lease shall not be deemed to have been a waiver of such breach. No provision of this Lease shall be deemed to have been waived by the Landlord unless such waiver be in writing signed by the Landlord. No consent or waiver, express or implied, by the Landlord to or of any breach of any agreement or duty shall be construed as a waiver of or consent to any other breach of the same or any other agreement or duty.

11.5 Acceptance of Partial Payments of Rent. No acceptance by the Landlord of a lesser sum than the Fixed Annual Rent and Additional Rent then due shall be deemed to be other than a partial installment of such rent due, and no endorsement or statement on any check, or letter accompanying such check or payment, shall be deemed an accord and satisfaction, and the Landlord may accept such payment without prejudice to the right of the Landlord to recover the remainder of such installment or pursue any other remedy under this Lease. The delivery of keys to any employee of the Landlord or to the Landlord's agent shall not operate as a termination of this Lease or a surrender of the Premises by the Tenant.

11.6 Interpretation and Partial Invalidity. If any term of this Lease, or the application thereof to any person or circumstances, shall to any extent be invalid or unenforceable, the remainder of this Lease, or the application of such term to persons or circumstances other than those as to which it is invalid and unenforceable, shall not be affected thereby, and each term of this Lease shall be valid and enforceable to the fullest extent permitted by law. The titles of the Sections and Subsections are for convenience only and are not to be considered in construing this Lease. This Lease contains all of the agreements of the parties with respect to the subject matter hereof and supersedes all prior dealings between them with respect to such subject matter.

11.7 Quiet Enjoyment. So long as the Tenant pays Annual Fixed Rent and Additional Rent, performs all other of the Tenant covenants under this Lease and observes all conditions hereof, the Tenant shall peaceably and quietly have, hold and enjoy the Premises free of any claims by, through or under the Landlord.

continued on page 10-44

continued from page 10-43

11.8 Brokerage. The Tenant represents and warrants that it has had no dealings with any broker or agent other than Milburn, Inc. in connection with this Lease and shall indemnify the Landlord for any claims for any brokerage commission, other than Milburn, Inc., arising out of Tenant's actions.

11.9 Surrender of Premises and Holding Over. The Tenant shall surrender possession of the Premises on the last day of the Term and the Tenant waives any right to any notice of termination or notice to quit. The Tenant covenants that upon expiration or sooner termination of this Lease, it shall, without notice, surrender possession of the Premises in the same condition in which the Tenant has agreed to keep the same during continuance of this Lease and in accordance with the terms hereof, normal wear and tear excepted, first removing therefrom all goods and effects of the Tenant and any leasehold improvements the Landlord specified for removal at the time the Landlord consented to their installation, and repairing all damage caused by such removal. Upon expiration of this Lease, or if the Premises should be abandoned by the Tenant, or this Lease should terminate for any cause, and at the time of such expiration, vacation, abandonment, or termination, the Tenant or Tenant's agents, subtenants or any other person should leave any property of any kind in or on the Premises , the fact of such leaving shall be conclusive evidence of the intent by the Tenant, and any individuals and entities deriving rights through the Tenant, to abandon such property. The Landlord shall have the right and authority without notice to anyone, to remove, destroy, sell, or use all or any part of such property and any proceeds from the property shall be compensation to the Landlord for the removal or disposition of such property.

If the Tenant fails to surrender possession of the Premises upon the expiration or sooner termination of the Lease, the Tenant shall pay to the Landlord, as rent for the period after the expiration or sooner termination of this Lease an amount equal to twice the Annual Fixed Rent and the Additional Rent required to be paid under this lease as applied to any period in which the Tenant shall remain in possession. Acceptance by the Landlord of such payments shall not constitute a consent to a holdover hereunder or result in a renewal or extension of the Tenant's rights of occupancy. Such payments shall be in addition to and shall not affect or limit the Landlord's right to collect such damages

continued on page 10-45

continued from page 10-44

as may be available at law, or any other rights of the Landlord under this Lease or as provided by law.

11.10 Security Deposit. Tenant has paid to the Landlord a security deposit equal to two months Annual Fixed Rent. The Landlord may commingle such deposit with its other funds and may apply such deposit upon default of the Tenant hereunder. If Tenant is not in default, Landlord shall return the then remaining portion of the security deposit to Tenant within thirty (30) days after the expiration of this Lease. If the Landlord applies any such funds, Tenant shall pay to the Landlord as Additional Rent within ten (10) days after invoice thereof, the amount of the security deposit applied by the Landlord, such that the remainder of the security deposit shall be restored to its original amount.

11.11 Financial Reporting. The Tenant shall from time to time (but at least annually) on the anniversary of the Lease provide the Landlord with financial statements of Tenant, together with related statements of Tenant's operations for the Tenant's most recent fiscal year then ended, certified to the Landlord by an independent public accounting firm.

Landmark Development
Corporation, Landlord

By_____________________________
Title:

Science Renters Club, Inc.,
Tenant

By_____________________________
Title:

As it is written, this lease may be acceptable from the vantage point of the landlord, but the tenant could have serious objections to its terms. For comments, analysis and alternative provisions in connection with the lease, see Chapter 13.

Chapter Eleven

Bank Loan Agreements

Things to Know Before you Borrow

Unless you are a bank attorney, you are unlikely to ever be called upon to draft a bank loan agreement. Nevertheless, it is important that the businessman understand the meaning of such agreements and be in a position to negotiate appropriate revisions.

Bank loan agreements are usually printed, giving the impression, to some extent, that the terms are fixed and non-negotiable. The impression may also be that the terms are mere boilerplate, used in all of the loan agreements of the bank, and need not be scrutinized by the businessman seeking a loan. Not so!

Of all the agreements I have ever studied, bank loan agreements are among the harshest, most unfair, and go the greatest distance beyond what could be considered fair play. But don't blame the poor loan officer for the agreement—blame the top management of the bank, who probably have never read it but merely said to the bank's attorneys: "Protect us."

Unless you have made arrangements with a bank well before the actual necessity for a loan arises, your negotiating position may not be too good. Nevertheless, you can probably be successful in negotiating the elimination of some of the more outrageous clauses.

First, when reviewing the agreement, do not confuse yourself by thinking of what the bank (a nice bunch of guys) will actually do: think only about what they have the power to do. Bank loans are arranged amid pleasant relationships between bank and client. But sometimes those relationships turn sour and the actual terms of the loan agreement become of paramount importance. So assume the mafia is going to take over the bank after you get your loan and are intent upon putting you out of business. Don't let them!

The typical bank agreement, as we shall see, is so onerous that if the bank insisted on its terms, it would do business only with fools and bad risks. Fools do not make good customers—even for a bank. Bankers sometimes seem to ignore the fact that an "airtight" agreement will not save the bank from the consequences of a bad loan. What it frequently does do is send the borrower who is fortunate enough that he does not need to grovel for a loan scurrying to another source for money. *The bank that insists on a one-sided stranglehold can make deals only with those with marginal qualifications, or who are so careless they will sign a loan agreement because it is the bank's "standard printed form."* Usually, the bank (always if it wants the business) will negotiate the terms by having the customer, or its attorney, meet with the bank attorney. Such negotiations can take four hours or four days—and the bank will insist the customer pay all fees of the bank attorney, whether a deal is made or not.

A Typical Bank Loan Agreement

It is important enough for you to understand just how bad bank agreements can be that I urge you to plow along with me as we review some of the provisions in an actual "standard agreement" of the United States Trust Company in Boston. In this case there are two documents: a demand note and a security agreement. First the note: (The bracketed numbers refer to the author's comments.)

COMMERCIAL DEMAND NOTE

$__________ ____________ 19____

________________________ Massachusetts

FOR VALUE RECEIVED, the undersigned (hereinafter the "Borrower" (jointly and severally if more than one) promise(s) to pay to the order of United States Trust Company (hereinafter, with any subsequent holder, the "Bank") at an office of the Bank, ON DEMAND, the sum of ________________________ Dollars $____________ with interest thereon as follows: (Check one) _____Floating Rate: Interest shall accrue on the unpaid balance at the aggregate of the Bank's Best Lending Rate, plus ______ percent per annum, with changes in the Bank's Best Lending Rate to take effect, for the purposes of determination of interest hereunder, when made effective generally to loans by the Bank. In no event shall the rate of interest be less than ______ percent per annum. [1] ____Fixed Rate: Interest shall accrue on the unpaid principal balance at _____ percent per annum. Interest shall be determined in all instances based upon a 360 day year and actual day months. After demand, interest shall accrue at a rate per annum equal to the aggregate of two percent (2%) plus the rate provided for herein. As used herein, Best Lending Rate means the rate of interest announced by the Bank from time to time as its Best Lending Rate. [2]

[1] Usually the "Bank's Best Lending Rate" is the same as or very near the prime rate, as that term is generally used. If you have any doubts, compare the current Best Lending Rate of your bank with the prime rate as published daily in the *Wall Street Journal.* If there is a difference of more than, say, one-eighth of a point, investigate further. The added interest is strictly a function of your credit, the market value of the collateral, and your skill in negotiating.

[2] When banks lend money, a year has 360 days; when they borrow money, a year has 365 days. This means the so-called annual interest rate is somewhat higher than the numbers indicate. It is a bit of a premium that means a lot of dollars to the bank, but not much to the small borrower. If several million dollars are involved, it is worth trying to get an admission from the bank that a year has at least 365 days. The bank has the power to increase the interest rate by two percent at any time merely by demanding payment. Since this comes into effect only upon default, it is probably not worth a fuss.

Unless and until demand is made, interest at the rate set forth above shall be paid monthly in arrears with the first such payment due on ________________ and each subsequent payment due on the like day of each calendar month thereafter. In addition to any interest payments to be made, unless and until demand is made, payment of $______ principal shall be made each month hereafter, commencing ____________, 19____.

Any payments received by the Bank on account of this Note prior to demand shall be applied first, to any costs, expenses or charges then owed the Bank by the Borrower, second, to accrued and unpaid interest, and third to the unpaid principal balance hereof. Any payments so received after demand shall be applied in such manner as the Bank may determine. [3] The Borrower hereby authorizes the Bank to charge any deposit account which the Borrower may maintain with the Bank for any payment required hereunder. [4]

[3] It is usual for money paid on a note to be applied in the sequence listed in the note. Why the bank wants the power to use some other sequence after demand is not obvious. Again, probably not worth a fuss.

[4] This gives the bank the right to remove money from any of the borrower's other accounts in the bank. Because the bank usually has clauses such as this, by which it has a right to claim anything it can get its hands on, it is a good general rule not to have your other bank accounts in the same bank where you have a demand loan with a clause of this type. It may never be a problem, but the bank has the power to demand payment, even if there is no default, and to remove all the money from other accounts to apply on the note—all without even notifying you that it is doing so.

The Borrower represents to the Bank that the proceeds of this Note will not be used for personal, family or household purposes. [5]

[5] This is a commercial loan and it is prudent for the bank to make sure the proceeds are not being used for non-business purposes.

The failure of the Borrower to pay when due any amount due hereunder shall at the Bank's option, also constitute a default under all other agreements between the Bank and the Borrower and under all other instruments and papers given the Bank by the Borrower. [6] Without limiting the demand nature of this Note,

continued on page 11-4

continued from page 11-3

upon the occurrence of any event of default under any other agreement between the Bank and the Borrower, whether such agreement, instrument or document now exists or hereafter arises (notwithstanding the Bank may not have exercised its rights upon default under such other agreement, instrument or paper), the entire unpaid principal balance of this Note and accrued and unpaid interest thereon, shall at the Bank's option, be immediately due and payable without demand, notice, or protest (which are hereby waived). [7]

[6] If a payment is late on this note, all other obligations of the borrower are, at the option of the bank, also in default. Suppose you have in addition to the note, a mortgage on your factory building payable over a long period at a fixed interest rate. If you are late paying on this note, the bank can declare the mortgage loan in default and demand payment of the entire balance. Of course, no bank would do that—would it? Suppose general interest rates have increased by several points since the mortgage was acquired. The bank then has a powerful incentive to enforce this clause in the agreement and force renegotiation of the mortgage at a higher interest rate. If the banker assures you they would never, never do that—why have it in the agreement?

[7] The situation is true also in reverse. If the borrower defaults on any other loan from that bank, this note, at the option of the bank, is also, at the option of the bank, automatically in default.

Any and all deposits or other sums at any time credited by or due to the Borrower from the Bank, or any of its banking and lending affiliates, or any bank acting as a participant under any loan arrangement between the Bank and the Borrower, and any cash, securities, instruments, or other property of the Borrower in the possession of the Bank, or any of its banking or lending affiliates, or any bank acting as a participant under any loan arrangement between the Bank and the Borrower, whether for safekeeping or otherwise, or in transit to or from the Bank, or any of its banking or lending affiliates, or any such participant, or in the possession of any third party acting on the Bank's behalf (regardless of the reason the Bank had received same or whether the Bank has conditionally released the same) shall at all times constitute security for any and all liabilities, obligations and indebtedness of the Borrower to the Bank, and may be applied or set off against such liabilities, obligations, and indebtedness, at any time, whether or not such liabilities, obligations, and indebtedness are then due or whether or not other collateral is available to the Bank. [8]

[8] This is merely an extension of the general principle that the bank is entitled to grab everything in reach—other bank accounts of the borrower, money in transit from an account of the borrower, money held by the bank to secure a payment to a vendor, etc. The bank can grab this money even if the borrower has made every payment on time and no payments are currently due. You may first learn about such a transfer from an irate individual inquiring about a bad check!

No delay or omission by the Bank in exercising or enforcing any of the Bank's powers, rights, privileges, remedies, or discretions hereunder shall operate as a waiver thereof on that occasion nor [sic] on any other occasion. No waiver of any default hereunder shall operate as a waiver of any other default hereunder, nor as a continuing waiver.

The Borrower and each endorser or guarantor of this Note, shall indemnify, defend, and hold the Bank harmless against any claim brought or threatened against the Bank by the Borrower, by any endorser or guarantor, or any other person (as well as from attorneys' reasonable fees and expenses in connection therewith) on account of the Bank's relationship with the Borrower or any endorser or guarantor hereof (each of which may be defended, compromised, settled or pursued by the Bank with counsel of the Bank's selection, but at the expense of the Borrower and any endorser and/or guarantor). [9]

[9] My general distaste for "hold harmless" clauses has already been expressed. This one may have some justification, but it is too broad and gives the bank undue power. For example, if some claim is made against the bank, the bank alone can select the lawyers for the defense, and it can settle a claim, even if groundless, all without the borrower's consent and at the borrower's expense.

The Borrower will pay on demand all attorneys' reasonable fees and out-of-pocket expenses incurred by the Bank in the administration of all liabilities, obligations, and indebtedness, of the Borrower to the Bank, including, without limitation, costs and expenses associated with travel on behalf of the Bank. [10] The Borrower will also pay on demand, all attorneys' reasonable fees, out-of-pocket expenses incurred by the Bank's attorneys and all costs incurred by the Bank, including without limitation, costs and expenses associated with travel on behalf of the Bank, which costs and expenses are directly or indirectly related to the preservation, protection, collection, or enforcement of any of the Bank's rights against the

continued on page 11-6

continued from page 11-5

```
Borrower or any such endorser or guarantor and against
any collateral given the Bank to secure this Note or
any extension or other indulgence, as described above,
with respect to any other liability or any collateral
given to secure any other liability of the Borrower or
such endorser and guarantor to the Bank (whether or not
suit is instituted by or against the Bank). [11]
```

[10] This is a blank check for legal fees and travel expenses for anything imaginable so long as it has to do with the "administration" of the loan. Since lawyers are human beings, one could hardly expect stringent self denial of fees when the client is not paying the bill. Bank attorneys can be expensive.

[11] This is another broad carte blanche for attorney's fees. It is only required that the charges be "directly or indirectly related to the preservation, protection, collection..." Moreover, the action can be taken by the bank against collateral for another loan and charged to this loan. If the borrower has previously negotiated a loan with the bank and removed this provision with respect to that loan, this provision puts it back in. A borrower in a strong negotiating position can insist that each loan be separate and that no provisions overlap. If the borrower is asking for a loan because it must, these provisions will remain.

```
The Borrower and each endorser and guarantor of this
Note, respectively waives presentment, demand, notice,
and protest, and also waives any delay on the part of
the holder hereof. Each assents to any extension or
other indulgence (including without limitation, the
release or substitution of collateral) permitted the
Borrower or any endorser or guarantor by the Bank with
respect to this Note and/or any collateral given to
secure this Note and/or to secure any other liability
of the Borrower or any endorser or guarantor to the
Bank. [12]
```

[12] Here, once again, the borrower waives "presentment, demand, notice, and protest." This is merely Legal Omelet for saying that the bank can take any action it wants without bothering to tell the borrower about it. This, and some other provisions are particularly important if you are merely guaranteeing a loan for someone else. The bank is not obligated to exhaust its remedies against the primary borrower before coming after the guarantor. In fact, the bank can completely forgive all liabilities of the borrower and seek payment from the guarantor. Perhaps the guarantor felt quite comfortable because of the collateral posted to secure the loan. Note however, the guarantor has consented to any "...indulgence (including without limitation, the release or substitution of collateral)..." The bank can release the collateral of the borrower and look to the guarantor for payment. If you have any inclination to endorse a note for someone else, read the note carefully and refuse to accept provisions such as this one.

This Note shall be binding upon the Borrower and each endorser and guarantor hereof and upon their respective heirs, successors, assigns, and representatives, and shall inure to the benefit of the Bank and its successors, endorsees and assigns.

The liabilities of Borrower and any endorser or guarantor of this Note are joint and several; provided, however, the release by the Bank of the Borrower or any one or more endorser or guarantor shall not release any other person obligated on account of this Note. [13] Each reference in this Note to the Borrower, any endorser, and any guarantor, is to such person individually and also to such persons jointly. No person obligated on account of this Note may seek contribution from any other person also obligated unless and until all liabilities, obligations, and indebtedness to the Bank of the person from whom contribution is sought have been satisfied in full. [14]

[13] This is redundant rhetoric reinforcing what was just said: Just because the bank lets the borrower off the hook doesn't mean the endorser is freed.

[14] This provision prevents the endorser from seeking collateral from the borrower before the bank is paid. Suppose an endorser becomes worried about having to pay the note and asks the borrower to give him a lien on the borrower's house. That would be a violation of the agreement. Not just getting the lien, but merely asking for it!

The Borrower and each endorser and guarantor hereof each authorizes the Bank to complete this Note if delivered incomplete in any respect. [15]

[15] This is a no-no. Banks have a habit of asking the borrower and the guarantors for an advance power of attorney to permit them to act in the name of the borrower or the guarantor. In this case all the bank asks is the right to complete any part of the note in any way it wants. The correct procedure, if the note is incomplete, is to return it to the borrower. Any modifications to the note after it is executed should be initialed by both parties.

This Note is delivered to the Bank at one of its offices in Massachusetts, shall be governed by the laws of the Commonwealth of Massachusetts, and shall take effect as a sealed instrument. The Borrower, and each

continued on page 11-8

continued from page 11-7

endorser and guarantor of this Note each submits to the jurisdiction of the courts of The Commonwealth of Massachusetts [16] for all purposes with respect to this Note, any collateral given to secure the respective liabilities, obligations, and indebtedness to the Bank, and their respective relationships with the Bank.

The above note is accompanied by the printed Security Agreement of United States Trust Company, a document printed in microscopic print on four pages, edge-to-edge and top-to-bottom. Some of the pertinent passages are reproduced below. The bracketed numbers refer to the author's comments.

SECURITY AGREEMENT

Inventory, Accounts, Equipment and Other Property

ARTICLE 1. GRANT OF SECURITY INTEREST

1-1. To secure the Borrower's prompt, punctual, and faithful performance of all and each of the Borrower's Liabilities (as the term is defined herein) to the Bank, Borrower hereby grants to the Bank a continuing security interest in and to, and assigns to the Bank, the following and each item thereof, whether now owned or now due, or in which the Borrower has an interest, hereafter, at any time in the future, acquired, or arising, or to become due, or in which the Borrower obtains an interest and all products, proceeds, substitutions, and accessions of or to any of the following (all of which, together with any other property in which the Bank may in the future be granted a security interest pursuant hereto, is referred to hereinafter as the "Collateral"):

(a) All Accounts and Accounts Receivable;

(b) All inventory;

(c) All Contract Rights;

(d) All General Intangibles;

(e) All Equipment;

(f) All Farm Products;

continued on page 11-9

continued from page 11-8

(g) All Goods;

(h) All Chattel Paper;

(i) All Fixtures;

(j) All books, records, and information relating to the Collateral and/or to the operation of the Borrower's business, and all rights of access to such books, records and information, and all property in which books, records, and information are stored, recorded and maintained;

(k) All instruments, Documents of Title, Documents, policies and certificates of insurance, Securities, deposits, deposit accounts, money, cash, or other property;

(l) All federal, state, and local tax refunds and/or abatements to which the Borrower is, or becomes entitled, no matter when or how arising, including but not limited to any loss carryback refunds;

(m) All insurance proceeds, refunds, and premium rebates, including, without limitation, proceeds of fire and credit insurance, whether any of such proceeds, refunds, and premium rebates, arise out of any of the foregoing (a through l), or otherwise;

(n) All liens, guaranties, rights, remedies, and privileges pertaining to any of the foregoing (a through m) including the right of stoppage in transit. [1]

[1] Now that is a demonstration of almost everything that is wrong with legal writing and bank greediness. For a start, on the scope of collateral, try to think of those assets of the borrower that are not posted as collateral for the loan. Real estate is the only one that comes to mind. If that is true, why does the agreement not simply say: "As collateral for the loan, the borrower assigns all of its assets to the Bank except for real estate." Real estate is not, at this point in the agreement, included directly in the collateral, but note that the title documents to any real property are included. If the borrower owns real estate on which there is a mortgage, the provisions of this agreement are likely in conflict with those of the mortgage note. The two should be compared carefully. For example, all receipts from fire insurance are part of the collateral, but the mortgagee probably has prior rights to such proceeds.

Note particularly that the agreement does not merely give the bank a security interest in the collateral, it "assigns" it to the bank! The bank is now the owner of all assets of the corporation, except for real estate. This assignment gives the bank, as we shall see presently, the absolute power to put the borrower out of business, even if the borrower is not in default on the loan. As we said before, no nice little banker would ever do such a thing. But what if the Mafia takes over the bank? The prudent borrower will not give title to these assets to the bank. It will give the bank a right to foreclose on those assets in the event of default, but then only after notice to the borrower.

Before agreeing to such an all-encompassing definition of collateral, the borrower should consider that once this agreement is executed, it has no further borrowing power other than with The Bank, no matter what the financial situation of the borrower. Even commercial companies are likely to be reluctant to extend credit to a company with no assets. A widely used form of credit is based on accounts receivable. The door is closed for that kind of financing because the accounts receivable have already been assigned to The Bank.

2-6. "General Intangibles" includes without limitation, "general intangibles" as defined in the UCC; and also all rights to payments for credit extended; deposits; amounts due to the Borrower; credit memoranda in favor of the Borrower; warranty claims; all means and vehicles of investment or hedging, including without limitation, options, warrants, and futures contracts; records; customer lists; goodwill; causes of action; judgements; payments under any settlement or other agreement; literary rights; rights to performance; royalties; license fees; franchise fees; licenses; franchises; permits; certificates of convenience or necessity, and similar rights granted by any government authority; copyrights, trade marks, [sic] trade names, service marks, patents, patent applications, patents pending, and other intellectual property; developmental ideas and concepts; proprietary processes; blueprints; drawings; designs; diagrams; plans; reports; charts; catalogs; manuals; technical data; computer programs, computer records, computer software, rights of access to computer record service bureaus, service bureau computer contracts, and computer data; proposals, cost estimates, and other reproductions on paper, or otherwise, of any and all concepts or ideas, and any matter related to, or connected with, the design, development, manufacture, marketing, leasing, or use of any and all property produced, sold, or leased, by the Borrower or credit extended or services performed, by the Borrower, whether intended for individual customer or the general business of the Borrower, or used or useful in connection with research by the Borrower. [2]

[2] We have already seen some examples of redundancy—but this must be the champion for downright childishness. For example, "Intangibles" as defined in the UCC include account and contract rights, leases, consignments, and "general intangibles" which include "copyrights, literary rights, goodwill, trademarks...patents." But having made reference to the UCC definition, the agreement repeats "copyrights, trade marks...patents." The simple expression "all intangible assets" would provide everything

the bank could legitimately expect. Generously, the bank makes no claim to the

```
3-7. There is not presently pending or threatened by or
against the Borrower nor shall there be threatened in
the future any suit, action, proceeding, or
investigation which, if determined adversely to the
Borrower would have a material adverse effect upon the
Borrower's financial condition or ability to conduct
its business as such business is presently conducted.
[3]
```

borrower's wife or eldest son!

[3] Evidently the lawyers who drafted this form for the U.S. Trust are privileged to read the future. Alas, most mere borrowers are mortal and haven't a clue as to what someone else may do next year. The borrower is asked here to declare, for example, that the government will not take over its plant by eminent domain. It is asked to declare that no suit will even be threatened by anyone which would, if the borrower lost, materially affect its business. Only God and lawyers could confidently make such a declaration. What happens if the borrower is wrong, and someone threatens him with a suit because

```
3-8. (c) The Borrower authorizes the Bank to verify the
Collateral or any portion thereof, including
verification with Account Debtors, and/or with the
Borrower's computer billing companies, collection
agencies, and accountants and to sign the name of the
Borrower to any notice to the Borrower's Account
Debtors or on any notice relative to the verification
of the Collateral. [4]
```

of, say, patent infringement? Is the borrower guilty of fraud for making a false representation to secure a bank loan? Even legal silliness ought to have some limit.

[4] Most business men (excluding lawyers and bankers for purposes of discussion) regard their customers as important and they take some care to see that the customer is a happy customer. The perceptions of its customers may be the most valuable asset a company has. Why should any sensible businessman give the power to a bank to willy-nilly interfere with this relationship? The bank wants the right not only to send notices to

```
3-10. Borrower shall have and maintain at all times
insurance covering... The Borrower shall advise the Bank
of each claim made by the Borrower under any policy of
insurance which covers the Collateral and will permit
the Bank, at the Bank's option in each instance, to the
exclusion of the Borrower, to conduct the adjustment of
```

continued on page 11-12

continued from page 11-11

each such claim. [5] Originals of all such policies shall be delivered to and held by the Bank. The Borrower hereby appoints the Bank as the Borrower's attorney to obtain, adjust, settle and cancel any insurance described in this section and to endorse in favor of the Bank any and all drafts and other instruments with respect to such insurance. The within appointment, being coupled with an interest, is irrevocable until this Agreement is terminated by a written instrument executed by a duly authorized officer of the Bank. [6]

the borrower's customers, but to sign the borrower's name to them! And this is not something that can happen only after the borrower has defaulted on its loan—it can happen anytime.

[5] The borrower is required to carry insurance on its assets. This is a reasonable request. But this Bank goes further—it demands the right to take over the settlement of any insurance claim, to the exclusion of the borrower. The borrower has no right even to attend meetings where discussions of settlement take place. The Bank can reach any settlement it desires with the insurance company and then release it from all further claims by the borrower. Suppose a borrower has a loss amounting to $100,000. The borrower owes the bank $50,000. How hard would this bank negotiate for full payment as the basis for a settlement? Would not its obvious course of least resistance be to take the fifty and sign off? The credit manager may argue that the bank doesn't operate that way. But that raises the question: Why have it in the agreement if the bank "would never do that?" Moreover, as we shall see presently, the bank has an absolute right to assign the agreement and be relieved of all further liability. Who knows what some assignee may do?

[6] This is just an extension of the same provision. The bank has now become the

3-16. The Borrower shall execute and deliver to the Bank such instruments and shall do all such things from time to time hereafter as the Bank may request to carry into effect the provisions and intent of this Agreement, to protect and perfect the Bank's security interest in and to the Collateral, and to comply with all applicable statutes and laws, and to facilitate the collection and/or enforcement of Receivables Collateral. [7]

borrower's attorney and can endorse any settlement checks, release the insurer in the name of the borrower, and even cancel the insurance. Moreover, this power is not revocable by the borrower. Even paying off the loan won't get rid of it! The bank can revoke it when and if it wants to.

4-1 At any time and whether or not an Event of Default has occurred hereunder, (a) The Bank may notify any of the Borrower's account or contract debtors, either in the name of the Bank or the Borrower, to make payment directly to the Bank or such other address as may be specified by the Bank, and may advise any person of the Bank's security interest in and to the Collateral, and may collect directly from the obligors thereon, all amounts on account of the Collateral; and [8]

(b) At the Bank's request, the Borrower will provide written notifications to any and all of the Borrower's account or contract debtors concerning the Bank's security interest in the Collateral and will request that such account or contract debtors forward payments directly to the Bank. [9]

[7] A provision of this kind is not wholly unreasonable, but it should be tempered. The borrower should not be required to do anything that is illegal or unreasonable. It might read "The borrower shall execute and deliver to the Bank all proper and reasonable instruments and shall do all reasonable and proper things ..."

[8] This clause gives the bank the right to write or call your customers and request them to make all invoice payments directly to the bank. And, please note, the borrower need not be in default for the bank to have this power. In most instances, it would be harmful to a business to have all of its customers notified by a bank to direct all payments to the bank.

4-2. Upon and after notification to the Borrower from the Bank (whether or not an Event of Default has occurred hereunder and whether or not any notification has been given the Borrower's contract and account debtors pursuant to Section 4-1 above), the Borrower shall hold all proceeds and collections of any of the Collateral in trust for the Bank and shall not commingle such proceeds or collections with any other funds of the Borrower. [10]

[9] This is just another phase of the same requirement, but in this instance the bank can direct the borrower to give written notification to its customers, telling them about the debt and the collateral, and instructing them to pay the bank directly. This builds confidence among the customers?

[10] The bank can at any time, for a reason or for no reason, even if the borrower has made every payment on the loan exactly on time, direct the borrower to hold all proceeds in trust for the bank. The borrower must keep those funds separate from all other money,

ARTICLE 5. DEFAULT

Upon the occurrence of any one or more of the following events (herein, "Events of Default") any and all Liabilities of the Borrower to the Bank shall become immediately due and payable, at the option of the Bank and without notice or demand.

5-1. The failure by the Borrower to pay upon demand (or when due, if not payable on demand) any of the Liabilities...[11]

not deposit them in its regular bank account, and turn them over to the bank. In the day-to-day operation of a business this would be more than just a damned nuisance.

[11] The agreement includes a whole list of defaults, but they aren't important. This is a demand loan. The bank can demand payment at any time, whether there is any occasion for it or not. So the recitation of defaults just further complicates the Legal Omelet. The

ARTICLE 6. RIGHTS AND REMEDIES UPON DEFAULT

6-3. In connection with the Bank's exercise of the Bank's rights under this Article, the Bank may enter upon, occupy, and use any premises owned or occupied by the Borrower, and may exclude the Borrower from such premises, or portion thereof as may have been so entered upon, occupied, or used by the Bank. The Bank shall not be required to remove any of the Collateral from the premises upon the Bank's taking possession thereof, and may render any Collateral unusable to the Borrower. In no event shall the Bank be liable to the Borrower for the use of occupancy by the Bank of any premises pursuant to this Article, nor for any charge (such as wages for the Borrower's employees, and utilities) incurred in connection with the Bank's exercise of the Bank's Rights and Remedies. [12]

6-4. The Borrower hereby grants to the Bank a nonexclusive irrevocable license to use, apply, and affix any trademark, tradename, [sic] logo, or the like in which the Borrower now or hereafter has rights, such license being with respect to the Bank's exercise of the rights hereunder including, without limitation, in connection with any completion of the manufacture or Inventory or sale or other disposition of Inventory. [13]

Bank has about the same rights whether or not the borrower is in default, and it has the right to call the loan at any time. No one except the lawyers should spend time and money worrying about the conditions of default. However, when the bank has called the loan—which (strange, indeed!) it can do without notifying the borrower, it has somewhat broader rights to wreck the business of the borrower.

[12] Upon default, which means not paying instantly upon demand, the bank can occupy the business premises, expel the borrower and run the plant. It can make shipments of the collateral, or make it unusable for the borrower, or do just about anything it wants. The agreement nowhere contains any requirement that the bank shall act in a reasonable or prudent manner. The bank need have no regard for the best interests of the borrower.

[13] The bank can also use the borrower's trademarks, applying them in its wisdom to products where they don't belong or using them in a generic sense and destroying the

7-2. (a) The Borrower WAIVES notice of non-payment, demand, presentment, protest, and all forms of demand and notice, both with respect to the Liabilities and Collateral. [14]

(b) The Borrower, if entitled to it, WAIVES the right to notice and/or hearing prior to exercise of the Bank's rights upon default. [15]

mark. It can use the company name in connection with the collateral. Remember, the collateral is the business—all of it. The bank can sell the business, it can sell the inventory, it can confiscate all money, bank accounts, and even take over legal claims the business may have against some other entity. Of course, this isn't important. Bankers are nice people and just because they insist on onerous provisions doesn't mean they are onerous people...

[14] This is just more redundancy to make sure the bank has no obligation to tell the

7-5. ...In the event the Bank assigns or transfers its rights under this Agreement, the assignee shall thereupon succeed to and become vested with all of the rights, privileges, and duties of the Bank hereunder and the Bank shall thereupon be discharged and relieved from its duties and obligations hereunder. [16]

7-13 The Borrower shall indemnify, defend, and hold the Bank harmless of and from any claim brought or threatened against the Bank by the Borrower, any guarantee or endorsor of any of the Liabilities, or any other person (as well as from attorneys' reasonable fees and expenses in connection therewith) on account of the Bank's relationship with the Borrower or any other guarantor or endorser of the Liabilities (each of

continued on page 11-16

continued from page 11-15

```
which may be defended, compromised, settled, or pursued
by the Bank with counsel of the Bank's selection, but
at the expense of the Borrower). The within
indemnification shall survive payment of the
Liabilities and/or any termination, release, or
discharge executed by the Bank in favor of the
Borrower. [17]
```

borrower what is going on. The borrower has no right to notice before the bank starts selling off the borrower's assets—or even the company itself. This is repeated time and again in the agreement, just so the borrower won't have any mistaken ideas.

[15] And to press the point home further, the borrower is not entitled to any notice or demand for payment by the bank, and is not entitled to any hearing before the bank moves in and takes over the business.

[16] We have already agreed the bank is a nice organization. But this provision says the borrower may not be dealing with the nice banker. The bank can assign the agreement to anyone, even a competitor of the borrower, and has no further liability or obligations to the

```
7-14. This Agreement shall remain in full force and
effect until specifically terminated in writing by a
duly authorized officer of the Bank. Such termination
by the Bank may be conditioned upon such further
indemnification provided to the Bank by or on behalf of
the Borrower as the Bank may request. [18]
```

borrower. Just in case the bank ever has any obligations hidden somewhere in this agreement, it would be well to provide that any assignment of the agreement does not relieve the bank of its obligations. Recommendation: Scratch this provision with indelible ink.

[17] We have discussed the nefarious hold-harmless clause before. If the borrower is forced to submit to some arm twisting by the bank, it should negotiate a milder hold

```
7-15. The failure by the Borrower to perform all and
singular the Borrower's obligations hereunder,
including, without limitation, those included in
Sections 3-14, 3-16, 4-1, 4-2, 4-3, and 4-5, above,
will result in irreparable harm to the Bank for which
the Bank will have no adequate remedy at law.
Consequently, such obligations are specifically
enforceable by the Bank. [19]

7-16. It is intended that:
```

continued on page 11-17

continued from page 11-16

...

(b) the security interest created by this Agreement attach to all of the Borrower 's assets now owned or hereafter acquired which are capable of being subject to a security interest; [20]...

(d) all costs and expenses incurred by the Bank in connection with the Bank's relationship(s) with the Borrower shall be borne by the Borrower; [21] and

(e) The Bank's consent to any action of the Borrower which is prohibited unless such consent is given may be given or refused by the Bank in its sole discretion. [22]

harmless, say, one that is limited to damages arising from negligent or fraudulent acts of the borrower.

[18] This clause should be unacceptable to a borrower who has any freedom of choice. The repayment of the loan in full to the bank ought to be an absolute termination of the agreement without the borrower having to fight a bureaucratic jungle to get a signed termination from a bank officer who has no interest in signing it. If the bank officer is as inhibited as some, he will send it to the legal counsel (at the borrower's expense, of course) for approval.

[19] The referenced sections deal with prohibitions on the acts of the borrower with respect to the collateral (which is the business) and with the bank's right to take over the business after default. The borrower is asked to agree in advance that any violation of any one of these provisions, or any other provision of the agreement, will "result in irreparable harm to the Bank." That statement is not likely to be true. A provision of the agreement could be violated by the borrower with no more damage to the bank than the price of a subway ticket. Such a breach could certainly be atoned with money—it would hardly be irreparable. What the bank wants is for the borrower to agree that any breach is irreparable and give the bank a right to demand "specific performance." Specific performance means that one party is required to perform a certain act, because the breach cannot be adequately compensated by money. For example, a contract for sale of a particular piece of land may be enforced by "specific performance," that is, requiring the seller to turn over that piece of land. This is because there is no other piece of land just like the one that was to be transferred. This is not likely to apply to any breach under this agreement.

[20] This is a catchall, just in case the bank overlooked any assets. It specifically states that every asset of the business that isn't already mortgaged by someone else, belongs to the bank. The bank may now even get its clutches on an interest in the real estate. This one sentence could replace a major part of the agreement.

[21] This convoluted language is trying to say that the bank is not obligated to give the borrower its consent to anything. It has absolute discretion and has the right to be as

unreasonable in its decisions as it is in proposing this agreement.

It seems apparent that this Security Agreement has a primary objective of so confusing and exhausting any borrower that he will give up and sign it without understanding it or attempting to renegotiate its one-sided terms. If the agreement said in clear plain

"The Bank specifically agrees that irrespective of any other provisions of this Agreement: (a) The Bank shall have no right to take any action in connection with the Collateral or in connection with the Borrower's business or in connection with any customers or suppliers of the Borrower, until and unless the Borrower is in default under this Agreement and (i) the Bank has given the Borrower a notice of the default, explaining the nature and circumstances of the default, and (ii) the Borrower has failed to cure such default within three (3) business days after such notice is received by the Borrower; (b) the Borrower shall not be liable for any damages to the bank except for acts resulting from knowing failure of the Borrower to abide by the terms of this agreement or negligent acts of omission or commission by the Borrower; and (c) upon repayment to the Bank of all monies owed to the Bank in connection with this Agreement and the accompanying Demand Note, including all accrued interest and other expenses, this Agreement shall cease and terminate and all Collateral shall be automatically released from any claim by the Bank, and the Bank agrees to promptly execute and deliver to the Borrower a release, in form suitable for filing, of all UCC filings previously made by the Bank.

language what it says in pages of legal jargon, few borrowers would be so pressed for funds as to sign it.

All of which brings us to the question of what the borrower is to do. The answer depends upon how desperate the borrower is for funds. If there is a choice, the borrower should start by finding another bank. Or it would be appropriate to tell the bank the agreement must be revised, but the borrower is unwilling to pay the expenses of the bank's attorneys to straighten out a mess that should never have existed. Alternatively, the following clause, added to the agreement and initialed by both parties, will alleviate some of the problem:

Until such time as the Bank shall notify Borrower of the revocation of such power and authority, Borrower (a) will at its own expense endeavor to collect, as and when due, all amounts due under Collateral, including the taking of such action with respect to such

continued on page 11-19

continued from page 11-18

collection as the Bank may reasonably request or, in the absence of such request, as Borrower may deem advisable and (b) — The Bank, however, may, at any time, whether before or after any revocation of such power and authority or the maturity of any of the Liabilities, notify any parties obligated on any of the Collateral to make payment to the Bank of any amounts due or to become due thereunder and enforce collection by suit or otherwise and surrender, release, or exchange all or any part thereof, or compromise or extend or renew for any period (whether or not longer than the original period) any indebtedness thereunder or evidenced thereby. Upon request of the Bank, Borrower will, at its own expense, notify any parties obligated on any of the Collateral to make payment to the Bank of any amounts due or to become due thereunder.

Borrower will (except as the Bank may otherwise consent in writing) forthwith, upon receipt, transmit and deliver to the Bank, in the form received, all cash, checks, drafts and other instruments or writings for the payment of money (properly endorsed, where required, so that such items may be collected by the Bank) which may be received by Borrower at any time in full or partial repayment or otherwise as proceeds of any of the Collateral. Except as the Bank may otherwise consent in writing, any such items which may be so received by Borrower will not be commingled with any other funds or property, but will be held separate and apart from its own funds or property and upon express trust for the Bank until delivery is made to the Bank, —

All items or amounts which are delivered by Borrower to the Bank on account of partial or full payment or otherwise as proceeds of any of the Collateral shall be deposited to the credit of a deposit account (herein called the "Assignee Deposit Account") of Borrower with the Bank, as security for payment of the Liabilities. Buyer shall have no right to withdraw any funds deposited in the Assignee Deposit Account. --

The Bank is authorized to endorse, in the name of Borrower, any item, howsoever received by the Bank, representing any payment on or other proceeds of any Collateral.

That addendum is not unreasonable and does not impact the just requirements of the bank in protecting its interest in the collateral. There are simply too many uncertainties in life to allow any bank to take action without notifying the borrower. It is not the intention here to pick on any one bank as being worse than others. It is just one of many. There are worse bank agreements, but there are many more that are less onerous.

Similar provisions are found in other respectable banks. The Continental Illinois National Bank and Trust Company of Chicago provided the following excerpt from its printed Security Agreement for accounts receivable financing. Under a section entitled "Collections, etc." the following provisions appear:

There are many more pages of equally confusing fine print, but the above is adequate to indicate the degree of care to be exercised when dealing with documents prepared by bank attorneys. Under the above terms, the bank has complete control of the accounts receivable of the business—even if the payments to the bank are maintained in current condition. The borrower is required to keep all money received from customers separate from its other moneys and to remit it to the bank in the "form received." If a check is received from a customer payable to the borrower, the borrower must endorse the check to the bank and forward it to the bank without cashing it. And this is true even though the borrower is not in default.

Moreover, the bank has the right, at any time, to have all payments from the customers of the borrower mailed directly to the bank. Such a procedure makes it more than just difficult for a company to keep current accurate records of its receivables. The money paid into the bank goes into a special deposit account from which the borrower cannot draw funds, even though the debt to the bank is not yet due.

The bank also has the power to settle accounts with the borrower's customers on its own terms and the borrower is bound by the settlement of the bank. Consider a situation where the borrower has paid off all indebtedness to the Bank except for $10,000. A customer owes the borrower $15,000, but the amount is disputed. The borrower is adamant that it is entitled to and intends to collect the full amount. The bank, however, has an interest only in its $10,000 and has therefore no incentive to seek a better settlement.

When such a security agreement is placed before you by a bank, one would hope that you have kept your borrowing options open to the extent that you can negotiate reasonable terms with the bank. Only a small change is required: a clause bringing the above provisions into force only when the indebtedness to the bank is in default.

The above terms are not unusual bank terms. The Bank of Boston, in its standard Loan and Security Agreement for accounts receivable, uses similar terms.

In addition to the rather brash grasping by the banks, most bank agreements also include provisions for grabbing small, perhaps unjustified, amounts of the borrower's money. For example, as previously noted, bank lawyers do not have calendars. They think a year has only 360 days. The difference isn't great. Suppose you owe the bank $100,000 on a fixed interest loan of 10 percent. The interest computed in the manner accepted by other businesses is $10,000 per year. But by the bank's method it is $10,139. Not much. But the bank knows it has a few hundred (or thousand) such accounts.

The Bank of Boston security form provides "The Bank shall credit the proceeds of collection of accounts receivable received by the Bank to the Loan Account, such credits to be entered as of the third business day after receipt thereof by the Bank." If the

Chapter Twelve

Releases, Promissory Notes, Assignments, and Bills of Sale

Releases

These widely used documents follow the same rules as other contracts. The following examples are intended to serve as a general guide and as reminders of clauses you may want to include. You should not follow the exact forms shown, but rather draft the document to meet your own particular needs. As always, these documents are no less subject to the stilted legalese of the lawyers. The following Release (names have been changed) was prepared by a downtown Boston law firm in settlement of litigation. It is an apt example of a Legal Omelet, suitable for reformation.

LIMITED RELEASE

GREETING: KNOW Ye, that Artificial Air Lines Corporation, a duly authorized corporation with a usual place of business located at 24 Bowery Street, New York, New York, for and in consideration of One Dollar ($1.00) lawful money of the United States of America, to it in hand paid this day by Artful Industries Inc., d/b/a American Merchandisers, a duly authorized corporation with a usual place of business at 327 Waltham Street, Brighton, Massachusetts, the receipt whereof is hereby acknowledged, has remised, released, and forever discharged, and by these presents does for itself and its successors, remise, release and forever discharge the said Artful Industries Inc. and its successors and/or assigns, of and from any and all action and actions, cause and causes of action, suits, debts, controversies, damages, judgments, executions, claims and demands whatsoever, in law or in equity, which against said Artful Industries Inc. said Artificial Airlines Corporation ever had, now has, or which it or its successors hereinafter can, shall or may have for, upon or by reason of and limited to the action entitled Artful Industries Inc., d/b/a American Merchandisers, v. Artificial Airlines Corporation, Middlesex Superior Court Department No. 12-8567 and not otherwise.

It is understood and agreed that the parties hereto intend that this release is limited only to the

continued on page 12-2

continued from page 12-1

incident herein referenced and is not intended to nor shall it operate to release in any way any other claims between the said Artificial Airlines Corporation and the said Artful Industries Inc. unrelated to said incidents.

It is understood and agreed that the parties hereto intend mutually to release each other as herein provided and the execution of this document by Artificial Airlines Corporation shall be construed to be simultaneous with the execution of its counterpart by said Artful Industries Inc. and shall become binding and effective upon the parties only upon the mutual exchange of the executed releases between the parties hereto.

IN WITNESS WHEREOF, the said Artificial Airlines Corporation, has caused its seal to be hereto affixed and these presents to be signed under seal by its duly authorized officer the 17th day of May, 1986.

ARTIFICIAL AIRLINES
CORPORATION

By____________________________

[Corporate Seal]

State of New York)
) ss.:
County of Clark)

On the 17th day of May, 1986, before me came Wilbur Heavenbent to me known and to me known to be the person who executed the foregoing instrument, did depose and say that he resides at 1236 Maiden Lane, Oxford, in the County of Westchester, New York, and that he is the Vice President of Artificial Airlines Corporation, the corporation described in, and which executed the foregoing instrument, that the seal affixed to said instrument is such corporate seal; that it was so affixed by order of the Board of Directors of said corporation; and that he signed his name thereto by like order.

____
Notary Public

My Commission Expires____________________

The above document was accompanied by an identical release with the names reversed. First, let us see if we can reduce the volume* by eliminating some redundancy and unnecessary words:

LIMITED RELEASE

GREETING: KNOW Ye, that [1] **Artificial Air Lines Corporation,** *a duly authorized* [1] *corporation with a usual place of business located at 24 Bowery Street, New York, New York,* [2] *for and in consideration of One Dollar ($1.00) lawful money of the United States of America, to it in hand paid this day by* [3] *Artful Industries Inc., d/b/a* [12] *American Merchandisers, a duly authorized corporation with a usual place of business at 327 Waltham Street, Brighton, Massachusetts,* [2] *the receipt whereof is hereby acknowledged,* [1] *has remised,* [4] *released, and forever discharged,* [1] *and by these presents* **does** *for* [1] *itself and its successors,* [5] *remise,* [4] **release** *and forever discharge* [6] *the said* [1] **Artful Industries Inc.** *and its successors and/or assigns, of and* [7] **from** *any and* [1] **all** *action and actions, cause and causes of action, suits, debts, controversies, damages, judgments, executions,* **claims** *and demands whatsoever,* [8] *in law or in equity,* [1] **which against** *said* [1] **Artful Industries Inc.** *said* [1] **Artificial Airlines Corporation** *ever had, now* **has,** *or which it or its successors hereinafter can, shall or may have for, upon or by reason of and* [6] **limited to the action entitled Artful Industries Inc., d/b/a American Merchandisers, v. Artificial Airlines Corporation, Middlesex Superior Court Department No. 12-8567** *and not otherwise.* [1]

It is understood and agreed that the parties hereto intend that this release is limited only to the incident herein referenced and is not intended to nor shall it operate to release in any way any other claims between the said Artificial Airlines Corporation and the said Artful Industries Inc. unrelated to said incidents. [1]

It is *understood and* [1] **agreed** *that* **the parties hereto intend** *mutually* [1] **to release each other as herein provided and the execution of this document by Artificial Airlines Corporation shall be construed to be simultaneous with the execution of its counterpart** [9] **by** *said* [1] **Artful Industries Inc. and shall become binding** *and effective* [1] **upon the parties only upon** *the mutual* **exchange of the executed releases** *between the parties hereto.* [1]

continued on page 12-4

**The deleted passages are italicized, the rest is embolded for contrast, and the bracketed numbers refer to the author's comments.*

continued from page 12-3

IN WITNESS WHEREOF, the said Artificial Airlines Corporation, has caused its seal to be hereto affixed and these presents to be signed under seal by its duly authorized officer the **[1] 17th day of May, 1986.**

ARTIFICIAL AIRLINES CORPORATION

By____________________________

[Corporate Seal]

State of New York)
) ss.: **[10]**
County of Clark)

On the 17th day of May, 1986, before me came Wilbur Heavenbent to me known and to me known to be the person who executed the foregoing instrument, did depose and say that he resides at 1236 Maiden Lane, Oxford, in the County of Westchester, New York, and that he is the Vice President of Artificial Airlines Corporation, the corporation described in, and which executed the foregoing instrument, that the seal affixed to said instrument is such corporate seal; that it was so affixed by order of the Board of Directors of said corporation; and that he signed his name thereto by like order.

____
Notary Public

My Commission Expires ______________________ **[11]**

[1] Redundant or unnecessary.

[2] The corporation is more precisely identified by the state in which it is incorporated. Because that description is sufficient to provide accurate identification, the inclusion of the address is optional. Sometimes it may be convenient as a way to preserve the mailing address. In this particular case, the corporation is sufficiently identified by the reference to the action in the Superior Court.

[3] This is part of a mutual release and no other consideration need be recited. There is emphasis on the payment being in lawful money of the United States. Imagine the tragedy of receiving a counterfeit peso!

[4] Redundant—remise means release.

[5] In most cases, a release by the principal party is sufficient. What the successors and assigns do is a matter of no import.

[6] Current release is satisfactory. Presently we shall make the release apply to present and future claims.

[7] Redundant—"of" means "from."

[8] Release from all "claims" is satisfactory. Perhaps "obligations" is a more suitable word. Surprising as it may be to some attorneys, it is possible to limit the redundancies without destroying the instrument.

[9] The use of two almost identical instruments is a typical example of legal "make work," presumably based on the theory that the more pages, the more money. We will use a single reciprocal release.

[10] This little "ss." is more persistent in notary headings than acne. It serves no purpose other than to add to the mystery perpetuated by the legal profession. If your attorney uses it, ask him what it means. If he doesn't know—he owes you a drink. If he does know, don't challenge him to a game of trivia. If he thinks it is important, find another lawyer.*

"ss" is probably from the Latin "sic subscributur" meaning "So it is subscribed."

[11] The entire notary procedure is unnecessary. I would prefer the personal warranty, as in the following example, to the notary. And it is free.

[12] "dba" is a commonly used abbreviation meaning "doing business as."

The following is an appropriate substitute for both of these releases.

LIMITED MUTUAL RELEASE

This is an Agreement, effective May 17, 1986, between Artful Industries Inc., a Massachusetts corporation, dba American Merchandisers, ("Artful") and Artificial Airlines Corporation, a New York corporation ("Artificial").

Background

The parties have been engaged in a legal action identified as Artificial Airlines Corporation v. Artful Industries Inc., dba American Merchandisers, Massachusetts Middlesex Superior Court No. 12-8567. The parties now desire to settle all disputes related to such action and to release each other from all related obligations and agree as follows:

Each party releases the other from all present and future obligations related to the above action.

Each party agrees to immediately take all appropriate steps to dismiss the above action with prejudice.

continued on page 12-6

continued from page 12-5

Each individual executing this Agreement on behalf of a corporation warrants that he is authorized to bind such corporation and that this Agreement is binding on that corporation.

Artificial Airlines
Corporation

By________________________
Title

Artful Industries, Inc.,
dba American Merchandisers

By________________________
Title

The following is a form release (No. 23 from Lawyers Stationery Co., Boston):

RELEASE

In consideration of ____________________________ dollars to it paid by ______________________________ the receipt whereof is hereby acknowledged, ________________ hereby remise, release and forever discharge the said ________________________ from all debts, demands, causes of actions, suits, dues, sum and sums of money, accounts, reckonings, bonds specialities, covenants, contracts, controversies, agreements, promises, doings, omissions, variances, damages, extents, executions and liabilities and any and all other claims of every kind, nature, and description whatsoever, both in LAW and EQUITY, which against the said ______________________ or ______ heirs, executors, administrators, successors or assigns ___________________________ now or ever had from the beginning of the world to this date and more especially on account of _______________________________
____
____ Executed as a sealed instrument this day and year above written.

By________________________

Signed in the presence of ________________________

This, another Legal Omelet, is obviously defective. The attorney failed to consult the thesaurus for additional synonyms: proceedings, litigation, lawsuits, challenges, burdens, loans, obligations, responsibilities, bills, fees, invoices, checks, exigencies, requirements, notes, altercations, arguments, disputes, contracts, settlements, indemnities, pledges, and commitments. See? All it takes to make like a lawyer is a thesaurus. But if you prefer to have better legal instruments, tailor the instrument to fit the needs of the moment. Don't try to use a standard form that is designed to cover every possible situation from the beginning of the world.* (This form also demonstrates the advantage of using pet names. Note the full name of the releasing party must be entered three times and the name of the party being released, twice.) If you need to release a debt for goods purchased and returned, the following might be suitable:

**In most cases, it might do just as well to limit the period to the last century or two.*

RELEASE

For valuable consideration, the receipt and adequacy of which are acknowledged, Jamestown Historical Society, Inc., a Virginia corporation, (the "Society") releases Milford Jones, an individual residing at 400 Seventh Street, S.W., Washington, D.C. 20590 from all claims of every kind which the Society now or ever has had against Jones. This release is especially in connection with Invoice No. 1298J covering goods sold to Jones and which have since been returned to the Society.

The party executing this Release on behalf of the Society personally warrants that he is authorized to execute this Release on behalf of the Society and that this Release is binding on the Society.

This release is effective as of January 15, 1989.

Jamestown Historical
Society, Inc.

By__________________________
Title:

On occasion when an employee terminates the employment, one or both parties may request a release. The release may be in favor of either party or it may be mutual. For example, an employee may have borrowed money from the employer which is being offset by reduced termination pay. A release of the following kind may be in order:

RELEASE

This is a Release Agreement between Howard McDougal ("Mac") and Disfar Corporation, a Connecticut corporation, ("Disfar").

Background

continued on page 12-8

continued from page 12-7

Mac has been employed by Disfar and is no longer so employed. During the employment, Disfar loaned $800.00 to Mac, as evidenced by a Promissory Note dated May 12, 1987. A balance of $675.50 remains unpaid. Mac's salary has been paid through the date of termination of Mac's employment.

Release

Disfar, in lieu of termination pay and all other obligations of Disfar to Mac, releases Mac from all further obligations on account of said Note. Mac releases Disfar from all obligations.

Exception

Nothing in this release shall in any way affect the obligations of Mac under the Agreement of Employment entered into on February 1, 1984 between Mac and Disfar, which agreement includes post-employment restrictions related to secrecy and competitive activities.

____
Howard McDougal

Disfar Corporation

By_____________________________

The following all-purpose form (Uniform Printing and Supply Form No. L-3857) seems to be directed toward the settlement of auto and other accidents. It suffers from the legalese to which we are becoming accustomed.

RELEASE OF ALL CLAIMS

KNOW ALL MEN BY THESE PRESENTS:

That the Undersigned being of lawful age, for the sole consideration of _______________________Dollars ($_________) to the undersigned in hand paid, receipt whereof is hereby acknowledged, do/does/ hereby and for my/our/its heirs executors, administrators, successors, and assigns release, acquit and forever discharge _____________________________________ and his, her, their or

continued on page 12-9

continued from page 12-8

its agents, servants, successors, heirs, executors, administrators and all other persons, firms, corporations, associations or partnerships of and from any and all claims, actions, causes of action, demands, rights, damages, costs, loss of service, expenses and compensation whatsoever, which the undersigned now has/have or which may hereafter accrue on account of or in anyway growing out of and all known and unknown, foreseen and unforeseen bodily and personal injuries and property damage and the consequences thereof resulting or to result from the accident, casualty or event which occurred on or about the _____ day of _________ 19____, at or near ______________________________________.

It is understood and agreed that this settlement is the compromise of a doubtful and disputed claim, and that the payment made is not construed as an admission of liability on the part of the party or parties hereby released, and that said releases deny liability therefor and intend merely to avoid litigation and buy their peace.The undersigned hereby declare(s) and represent(s) that the injuries sustained are or may be of a permanent and progressive nature and that recovery therefrom is uncertain and indefinite and in making this Release, it is understood and agreed, that the undersigned rely(ies) wholly upon the undersigned's judgment, belief and knowledge of the nature, extent, effect and duration of said injuries and liability therefor and is made without reliance upon any statement or representation of the party or parties hereby released or their representatives or by any physician or surgeon by them employed.The undersigned further declare(s) and represent(s) that no promise, inducement or agreement not herein expressed has been made to the undersigned,and that this Release contains the entire agreement between the parties hereto and that the terms of this release are contractual and not a mere recital.

THE UNDERSIGNED HAS READ THE FOREGOING RELEASE AND FULLY UNDERSTANDS IT

Signed, sealed and delivered this ___ day of ______, 19___.

CAUTION READ BEFORE SIGNING BELOW

______________________________ ________________________LS*
Witness

______________________________ ________________________LS
Witness

continued on page 12-10

continued from page 12-9

STATE OF ______________________)
)
SS.COUNTY OF_____________________)

On the ______ day of __________________, 19_____, before me appeared ____, to me known to be the person(s) named herein and who executed the foregoing Release and _________ acknowledged to me that _________ voluntarily executed the same.

My term expires________________, 19______

____
Notary Public

The note of caution to read before signing, might well read "Rewrite before Signing"! Nevertheless, it will serve as a starting point in preparing a release for a particular accident situation. The purpose of the wording of this particular release is an attempt to prevent the party signing the release from later making claims based on an injury, the extent of which was not known at the time of the release. Such releases should be framed with care and, if the potential damage is large, should be reviewed with an attorney skilled in negligence law before relying on the effectiveness of the release. You can, however, readily rewrite the release to improve the wording and direct it more specifically to the particular situation at hand.

Promissory Notes

Promissory notes are no more than a specialized form of agreement by which one party agrees to pay money at some future time to the other party. The actual format may be from the very simple to the very complex. We have already seen that banks opt for the complex. Here is a simple form published by American Blank Book Company, Boston.

$____________ ____________________19_____

______________________ after date _____ promise to pay to

the order of ______________________________________ Dollars

Payable at ____

Value received ____

No.________ Due______________ ____________________________

That simple form is adequate for some occasions, but generally you will be better off to draft the form of the note to fit the particular circumstances. The above form, for instance, has no convenient way of including interest or in providing for periodic payments and there are no conditions for default. We'll consider some others with varying degrees of complexity.

The instruction "pay to the order of" makes the note into a negotiable instrument that can be sold or discounted at a bank. In other words, the note is payable to anyone who is designated by the note holder. Without these key words or some equivalent, the note is payable only to the original payee or to his estate.

The following rather more complex form of note covers many things that are omitted in the simplified form above. It is from the word processor of a large Boston law firm. Only the names and dates have been changed. You may wish to model a note after this one, or after the author's simplified version that follows the "real thing."

PROMISSORY NOTE

Date October 19, 1987.

FOR VALUE RECEIVED, THE UNDERSIGNED, MASTER SCIENCE CORP., a Delaware corporation (hereinafter, together with its successors in title, called the "Borrower"), by this promissory note (hereinafter called the "Note"), absolutely and unconditionally promises to pay to the order of Elmer Braidy (hereinafter, together with his successors in title and assigns, called the "Lender") [1]) or the holder hereof, the principal sum of Seventy-Two Thousand Four Hundred Thirty-Six and 32/100 Dollars ($72,436.32), and to pay interest on the principal sum outstanding hereunder from time to time from the date hereof until the principal sum or the unpaid portion thereof has been paid in full, at the rate of eight percent (8%) per annum. This note (the "Note") shall be payable in twenty-four equal installments of Three Thousand Eighteen Dollars and 18/100 ($3018.18), plus interest in arrears, on the first day of each month commencing hereafter.

Each overdue amount (whether of principal, interest or otherwise) payable on or in respect of this Note or the indebtedness evidenced hereby shall (to the extent permitted by applicable laws) bear interest, from the thirtieth day following the date on which such amount shall have first become due and payable in accordance with the terms hereof to the date on which such amount shall be paid to the holder of this Note (whether before or after judgment), at the rate of interest equal to (a) the rate of interest announced by the Chase Manhattan Bank N.A. from time to time as its prime rate plus (b) two percent (2%) per annum. The unpaid interest accrued on each overdue amount in accordance with the foregoing terms of this paragraph shall become absolutely due and payable by the Borrower to the holder hereof on written demand. Each

continued on page 12-12

continued from page 12-11

such written demand shall state the aggregate amount of accrued but unpaid interest payable to the holder hereof on the date of the demand. Interest on each overdue amount will continue to accrue, as provided by the foregoing terms of this paragraph, until the obligations of the Borrower in respect of the payment of such overdue amount shall be discharged (whether before or after judgment).

All payments of principal, interest and other amounts payable on or in respect of this Note or the indebtedness evidenced hereby shall be made to the holder hereof in dollars, at such address of the holder as the holder shall have designated in a written notice to the Borrower, by the Borrowers check or, if the holder hereof shall so request, by certified bank or cashier's checks. All payments on or in respect of this Note or the indebtedness evidenced hereby shall be made to the holder of this Note without set-off or counterclaim and free and clear of and without any deductions of any kind.

This Note evidences the obligations of the Borrower (a) to repay the principal amount of all loans made by the Lender to the Borrower hereunder, (b) to pay interest on the principal amount hereof remaining unpaid from time to time, and (c) to pay all other amounts which may become due and payable hereunder as herein provided. For all purposes of this Note, the term "holder" shall mean the Lender in possession of this Note or any other person who is at the time the lawful holder in possession of this Note.

The Borrower will have the right to prepay the principal of this Note in full or in part at any time or times without premium or penalty. All computations of interest payable as provided in this Note shall be made by the holder hereof on the basis of the actual number of days elapsed divided by 360.

The failure of the holder of this Note to exercise all or any rights, remedies, powers or privileges hereunder in any instance shall not constitute a waiver thereof in that or any other instance. Should all or any part of the indebtedness represented by this Note be collected by action at law, or in bankruptcy, insolvency, receivership or other court proceedings, or should this Note be placed in the hands of attorneys for collection, the Borrower hereby promises to pay to the holder of this Note, upon written demand by the holder hereof at any time, in addition to the principal, interest and all other amounts payable on or in respect of this Note or the indebtedness evidenced hereby (if any), all court

continued on page 12-13

continued from page 12-12

costs and all reasonable attorneys' fees and other reasonable collection charges and expenses incurred or sustained by or on behalf of the holder of this Note.

The Borrower and every endorser of this Note hereby absolutely and irrevocably waive notice of demand, notice of non-payment, protest, notice of protest, suit and all other conditions precedent in connection with the delivery, acceptance, collection and/or enforcement of this Note.

All notices, demands and other communications to or upon the Borrower pursuant to this Note shall be in writing, either delivered by hand or sent to the Borrower by first class mail, postage prepaid, or by Telex or telegraph, addressed to the Borrower at 65 Almer Avenue, Cambridge, MA 02139, or to such other address of the Borrower as the Borrower shall have designated in a written notice to the holder of this Note. This Note is intended to take effect as a sealed instrument. This Note and the obligations of the borrower hereunder shall be governed by and interpreted and determined in accordance with the laws of the State of New York.

IN WITNESS WHEREOF, this PROMISSORY NOTE has been duly executed by the undersigned MASTER SCIENCE CORP., on the day and year first above written.

MASTER SCIENCE CORP.

By____________________
Title:

This Legal Omelet is even more interesting when one considers its origin. The borrower offered to accept a note bearing interest at eight percent payable monthly over two years. The lender accepted this offer. No other terms were discussed. The borrower then had its Boston law firm draw up the note. It was signed and forwarded to the lender. Of course, the lender accepted it. These elements had not been discussed and the lender had never asked for them:

- interest at two percent over prime on overdue amounts;
- an obligation on the borrower to pay with certified or cashier's checks;
- no right of set-off by the borrower;
- cancellation of waivers;
- reimbursement of lender's expenses associated with collection of the note including attorneys' fees, court costs and other expenses;

- waiver of notice of demand, etc.;
- execution of the note as a sealed instrument;
- calculation of the interest on the basis of a 360-day year.

One might wonder just who the attorney was representing. Did he become confused and imagine he was representing the lender? Not likely. It is more likely the note came straight out of the word processor. The business man should be aware that neither an attorney nor a word processor is a substitute for thinking.

There are several clues in the note to indicate the word processor did the thinking in this case. For example, the note is to be "interpreted and determined in accordance with the laws of New York." The lender and borrower each do business only in Massachusetts; the loan and the note were both made in Massachusetts; the borrower is a Delaware corporation; and neither party has any business affiliations in New York. Nevertheless, the word processor thought New York would be an appropriate state. Also, note the suggested notice by "telegraph." It is obviously an old word processor program. And it doesn't even mention FAX.

If one is going to install a standard promissory note in the word processor for use on all occasions, it would be desirable to have two versions, depending upon whether the interests of the borrower or the lender are to have priority. Moreover, since the program will produce many notes, it might be worthwhile to pay just a little attention to the wording.

Consider these possible revisions:

"THE UNDERSIGNED": There is no need to refer to the undersigned. The name of the borrower is sufficient in the first instance and after that the "pet" name can be used.

"(hereinafter called the 'Note')": This doesn't save much. The words "this Note" will not be confused with some other obligation. The "hereinafter" as used herein and hereinafter ought to be reserved for TV evangelists.

"absolutely and unconditionally": Legal Omelet. A promise to pay is quite sufficient. Even under New York law.

"(hereinafter, together with his successors in title and assigns, called the 'Lender')": It is not necessary to refer to successors in title or assigns.

"or the holder hereof": The note is payable to the "order of ..." Subsequent references to the holder are superfluous.

"... until the principal sum or the unpaid portion thereof has been paid in full...": If the principal sum is paid, what could be the "unpaid portion thereof"? It is enough to state that payments of so much per month will be made until the note is paid.

"This note (the "Note")..." As we mentioned above, to refer to the note by the pet name "Note" is foolish. To do it twice is absurd.

"...on the first day of each month commencing hereafter": It would be just as clear and simpler to state: "...on the first of each month beginning on November 1, 1987."

"Each overdue amount (whether of principal, interest or otherwise)...": This is superfluous. "All overdue amounts..." is enough.

"...payable on or in respect of this Note or the indebtedness evidenced hereby...": These words do serve a function: they make the document longer. It might say only: "payable on this Note." It is not at once clear to me how a payment could be made on the note and not on "the indebtedness evidenced hereby." Or how a payment could be made on the "debt evidenced hereby" and not on the note. But then, I don't work downtown.

"...bear interest, from the thirtieth day following the date on which such amount shall have first become due and payable in accordance with the terms hereof to the date on which such amount shall be paid to the holder of this Note (whether before or after judgment), at the rate of interest equal to (a) the rate of interest announced by the Chase Manhattan Bank N.A. from time to time as its prime rate plus (b) two percent per annum."

More words. Longer document. More money. This is a note at a fixed rate of eight percent. It is ridiculous to complicate it by relating the overdue interest to the prime rate of some New York bank. This is all that is needed: "Overdue amounts on this note shall bear interest at the rate of ten percent per year." This doesn't specifically state that the interest shall accrue until the overdue amount is paid, but most people are ingenious enough to figure that out. There is no reason a judgment should cut off the interest, so why mention it? And if a judgment did cut off the extra interest, the lender will have bigger things to worry about than the lousy extra interest.

"The unpaid interest accrued on each overdue amount in accordance with the foregoing terms of this paragraph shall become absolutely due and payable by the Borrower to the holder hereof on written demand." A Legal Omelet, but it does add more words. Nevertheless, it is nonsense. The note should merely provide that the principal and all accrued interest is payable each month. No special reference to the overdue interest need be made. There is no need for a special written notice from the holder of the note.

"Each such written demand shall state the aggregate amount of accrued but unpaid interest payable to the holder hereof on the date of demand." The demand is needless. There ought to be a presumption that a corporation that borrows seventy plus thousands of dollars has someone who can count. Even without the recital in the note, there is no law prohibiting the lender from notifying the borrower: "Hey, you haven't sent me enough interest ..."

"Interest on each overdue amount will continue to accrue, as provided by the foregoing terms of this paragraph, until all obligations of the Borrower in respect of the payment on such overdue amount shall be discharged (whether before or after judgment)." Of course. It doesn't need to be stated again.

"All payments of principal, interest and other amounts payable on or in respect of this Note or the indebtedness evidenced hereby shall be made to the holder hereof in Dollars ...": Let's see if we can't condense that just a bit. No need to refer to "principal, interest and other amounts payable..." We can just say "All payments..." Even a lawyer can figure out we are talking about payments on the note. There is no need to say "on or in respect of this Note." Payments on the note will be enough. If a payment is made on the note, we can assume it is "in respect of this Note." There is no need to refer to the "indebtedness evidenced hereby." Payments made on the note are paid on the "indebtedness evidenced" by the note. The note is made in Massachusetts. The parties are both resident in Massachusetts. No foreign transactions are involved. The note states the borrower will pay such and such "Dollars." So we don't need say anything more about paying in dollars. There, we have successfully shortened this section to obliteration.

"...if the holder hereof shall so request, by certified bank or cashier's checks...": We lawyers must be very careful. The lender loaned seventy plus thousands of dollars to the borrower on a two-year promissory note. Of course, he is worried about a bad check! In fact, the borrower would be better off to receive a bad check than to receive no check. Utter nonsense. Leave it out.

"All payments on or in respect of this Note or the indebtedness evidenced hereby shall be made to the holder of this Note without set-off or counterclaim and free and clear of and without deductions of any kind." We have already considered the extraneous words such as "or in respect of" or "the indebtedness evidenced hereby..." The release of the right of set-off means that if the lender owes some money to the borrower, the borrower cannot deduct it from the payments on the note. In this case, the set-off limitation was a gift to the lender. Sometimes it is required, but there should be some good reason or the borrower should not consent to it. The whole thing might have been said this way: "All payments on this note shall be without set-off or deductions for any counterclaim."

"This Note evidences...the lawful holder of this Note." This entire paragraph is unnecessary. A note in itself is evidence of an obligation to pay the items enumerated in this paragraph. Chewing the cud twice doesn't increase its weight. The reference to the "lawful holder" here and at other places in the note is superfluous. A note payable "to the order of..." is contemplated to be held by someone other than the original payee. Any holder "in due course" has a right to be paid in the manner specified in the note. "In due course" means someone who acquires the note in a lawful manner.

"All computations of interest shall be made by the holder hereof on the basis of the actual number of days elapsed divided by 360." These words represent a malapropos attempt to copy the banks and reduce the year to 360 days. It is not clear that is accomplished: Suppose the number of days elapsed is 180. The note then reads "All computations of interest ... shall be on the basis of one-half." And who cares whether it is the holder or someone else who makes the interest computations? If you are the lender, you might want to say simply: "Interest computations shall be on the basis of a 360-day year." If you are the borrower, don't say anything.

"The failure of the holder of this Note to exercise all or any rights, remedies, powers or privileges hereunder in any instance shall not constitute a waiver thereof in that or in any other instance." Aside from the redundancies of "rights, remedies, powers and privileges", a waiver clause has little utility in a promissory note. The fact that a lender took no action when the borrower missed a payment would not be considered a waiver of the obligation to make future payments. If the lender does nothing until the statute of limitations has run its course, he is in trouble. But then the waiver clause wouldn't help him. My option is to avoid cluttering the note with a waiver clause. If one is to be included, it might state: "The failure of the Lender to exercise any right hereunder is not to be construed as a waiver of such right."

"Should all or any part of this Note be collected by action at law...on behalf of the holder of this Note." This major part of the paragraph merely makes the borrower responsible for the costs of collection. It isn't necessary to refer to "any part of this Note." Maybe the lawyer who wrote that was referring to any unpaid balance, not to a piece of the written note. Did the lawyer make a grievous error in referring to the Note without "or the indebtedness evidenced hereby"? What if the lender brought suit on the note, but not on the indebtedness evidenced thereby? Enough lawyer bashing. The whole thing can be boiled down a bit to: "If legal or other action is taken to collect this Note, the Borrower agrees to pay all expenses of such collection attempt including reasonable attorneys' fees."

"The Borrower and every endorser of this Note hereby absolutely and irrevocably waive notice of demand, notice of non-payment, protest, notice of protest, suit and all other conditions precedent in connection with the delivery, acceptance, collection and/or enforcement of this Note." Before discussing the desirability of this paragraph, consider some of the words: "and every endorser." There were no endorsers but, of course, the word processor did not know that. "hereby absolutely and irrevocably waive notice." Why can not the borrower simply "waive notice"? Once having waived notice it is "absolutely" and it is (in the absence of something in the note to the contrary) "irrevocable." And what exactly is the borrower waiving? First, it is waiving demand. Presumably this means a demand for payment. But this is not a demand note, so no demand is required. A demand before filing suit? Who files a legal action without first demanding that the other guy pay up? The borrower also waives "notice of non-payment." The lender has no obligation to tell the borrower he failed to pay. But no matter—human nature being what it is, the lender will tell the borrower when he fails to pay! The borrower also waives not only "protest" but "notice of protest." This is archaic legal jargon. A "protest" is a formal declaration made by someone concerned about an act about to be done (or already performed) by which he expresses his disapproval. The object of the protest is to preserve some right that might be lost if an implied consent resulted from silence. It also refers to a formal statement prepared by a Notary Public, at the request of the holder of a note, declaring the note was presented for payment and was not paid, perhaps embellished with the details of the presentment and the reasons for non-payment. The holder of the note has no obligation to present it for payment or to protest its non-payment. This sort of garbage is used by lawyers because most clients don't know what "protest" means, and may think it has some deep hidden legal meaning. It helps keep clients from trying to write their own promissory notes. Omitting this paragraph will reduce the document by about five lines and save a few dollars of legal fees.

"All notices, demands, and other communications to or upon the Borrower pursuant to this Note shall be in writing...by first-class mail, postage prepaid, or by Telex or telegraph..." "Communications" could be used to include notices and demands. As a practical matter the word "notices" will be sufficient. If it is sent by first-class mail, it is difficult to send it postage-collect. It isn't sent by first-class mail unless the postage is prepaid. The telegraph is passe. The Telex is almost passe. Certified mail and facsimile are in. How about: "All notices to either party shall be in writing and sent by certified mail, return receipt requested, or by facsimile..."?

Incorporating these changes, the above note might be rewritten as follows:

PROMISSORY NOTE

Date: October 19, 1987.

For value received, Master Science Corp., a Delaware corporation, (the "Borrower") promises to pay to the order of Elmer Braidy (the "Lender") Seventy-two Thousand Four Hundred Thirty-six and 32/100 Dollars

continued on page 12-18

continued from page 12-17

($72,436.32) with interest at eight percent (8%) per year, computed on the basis of 360-day years. This Note shall be payable in twenty-four (24) monthly installments of Three Thousand Eighteen and 18/100 Dollars ($3018.18), plus interest in arrears, on the fist day of each month commencing on November 1, 1987. All amounts overdue by thirty days or more shall bear interest at ten percent (10%) per year. The Borrower shall have the right to prepay all or any part of this Note at any time without penalty.

If the Lender takes any legal or other action to collect this Note, the Borrower agrees to pay all costs of such collection including reasonable attorneys' fees.

The individual executing this Note on behalf of the Borrower personally warrants that he is authorized to execute this Note on behalf of the Borrower and that this Note is binding on the Borrower.

Master Science Corp.

By______________________

Title:

As with other forms of agreements, you can tailor a promissory note to meet the particular needs of the current situation. For example, if an employer loans money to an employee, it is desirable to provide for a right of setoff in the note. The company, might for example, owe the employee termination or vacation pay and would obviously want to set this debt off against the amount owed on the note. The following is suitable for such situations:

PROMISSORY NOTE

$ ____________

FOR VALUABLE CONSIDERATION, the receipt and adequacy of which are acknowledged, I promise to pay to the order of ____________________, __________Dollars ($_____.__), with interest at ________ percent (__%) per year, in equal monthly payments of $____________ beginning on _______________________, 19___, and a final payment of $___________ on or before ____________________, 19___.

If I am late in making any payment hereunder, the entire balance shall become immediately due and payable

continued on page 12-19

continued from page 12-18

without demand. Any amounts not paid when due shall thereafter bear interest at the maximum legal rate per year, but in no event more than ____% per year. The payee shall have complete right of setoff, and I hereby grant to the payee the right, without notice to me, to deduct, from any amount owed to me, whether for wages or otherwise, all amounts then due on this obligation. I further agree to pay all reasonable costs of collection of amounts due hereunder, including attorneys' fees, court costs, and all other associated costs.

____

Date ______________, 19___

Assignments and Bills of Sale

An assignment is the transfer of something from one entity to another. The something may be either tangible or intangible. We have already seen examples of assignments of patent rights. Other intellectual rights, such as copyrights and trademarks can be assigned in a similar manner. In some instances, there are limitations on the assignment. For example, a trademark is not by itself assignable, but can be assigned with the articles or services with which it is used. Promissory notes that are payable to "the order of" are assigned by endorsement. A promissory note that is payable only to the lender can be assigned, but the assignee may not have direct rights of collection from the maker of the note. Real property can be assigned, but the assignment is usually referred to as a "deed." Personal property can be assigned. Stocks and other securities can be assigned by written instrument or by endorsement directly on the certificate evidencing the security. There are no specific rules for assignments—they follow the general rules and formats of other forms of agreements. Sometimes, however, an assignment must have a particular format. For example, a deed to real property must meet certain requirements in order for it to be recorded by the Register of Deeds. These include a proper description of the property and, in most states, a notarial acknowledgement. In some states, the transfer of an automobile must be in a prescribed format before the transfer can be recorded in the registry of vehicles.

An assignment should identify the assignor and assignee in the same manner as in other agreements. The thing being assigned should be clearly identified: Material things can often be identified by serial number, model number, location, or by any description sufficient to uniquely identify the property. Intangible properties can often be identified by an exhibit to the assignment. For example, the assignment of a contract may include a copy of the contract as an exhibit to the assignment ("exhibit" means something attached to and forming part of the document). Official registration numbers are sometimes effective. Patents, patent applications, and registered trademarks can be identified by official registration numbers. Delivery is an important step in the assignment. When appropriate, the assignment should state the place and time of delivery. In some cases, both parties should sign the assignment and the assignee should acknowledge the receipt of the transferred property.

Bills of Sale

A bill of sale is merely a record of a sale that has been completed; it is evidence of the transfer of title as a result of a sale. Here is a typical bill of sale for an automobile:

Bill of Sale for Motor Vehicle I [we]

______________________ of ______________________

in consideration of ______________________Dollars, the receipt of which is acknowledged, sell to ______________________ of ______________________

the following vehicle:

One [Name of manufacturer and type, model, engine number, manufacturer's number] and I [we] warrant that I am [we are] the true and lawful owner[s] of such vehicle, that I [we] have full power to lawfully dispose of said vehicle.

____
Seller[s]

Date______________________

____
Witness

A bill of sale for any property, usually tangible, can be prepared following the general format for an assignment set forth earlier in this chapter.

Chapter Thirteen

"What-iffing" the Contract

When you have completed a draft of an agreement, it is well to consider what would happen under various imaginary circumstances. What if? One party fails to make payments when due? What if? One party goes bankrupt? What if? The goods are delivered late or fail to meet specifications? What if? The seller of goods or property does not have a clear title to the goods? What if? Something goes wrong: Does the other party have financial assets to repair the loss? What if? The goods fail to function in the particular application for which they were purchased? What if? An employee under a non-competition employment agreement does not go to work directly for a competitor but acts as a consultant for the competitor to the detriment of the former employer? Assume a corporation of limited ownership has agreed to refrain from certain acts for some period of time. What if? The owner or owners of the corporation merely establish a new corporation to perform the prohibited acts?

These and many other questions will occur to you as you read through your draft. In preparing any document of importance, it is a good practice to prepare the draft and put it away for a day or two, giving your subconscious a chance to do its work. Then again review and what-if the document. We will now review some of the earlier examples of agreements and do some typical what-iffing on them.

What-iffing the Polly Pie Agreement

Consider the consulting agreement of Chapter 4 between Polly Pie Corporation and Machine Design Company, Inc. What if? The services of the consultant are unsatisfactory? Does Polly have a right to discontinue the services? If so, is any advance notice required? What if? The equipment produced by MDC fails to meet the specifications? Can MDC be forced to revise the equipment? What if? MDC takes too long in revising the equipment and Polly suffers losses because of it? What if? The equipment meets the specifications, is paid for by Polly, and then breaks down in production? Is there a warranty beyond meeting the specifications? Does MDC have resources to carry out any implied or express warranty? What if? MDC violates its pledge of confidentiality? What would be the damage to Polly and how can those damages be proved? What if? An MDC employee makes an important invention while working on the project and refuses to assign the invention to MDC? MDC is restricted from working for a competitive company for a period after the conclusion of the consulting agreement. What if? MDC immediately sets up a subsidiary corporation and that corporation undertakes work for a competing company?

In connection with Section 3, Termination by Polly, Polly has a right to discontinue the services of MDC at the end of any Phase or at any time by assuming the costs of labor that is not reassigned to another job. To provide some further protection to Polly if MDC proves grossly incompetent, the following could be added to Section 3:

```
If at any time Polly reasonably determines the Project
is not being conducted by MDC at a level of competency
or effort consistent with the general standards or
customs of the industry, Polly shall have the right to
terminate the project without advance notice and
without responsibility for any charges accruing
subsequent to the date of such notice.
```

That language contains enough room for disagreement in interpretation that the machine designer may, with considerable justification, resist its inclusion.

With respect to Section 4, Delivery and Warranty Limitations, there is no warranty that any particular specifications will be met. This is typical of machine development contracts and is not unreasonable if compared with one alternative available to the one assigning the project. That alternative is to have the development done internally by engineer employees. Under those circumstances, it is not the usual practice to expect the engineer to take financial responsibility for failure to meet specifications, cost overruns, or late delivery. The remedy usually consists only in terminating the services of the engineer. This is analogous to the situation with an outside development concern. The businessman with experience in this field will be wary of an offer to develop a new machine at a fixed price with a guarantee of operating specifications or delivery date. As a practical matter, the right to terminate is about the only protection available from competent design firms.

The question of revising or modifying the machine after delivery is a new subject and may be arranged on a somewhat different basis from the original development agreement. More is known about the machinery at that time and a fixed price contract with performance specifications may be a reasonable possibility.

Section 5, Operational Responsibility, raises serious questions for the manufacturer. Under the terms of the agreement, the user assumes complete responsibility for any accident. What if? An employee of Polly is injured on the machine made by MDC? What if? The injury results from a design error or faulty material used in the construction?

In the usual course, Polly would carry Workers' Compensation insurance that would protect it from damages in excess of those provided by statute and resulting regulations. Lawyers for employees that are injured go looking for deeper pockets, and the machine manufacturer is one of the first places to look. Even if the machine manufacturer, in fact, made no design error, or made one unrelated to the accident, and there were no defects in workmanship or materials, our system of jurisprudence, in which the courts and the juries more and more regard manufacturers as insurers, damages are frequently assessed in spite of no proof of wrong doing. If that happens, the user of the machine, in addition to the cost of maintaining Workers' Compensation insurance, may have to reimburse the machine manufacturer for its expenses. The operative word here is "may," because in some states a hold harmless clause of this kind is unenforceable against the employer, presumably because it is an abrogation of the basis for Workers' Compensation insurance.

In many such cases there is more than one at fault. The employee may be negligent; the user may have permitted the removal or bypassing of safety devices; and the machine manufacturer may have made an error in design or workmanship. Some protection of the machine designer and builder is appropriate, at least to the extent that others contribute to the injury or damage. The liability in this regard is more poignant because the user has complete control over the machine once it is placed in production and a duty (at least implied) to take reasonable care to discover and correct errors in the machine design or construction. One possible compromise is to revise the first paragraph of Section 5 to read:

```
Polly shall have complete responsibility for the instal-
lation, operation and safety of the machinery. Polly
agrees to provide insurance relating to the operation of
the machinery, or any product made on or processed by it,
in sufficient amount and with appropriate terms to pro-
tect MDC from all claims of damage, personal injury or
death relating in any way to the operation of the machin-
ery. If such insurance is inadequate to protect MDC,
Polly agrees to hold MDC, its officers and employees,
harmless from liability from any cause, resulting from
the operation of the machinery, provided, Polly or its
employees or agents contribute in any material way to
such damage, personal injury or death. Polly agrees to
hold MDC, its officers and employees, harmless from lia-
bility from any cause resulting from any product made or
processed on the machinery.
```

The hold harmless clause has been modified by limiting liability from operation of the machine. The responsibility for liability for products made or processed on the machinery would seem to rest logically with the user of the machinery, for it has complete design and production control over the product. However, the user may share my general aversion to hold harmless clauses and limit the agreement to "being responsible for all liability arising from any product made or processed on the machinery."

This entire subject is difficult and the result depends in large measure upon the negotiating strength and sense of fairness of both parties. For successful negotiations, it is necessary for each of the businessmen to know precisely what the language of the agreement means, for only then can they assess the potential liabilities and benefits.

What if? The machinery, after it is installed and in use, is found to infringe a U.S. patent? The machine designer takes no responsibility if he was unaware of any infringement at the time of development and the burden of infringement falls entirely upon the user. This is as it should be. It would cost many thousands of dollars to make an infringement search and there can never be any certainty that it is complete. If a machine manufacturer sells repeat machines as a standard line, it is usual and proper for the seller to provide either an express or implied warranty of non-infringement. Not so with a newly-developed one-of-a-kind machine.

The agreement does not assign to Polly all inventions made on the project. It does give Polly a free, exclusive license to use the machine under any patents owned by MDC. The coverage can be broadened a bit by including all patent rights that MDC has power to license. A further step would be to require an exclusive license in the field under all patents resulting from inventions made on the project, whether or not embodied in the machinery. The ultimate is an outright assignment of all inventions conceived or first reduced to practice on the project. Generally, a machine design company that has plans for longevity will not agree to the latter provision.

In connection with Section 7, Proprietary Information, there are a number of ways to tighten the restrictions short of making the receiving party absolutely liable for any leak of information. One reasonable request is that the party receiving confidential information be required to obtain from any employee, or other party to whom the information is to be transmitted, an agreement to abide by the requirements of the development agreement.

This clause, of course, introduces the never-ending negotiations with respect to the period of time of confidentiality and whether the confidential information is limited to written material. These are things to be negotiated between the principals, not between lawyers.

What-iffing the Sharleen Sales Rep Agreement

It might be good practice to what-if the simple Sales Representative Agreement between Sharleen Corporation and George Smith of Chapter eight. What if the sales representative is unsatisfactory? What are the conditions of termination? How much notice must be given? Can any commissions be withheld until the sales representative has complied with all terms of the agreement including the return of all company materials? What if commissions are paid on a sale and the goods are later returned for credit? What if the sales representative exceeds authorized expenses? What if the sales representative fails to spend adequate time in promoting and selling the company products? What if the sales representative binds the company to obligations the company considers undesirable? What if the sales representative is habitually late in reporting sales activities and leads to the company? You will think of many more in a real-life situation.

If it is immediately apparent the representative is incompetent or is not making a reasonable effort, the agreement as now written requires Sharleen to give Smith 30 days notice of termination. In addition, the representative is still entitled to the minimum payment of $28,000 for the first year under paragraph (6). In some instances, a provision such as the following could be included:

If in the reasonable judgment of Sharleen, at any time within the first three months of this Agreement, Smith is not exerting his best efforts in the promotion and sale of products manufactured by Sharleen, then Sharleen shall have the right to terminate this Agreement on five days notice, and Smith shall be entitled only to receive commissions on Net Sales initiated by and resulting directly from the efforts of Smith, and the provision for a minimum payment set forth in Paragraph (6) hereof shall be void.

In the event of termination, can commissions be withheld until all materials in the possession of Smith are returned to Sharleen? There is no specific provision for the return of any materials by Smith and, although there may be an obligation on Smith to return any company materials, Sharleen would be on shaky ground in withholding commissions. With a provision something like the following, things would be different:

Upon termination of this Agreement, for any reason, Smith agrees promptly, and without further request, to return to Sharleen all materials relating to the business of Sharleen including, without limitation, all product samples, display materials, and all copies of literature, written materials, correspondence, customer lists, and the like.

What if goods are returned for credit? Sharleen is not obligated to pay commissions because the definition of Net Sales excludes "returns and allowances." If Sharleen has already paid the commission, it is entitled to deduct the commissions on returned goods from future commission payments.

What if Smith signs a quote on behalf of Sharleen that Sharleen disavows? Nothing in the agreement overtly gives the representative the right to bind Sharleen to any agreement or makes Smith an employee of Sharleen. The situation would leave, however, an open question of whether the quotation binds Sharleen. Prudence would suggest a provision something like the following:

Smith shall at all times be an independent contractor and not an employee of Sharleen and shall have no power to make any commitment binding upon Sharleen unless authorized in writing in advance by Sharleen in each particular instance.

What if Smith is habitually late in reporting sales activities and leads to Sharleen? There is nothing in the agreement that requires Smith to make any such reports to Sharleen. If such reports are to be a part of the agreement, they must be specifically provided for:

Smith agrees to provide to Sharleen, in such detail and in such format as Sharleen may reasonably request, monthly reports listing all sales activities of Smith for the preceding month, the names and addresses of all prospective customers known to Smith, copies of all correspondence with customers or prospective customers, and Smith's best estimated forecast of likely sales of Sharleen products by Smith during the next three month period.

What-iffing the Science Renter's Lease

A commercial real estate lease is usually a major undertaking for a business and considerable care should be taken in studying a lease agreement before it is executed.

Here are some possibilities in connection with the lease of the Science Renter's Club in Chapter 10.

This is a more or less conventional lease that was prepared by a large property owners' association with rental properties in the Midwest and East. The lease is clearly biased in favor of the landlord, so we'll consider possible objections from the standpoint of a prospective tenant.

Section 2.4. The monthly parking charges are not specified, it is only the amount set by the landlord for all tenants and users of the parking facilities. In most instances, this provision will be acceptable. It may be preferable, however, to include an upper limit, for example, by adding at the end of the first sentence of the second paragraph of this Section:

> ...provided the monthly parking charge per auto parking space shall not exceed $xx per month.

Section 2.5. What if the tenant gives the landlord notice of an extension of the lease some eleven months before the expiration of the first five-year term? It has lost the right to require the landlord to extend the lease. This is emphasized by the statement that "time is of the essence in the giving of the notice of extension." In this case, it may not be of great importance because the rent for the extended period is to be at market rate. It could be of more importance if the rate were pre-set at a level substantially lower than the going market rate. From the viewpoint of the tenant, a six-month period of notice to extend is much to be preferred.

What if the tenant and the landlord cannot agree on a fair rent and the appraisers come in with a rental price well above what the tenant is willing to pay? As now written, the tenant would have the five-year extension. A possible compromise is to require agreement between the tenant and the landlord at least nine (or six) months before expiration of the lease. If there were no agreement, the matter would go before the appraisers in such time that the new rate would be established well before the expiration. The lease could then provide:

> The Tenant shall have ten (10) days after the determination of the Fair Rental Value to elect, by notice to the Landlord, to refuse the extension in which event (i) the Lease shall terminate at the end of the original Term, and (ii) the Tenant shall pay all the costs of the three appraisers.

Section 3.6. What if during the term of the lease, the landlord agrees to pay the tenant $3,000 to install a permanent alarm system in the premises and, after the installation, fails to pay the tenant? Can the tenant deduct the $3,000 from the rent? No. The tenant cannot offset against the rent or other charges, It must pay full rent even if the landlord never pays the $3,000. This provision is probably in the lease at the insistence of a

mortgagee or ground lessor and probably cannot be changed. No big deal—the tenant just makes certain by other means that it will get paid for any obligations of the landlord.

Section 4.2. What if the tenant suspends an expensive display case by securing it to the ceiling girders? May the tenant remove the case at the end of the lease? Not unless the landlord agreed to such removal before the display case was installed: otherwise it belongs to the landlord.

Section 5.3 What if? A truck backs into the building and makes the premises unusable for the tenant? The truck drivers are on strike in the area and the landlord cannot repair the damage for two months. The tenant must continue to pay full rent even though it cannot use the premises. The prudent answer is a provision that limits the time for repairs. The following sentence could be added to Section 5.3:

Notwithstanding the foregoing, if thirty percent (30%) or more of the Premises are made unusable for the purposes of the Tenant and such condition continues for thirty (30) days or more, the Fixed Annual Rent and the Additional Rent shall be abated for the period when the Premises are of reduced utility in accordance with the percentage of the area of the Premises that are unusable. If the Premises are not restored to the condition existing prior to the start of the period of reduced utility for a period of 60 days after notice to the Landlord, the Tenant shall have the right to terminate this Lease.

Section 6.2. This Section permits the landlord to examine the books and accounts of the tenant to determine whether the tenant has complied with all laws and regulations. This is a broad power and one that could provide a leak for confidential information. From the tenant's standpoint, the provision for examination of the tenant's books should be deleted. At the very least (a) the "determination by the landlord" should be modified by the word "reasonable"; (b) the access to the tenant's books should require advance notice to the tenant; and (c) the landlord should agree to keep in confidence all information about the tenant's business.

Section 7.1 This is another of those troublesome hold harmless clauses. The tenant should negotiate it out if possible and replace it with:

Section 7.1. Indemnity. With respect to the Landlord, the Tenant agrees to be responsible for any act or omission by the Tenant, or by its contractors, agents and employees while engaged in activities on behalf of the tenant, resulting in personal injury or property damage during the term or while the tenant occupies any part of the Premises.

The tenant should not be forced to pay all of the landlord's costs just because someone "claims" the tenant or its agent has misbehaved. So the second back-up position is to strike the words "from claims" and also the words "or claimed to have arisen from."

Section 8.3. This Section grants the primary right of termination in the event of a casualty to the landlord. The tenant can probably live with this provision if its negotiating position is not strong. But the preferred revision would be to eliminate Section 8.3 and provide in Section 8.2 that either party shall have the same right to terminate. As now written, the tenant could find itself paying rent, although reduced under Section 8.6, on crippled premises for as long as 18 months.

Section 8.7. What if? The premises are taken over for six months by eminent domain? The tenant cannot use the premises, but must continue to pay full rent to the landlord. The tenant can only hope for a full recovery, perhaps at a much later time, from the authority taking the property. Generally, the landlord is in a better position to obtain a satisfactory recovery than is the tenant. The tenant, if possible, should negotiate for a provision providing for an abatement of the rent during any such period, perhaps with an agreement to reimburse the landlord to the extent the landlord is unable to recover from the eminent domain authority.

Section 9.1. This Section provides for the dire consequences if the tenant does not meet its obligations. But the landlord also has obligations. What if? The landlord defaults? The lease is silent on that. The failure of the landlord to perform its obligations should also be defined as an Event of Default of the landlord, with appropriate remedies for the tenant. What if? The landlord fails to remove the snow from the parking area or repair an elevator? From the standpoint of the tenant, subparagraph (b) of Section 9.1 should be made reciprocal, with the same right of termination by either the landlord or the tenant.

Section 9.2. This Section as written is highly biased toward the landlord. What if? The lease is terminated by the tenant because of a breach by the landlord? As written, no reason for termination is stated. Because this is a subsection under a section entitled "Tenant's Default", it might be assumed that Section 9.2 refers only to the situation where the landlord is terminating because of a default by the tenant. But that leaves open the kind of ambiguity that makes for disputes. The interpretation is made more nebulous by Section 11.6 which says that titles don't count. As a very minimum the opening sentence of Section 9.2 should start: "If this Lease is terminated because of an Event of Default by the Tenant..."

Consider a situation in which the lease is terminated prior to the end of the term, either by the tenant or by the landlord for any reason. The language is complex and it is difficult to determine just what it means, so we'll take it one step at a time. What is meant by the expression: "...discounted present value of the total rent reserved for the remainder of the Term"? This means the present value of all of the rent payable for the remainder of the lease term. Suppose the lease has two years to run and the monthly payment (including Annual Fixed rent and Additional rent) is $12,000. During those two years the payments would total $288,000. But we are talking about a single advance payment. The present discounted value depends upon the interest rate which is not stated in the lease. If we assume it is eight percent, then the discounted present value is $266,963. That amount, deposited at eight percent interest, would make the 24 monthly payments of $12,000 each. (Don't ask me about the calculations. If I could figure that stuff, I wouldn't have wasted all this time trying to be a lawyer.) We'll call that amount the "Present Value." Suppose also that the fair rental value of the premises, at this point in time, amounts to only $9,500 per month. The present discounted value, on the same basis is some $211,345. We'll call that the "New Rent." The Lump Sum Payment is the excess of the Present Rent over the New Rent or $55,618. The first step then is for the tenant to give the landlord a check for that amount.

The next step is that the tenant, in addition to the above payment, continues to pay the same rent as in the past—$12,000 per month. If the landlord relets the premises, then the payments are reduced by the amount the landlord receives from the new tenant less the landlord's expenses in connection with the reletting including advertising, brokerage commissions, legal fees, and preparing the premises for the new tenant. According to the lease, the tenant can deduct the lump sum payment from the last rent payment. In this case the lump sum payment was $55,618, and the last payment is only $12,000. The lease should be revised to state the lump sum payment is deducted from the "final Periodic Payments" rather than the "last Periodic Payment."

If the landlord elects not to lease the premises or to give free rent, there may be no credits for the tenant. The lease should require the landlord to make its best (or at least reasonable) efforts to relet the property and to minimize the expense to the tenant.

Section 9.4. This is a reasonable provision but, the tenant should try to have it made reciprocal. If the landlord fails to clean the joint, the tenant should have the right to do so and charge the landlord. The same comment applies to Section 9.5. If the tenant incurs legal fees in getting the landlord to fly right, it should be entitled to reimbursement.

Section 9.6. The charge for being late with the rent payment is high. This is a matter for negotiation, but usually the landlord wins.

Section 10.1. This is a bad one. What if? A mortgagee or ground lessor forecloses on the property? Then the tenant's lease can be vacated because this Section states that the lien of a mortgagee or ground lessor is "superior to all rights vested in the Tenant." It is most important that the lease require the mortgagee or ground lessor to recognize the rights of the tenant under the lease. A provision like the following is suitable:

"In the event of any mortgage or ground lease on the property (present or future) this Lease shall, at the election of the holder of any mortgage or ground lease on the Property, be subordinate to such mortgage or ground lease on the Property, so that the lien of such mortgage or ground lease shall be superior to all rights vested in the Tenant, provided, the holder of each such mortgage or ground lease shall execute and deliver to the Tenant a recordable agreement to the effect that in the event such mortgage or ground lease is foreclosed by entry or sale, the Tenant, so long as it performs its obligations under this Lease, shall enjoy the Premises for the remainder of the unexpired Term and any extension thereof upon the same terms as are set forth herein without hindrance or interruption from any such holder or its successors or assigns."

What-iffing is an important step for all agreements, but it can be carried to extremes. Over-zealousness can kill a deal. The businessman, not the lawyer, must decide when the matter is of significant importance or when it is merely a matter of principle.

Chapter Fourteen

Negotiations and Creeping

Who Negotiates?

The fine art of negotiating is beyond the scope of this book, but there are certain aspects of it you should be aware of. One of the most important guidelines, in the opinion of this author, is never, never, allow your attorney to negotiate the terms of an agreement with another attorney representing the other party. Disaster is the rule—not the exception. You, as the businessman, should decide independently which terms are acceptable to you and which are not. When you have reached a decision on the terms, then ask your attorney about the consequences of your conclusions and whether there are other terms that should be included. Do not think of your attorney as some oracle that knows better than you what should be in an agreement—consider each provision for yourself and then discuss it with your attorney. Do not buy a suggested provision unless you understand it and the possible consequences.

Success in any negotiation, no matter how skillfully conducted, is in large measure a matter of the relative need of each of the parties for an agreement. For example, an individual or a corporation that comes to a bank desperately needing money is in a weak position to negotiate the most favorable terms. Bankers know this and take advantage of it. Who else can require one party to an agreement to pay the legal expenses of both parties? Banks do. Not because it is fair or equitable, but because the pressures are such they can get away with it. You can negotiate successfully with a bank only when you have a viable alternative. It is wise to shop for loans well before any loan is required and to make sure each bank is aware of its competition. This is, of course, not always possible, making your skills at negotiating even more important.

Some Thoughts on Negotiating

The following comments are intended to apply primarily to ordinary business negotiations. They may not be applicable to divorce, labor or other classes of negotiations. This author has spent many hours negotiating with the Department of Defense and the comments made here are definitely not applicable to negotiations with the military. Martinis have no place in most commercial negotiations.

Perhaps, the very word "negotiation" carries a negative connotation. It sounds as though one party were trying to get the better of the other. That may be true in many instances, but it may be better to refer to a proposed meeting as an attempt to arrive at an equitable deal rather than entering negotiations. It may sound better to the other party to say: "Let's see if we can put that in terms we can agree on" rather than "Let's negotiate it."

Before starting any discussion about terms, you should be certain in your own mind of your aims and objectives. You should have a very clear idea of what you would like to have, what you would be willing to settle for and what is unacceptable. You should also, figuratively, walk around to the other side of the table and try to understand the perspective from the viewpoint of the other party. Try to understand just what he would like to achieve, just what you think he will settle for and what he will find unacceptable. This may help you to structure the deal in such manner that it is more acceptable to the other party, while meeting your own objectives.

Part of understanding the viewpoint of the other party is to discover as much as possible about the other party before you begin negotiations. This may mean gathering information about his finances, how long his lease has to run, the profitability of his operation, past deals he has made, how many law suits he has been involved in, or details about his personal life style. Just which kinds of information are pertinent depends upon the particular deal you are trying to put together.

Before you arrange a timetable, select a time when you will be in good form. If Monday mornings are a bad scene for you, negotiate on some other day or at some other time. Don't expect to be at your sharpest with a hangover.

There may also be differences in such factors as dress and environment, depending upon whether you are "buying" or "selling." Sometimes it is of little or no import to you whether a deal is made. If it is more important to the other party that a deal be made, you have the advantage and you can afford to be a bit careless about your necktie. At other times you will be "selling" when the slightest detail should not be overlooked in preparing the environment.

General conversation at the outset may be appropriate. This is a personal matter and depends upon the other party and your relationship with him. It may be appropriate to inquire about his family, or his golf game, or his latest business venture—only you can judge whether any such overtures are appropriate. In some instances you may want to give the other party a preview of your company or yourself and in broad terms what you are trying to accomplish. Do not spend time telling the other party how honest you are—every crook does that.

Usually, negotiating sessions should be short. There may be times when you will be able to wear the other party down to an agreement with a marathon, but it is less likely to be an agreement that will benefit both parties over a period of time.

It is often said that the party with the fewest number of representatives at a negotiating session is at a disadvantage, and sometimes that is true. But not always. One competent person can negotiate with a roomful if he has the requisite skills. The truth is that nearly always, there is one person on the other side who has the final authority. That is the person you are negotiating with. It may not be easy initially to identify that person—he may not be the one with the biggest title. However, as the meeting progresses, you can usually determine the one person that you must convince in order to make a deal. When you have made that determination, you will want to address your remarks to that person, even though you are looking at someone else. Of course, both sides are playing the same game—the other party is looking at your body signals. *What* you say may not be as important as *how* you say it.

Which brings us to another important don't: Don't try to negotiate an important deal over the telephone. The telephone only transmits part of what the other party is saying—the body language is lost. A statement is interpreted differently if made with a frown rather than with a smile. A clenched fist may tell you more about the other party's position than words alone. It is important to pay attention to their actions as well as their words.

Remember, too, that while you have been sizing up the other side and looking into the background, the other side has been doing the same to you. You may spoil a deal if you appear too "slick" or too knowledgeable. In some circumstances, a bit of ignorance is an asset. Questions indicating a lack of understanding about something you are perfectly familiar with can be powerful tools. Such questions will not only put you in the "common" category, the answers will reveal much about the sophistication of the other party.

I don't intend to suggest that you should appear to be something you are not. Don't pretend you are there only to negotiate a deal that is in the best interests of the other party. Those tactics are properly reserved for the con man—and if you are a typical businessman, you can never compete with a skilled con man. Similarly, if the other party makes an attempt to impress you with his ever-loving intentions to act only in your best interests, a very short negotiating session is in order.

Don't start negotiations with a rigid format for objectives and structure. That amounts to a "take-it-or-leave-it" situation. That doesn't call for negotiations—you can make that offer on the telephone. A satisfactory deal may be structured in a number of different formats. For example, a deal with the same practical results might be described in terms of a license, franchise, sale, or lease.

Negotiating a deal is nothing more or less than selling. Being a good salesman is being a good negotiator. However, in negotiating a deal, you have much more flexibility than most salesmen. Timing is all important. Select with care the opportune time to make a critical proposal, to say, "Oh, by the way..." You should certainly stress the plus factors of the deal from the standpoint of the other party, but you should not try to profit from a deal that will prove too onerous for the other party. If the deal doesn't have benefits for both parties, it is a lousy deal.

Try to win agreement on the major terms of the deal, don't get bogged down in details before the broader guideposts have been established. When you have reached agreement on the general terms, do not adjourn until you have made a written record of those points and each person receives a copy. You can then continue with discussion of ancillary details, or you can than propose a written agreement for discussion. When the parties have agreed upon the general terms of an agreement, the agreement is then drafted either by one of the parties or its attorney.

Creeping

One of the most insidious practices of attorneys (and others) is "creeping." Creeping is the practice of slanting the terms to be more favorable to the party drafting the agreement without specifically violating the general terms of agreement. It will be to your advantage to be the one to prepare the first draft of the agreement. Better to be the creeper then the creepee. This inhibits creeping by the other side.

For example, two parties agree as follows: Developer Company agrees to develop a new "Hydromixer" for Customer and to supply the units to Customer for not more than $65 each. The first deliveries are to be started in September. Developer will not supply the units to anyone else for a period of five years. Customer agrees to pay Developer $600 to cover development costs.

The parties have reached a general agreement, but the draft of the contract will be quite different depending upon who prepares it. Assume, first, that Developer or his attorney is assigned the task of preparing the draft, the critical provisions might go something like this:

Customer agrees, upon the execution of this Agreement, to pay to Developer the sum of $600 for the development of a new Hydromixer.

Developer agrees to make reasonable efforts to meet the objectives set forth in Exhibit A and to have a model demonstrating the proof of principle ready for demonstration by September 30, 1988. Developer makes no warranty as to any delivery date and does not warrant that any unit will meet the objectives set forth in Exhibit A.

Developer agrees to provide Hydromixer units to Customer at an FOB cost not to exceed $65 each unless unforeseen costs make a higher price necessary, in no event more than 20% higher than the actual cost to Developer. Developer further agrees it will not sell Hydromixer units, substantially identical to those developed by Developer for Customer, to anyone else for a period of five years from the date of this Agreement, provided, Customer purchases from Developer and pays for at least one hundred Hydromixers in each twelve month period beginning with the date of this Agreement. Customer agrees it will not purchase Hydromixers from any other source during the foregoing five-year period.

Now lets look at corresponding provisions when prepared by Customer or his attorney:

Developer agrees to develop a new Hydromixer for Customer and to deliver a production model of the new Hydromixer to Customer not later than September 1, 1988. Customer warrants the Hydromixer will meet all specifications as set forth in Exhibit A. Upon delivery of the Hydromixer to Customer, Customer agrees to pay the sum of $600 to Developer, provided the Hydromixer meets all specifications set forth in Exhibit A and is delivered to Customer not later than September 1, 1988.

Developer agrees to deliver Hydromixers to Customer, meeting the specifications set forth in Exhibit A, within thirty days after each order is placed with Developer. The delivered price of such Hydromixers shall be not more than $65.00.

Developer agrees it will not manufacture for or sell to others any Hydromixers for a period of five years following the delivery of the first production order for Hydromixers to Customer. Developer further agrees it will not disclose any manufacturing techniques or in any way assist any other entity in the design or manufacture of Hydromixers during such five-year period.

There is a wide difference between the two documents and further negotiations between the principals are clearly in order. This is a rather exaggerated example of creeping, but it makes the point.

The Relationship between Form and Substance

The "window dressing" of an agreement can also be important. For example, a formal agreement may be prepared on legal paper (which won't fit any business file), with much use of Witnesseth and Whereas. The signature may provide for the corporate seal and a witness. Such a formal document might well cause the other party, alas, to consult his attorney. The same agreement couched in informal terms and submitted as a letter agreement might be executed with fewer complications. Consider the following two agreements.

TERMINATION AGREEMENT

This agreement entered into this 22nd day of January 1990 by and between Cisco Products Corporation, a Delaware corporation, (hereinafter referred to as "Cisco") and Bates Incorporated, a Georgia corporation (hereinafter referred to as "Bates")

WITNESSETH:

WHEREAS, the parties hereto have entered into an agreement dated June 22, 1986 whereby Bates agreed to provide its services in an attempt to arrange a merger of Cisco into another company (the "Agreement"), a copy of which is attached hereto as Exhibit A hereof;

WHEREAS, the efforts of Bates have been unsuccessful to the present time; and

WHEREAS, Cisco desires to terminate the Agreement and to effectuate a possible merger without the assistance of Bates;

NOW, THEREFORE, for good and valuable consideration, the receipt and adequacy of which are hereby acknowledged, the parties have agreed as follows:

(1) Upon execution of this agreement, Cisco agrees to pay to Bates the sum of Twelve Thousand Dollars ($12,000.00).

(2) The Agreement is hereby terminated and of no further force or effect, provided, the provisions in the Agreement relating to the obligations of Bates to retain in confidence all information about Cisco shall survive this termination.

(3) Bates agrees promptly to turn over to Cisco copies

continued on page 14-6

continued from page 14-5

of all documents in its possession relating to its endeavors under the Agreement.

(4) Each of the parties hereto releases the other from all liability and obligations in connection with the Agreement, except those specifically set forth herein. In addition Bates waives all rights to any future payments, fees or commissions in connection with any sale, acquisition or merger of Cisco, irrespective of whether such transaction involves a party or parties previously communicated with by Bates.

WHEREFORE, the parties have hereunto set their hands and seals this ____ day of ________________, 1989.

[Corporate Seal] | Cisco Products Corporation

Witness: ___________________ | By________________________
Title:

[Corporate Seal] | Bates Incorporated

Witness: ___________________ | By________________________
Title:

This termination might be accomplished with equal effectiveness by the following letter with less chance of interference by some attorney who thinks it is unethical to approve a document he doesn't amend.

BATES INCORPORATED
230 Peachtree Row
Atlanta, Georgia 30304

January 22, 1990.

Cisco Products Corporation
Att: Joseph Lauder, President
210 Park Avenue
New York, NY 10169

Re: Termination of Agreement of June 26, 1986.

continued on page 14-7

continued from page 14-6

Letter Agreement

Dear Joe,

This will confirm our agreement reached by telephone earlier today.

(a) Within two business days after receiving your executed copy of this letter agreement, we will send you our check for $12,000.00.

(b) The agreement between Cisco Products Corporation and Bates Incorporated dated June 22, 1986 (the "Agreement") is terminated except for the provisions by which you agreed to keep information about Cisco confidential. Your obligations under those provisions will survive this termination.

(c) You will immediately turn over to us copies of all pertinent records relating to your activities under the Agreement.

(d) We release each other from all liabilities and obligations under the Agreement, and you agree that you are not entitled to any commissions or other payments in connection with the Agreement or from any future sale, merger or acquisition of Cisco Products.

If the above is in accordance with your understanding of our agreement, please sign the enclosed copy of this letter and return it to me.

Best regards,

Cisco Products Company

By______________________________ President

Accepted and Agreed to:

Bates Incorporated

By______________________________ Date_________________________

President

In negotiating, much revolves around the particular wording. This is particularly true when attorneys are attempting to reach agreement, for each has his own style and pet provisions. The general approach is to give in reluctantly on something that is completely unimportant and try to exchange that concession for something that is worthwhile. You may be surprised how often a desirable provision can be gained merely by asking.

Chapter Fifteen

Effective Use of Attorneys

Look Over the Lawyer's Shoulder

Strange as it may seem, attorneys can be useful—under strictly controlled conditions. The few minor criticisms mentioned in these writings about the conduct of attorneys gives only an inkling of the enormous economic damage being inflicted on this country by the legal profession. The problem is not limited to minor, incompetent country-town lawyers—it is rampant in the largest and most prestigious firms in the country. No matter how large or complicated the task, or how prestigious the firm, keep a short rein on the activities of the attorneys. By and large, lawyers are not managers, so don't expect them to manage.

When A.H. Robbins Co. was forced into bankruptcy in 1985 by liability claims, the attorneys for the litigants presented invoices for legal fees for services between August 1985 and November 1987 in excess of $12 million and the case was not over. (Berlack Israels & Liberman, shareholders counsel, claimed $918,000; Cadwalader Wickersham & Taft, counsel for claimants, invoiced for $2,790,000; Mays & Valentine, general counsel for Robbins, $2,390,000; Skadden Arps Slate Meagher & Flom, bankruptcy counsel for Robbins, $5,520,000; and Wachtell Lipton Rosen & Katz, trade creditors' counsel, $467,000.) At that point Judge Merhige, the judge in charge of the bankruptcy proceedings, ordered further fees held up pending the conclusion of the case. That judge is to be commended—most judges ignore the absurd fees of the attorneys.

Why are the fees so high? One reason is that it is common practice to use a mob approach to litigation. More often than not, law firms "double-team, triple-team and quadruple-team" routine assignments. Lawyers are not managers. Who was at fault in the Robbins case? Clearly, it was the management of the litigants who failed in their duty to oversee the activities of their lawyers. It would have been wise for each of the claimants to provide a manager, and not one selected from the various law firms that participated in the scam. Such a manager's primary objective should be to see that each necessary task is performed effectively, efficiently and at minimum cost. Clearly, this takes a skilled manager, but there was plenty of money in the Robbins case to pay many managers and still achieve phenomenal savings. Just the lawyer's awareness that a knowledgeable manager is looking over his shoulder and asking questions will cause a major curtailment in legal fees. The lesson is clear: Even though you are an executive in a large corporation with access to the most prestigious law firms, don't overlook your duty to monitor carefully the activities of the lawyers. It can save millions!

Maybe you are not an executive in a large corporation, maybe you are a businessman in a small struggling company. The lesson is the same. Tell the attorney specifically what you want done and find out in advance what it will cost, at least within some tolerable brackets. Keep a lid on the charges.

Those are general pieces of rather obvious advice, but putting things into actual practice is far from easy. There are books and books on how to select and make use of an attorney. Most of it is garbage.

Selecting an Attorney

One frequent suggestion is to interview the attorney, learn about his hourly rates, and find out what success he has had in the past. An interview with the attorney is, of course, a necessary step in selecting counsel. But the interview should not be directed to asking about the hourly fee or investigating the past efforts of the attorney. The hourly figure isn't in itself a very meaningful criterion. One attorney may spend considerably more time doing a specific job than another. One attorney may do a conspicuously better job than another. One attorney may charge for time actually spent on the job and exclude trips to the bathroom, interruptions from associates, telephone calls from others, etc. Another may lump all of this time onto the job at hand. These are all things you will learn at a later time. Until you know something about the attorney, put off the interview.

Step One—Scouting the Turf

If you are looking for an attorney to handle business problems, select an attorney who specializes in business problems. Avoid the jack of all trades—if the attorney handles negligence suits, or divorce cases, or maritime litigation, or labor disputes, don't consider him as a possible attorney to handle your business problems. If you want to get a divorce, go to a divorce lawyer. If you want to file a patent application, talk to a patent lawyer. The same precautions apply to larger firms that attempt to cover the waterfront. Generally, you will be better advised to go to a firm that specializes in patent law than to a large firm that has a "patent department."

You can ascertain something of the scope of the practice of an attorney by a simple telephone call. The secretary who answers the telephone may respond to questions about the kind of cases the attorney handles. If you want an attorney to handle business matters, perhaps the best place to start is to ask other businessmen. These may be people you know, or you may even call strangers, introduce yourself and tell them what you are looking for.

Another possible approach is to call the attorney and, after ascertaining that he does, indeed, specialize in business matters and doesn't handle divorce cases, explain that you would like to consider the possibility of working with him and would like the names of several present clients he has worked with over a period of time. Even more informative will be the names of former clients. If you get some names, the next ploy is to call them, introduce yourself without saying that Attorney X sent you, and ask for recommendations for an appropriate attorney. If Attorney X is not mentioned, you have a clue, however faint. In any event, you will downplay any direct recommendation. Be sure to ask whether he knows anyone else who is acquainted with Attorney X. The secondary name is entitled to more credence than the first. After satisfying yourself that Attorney X is at least a good prospect, an interview might be in order.

Step 2—The Interview

Don't open the interview by asking about hourly rates and work habits. Tell the attorney something of what you are looking for and ask whether this fits in with his plans of operation. If the attorney is good—he's likely busy. If he is busy, he hasn't much time for questions about rates. His answer should be something like, "I try to charge a reasonable rate, everything considered. If a client thinks I am too expensive, he is welcome to go somewhere else."

If you contemplate the attorney will be doing any significant amount of travel in handling your affairs, it may be thought appropriate to ask about travel expenses. Does he travel first class? Does he stay only at the Meridien or its equivalent? I would not ask those questions. If the travel is too expensive, I'll find it out soon enough, and I don't want to alert the attorney that I will be looking at these things carefully. Why encourage him to bury travel charges somewhere else?

Questions about billing procedures are in order. It is preferable to have monthly billings rather than job billings. You are better able to judge the reasonableness of the charges on a monthly basis and you can get out before the mire gets too deep.

This interview will tell you something about the personality of the attorney and how he might fare in accompanying you in negotiations. From the general conversation, you will be able to get some feel for his abilities and his intelligence. Don't ask him for his academic background, etc. It's not likely to be relevant, since most academic records do not distinguish between memory and reasoning power, particularly in subjects such as law where memory is the primary measure. However, one background area of investigation is important: Has the attorney had any actual business experience aside from law? Probably not, but if he has, it may be a plus.

Step 3—Integrity

Honesty is important. Personally, I don't know how to judge it from an interview, but you may well have the kind of insight that will enable you to draw a conclusion that would be beyond me. Now, I say honesty is important on the assumption that you are reasonably honest in your business practices. If you are looking for an attorney who will join you in deceptive or illegal practices, then honesty may not be a requirement for you. But beware—the attorney who will help you cheat will also be likely to cheat you!

It may seem superfluous to talk about honesty among lawyers! It ain't. In many of the larger law firms with immaculate reputations, fraud is commonplace. I do not say this from any statistical study or from anything I have read. I say it from personal observation. Not long ago, a law suit was filed against one of my clients and was being handled by a major downtown litigating firm. In response to a requirement to produce certain documents, I gathered all relevant documents from my client's files and took them to the lawyer handling the litigation. While I sat in his office, he went through the documents and extracted some six or seven papers which he put in his desk drawer. When I inquired whether he considered those documents to be relevant his reply was something like: "Hell yes, they are relevant, but I sure as hell don't want those guys to find out about them." The withholding of these documents was a criminal offense. Even more, it undermines the very foundation of the process of discovery that was designed to decrease court time and to bring about fairer decisions. It didn't work.

In another instance, an attorney specializing in employee retirement matters, perceived that an annoying, or even expensive, situation would not exist if a certain parcel of property had been transferred in the preceding year. "No problem," said the attorney, "we merely back-date the deed."

He prepared the deed as of the previous year, had the client sign it, and had it notarized by a secretary in his office. That attorney committed fraud as did the secretary who was the notary public.

I do not mention these instances as isolated one-of-a-kind situations. They are representative of usual and ordinary actions by many (not all) attorneys. So if you want to engage in such activities, it won't be too hard to find attorneys to assist.

I have higher regard for the ethics of judges than lawyers. At least, judges made a recent list of 10 occupations regarded by the public as having the highest ethics. Lawyers didn't. However, my respect for the ethics of judges is limited to a majority of those states where judges are appointed—not where they are elected. As I view the election states, my respect for the judiciary rapidly dwindles, reaching a bottom in the otherwise great state of Texas.

Step 4—The Litigation Negative

In selecting an attorney to assist in business deals, it is important to avoid attorneys who specialize in litigation. Conducting litigation in the present day convoluted court system results in a mind warp of litigating attorneys that makes it difficult for them to consider or understand the practicalities of a business deal. The usual result is that all provisions of an agreement are written in the manner the litigating attorney would like to have if it he were litigating a dispute. This premature assumption of litigation can sour a contract. For example, a provision of an agreement might read:

The Fiscal Corporation agrees to deliver to the Beetle Company, on or before December 1, 1988, one ton of Millaget Material meeting the specifications set forth in Exhibit 4 hereof.

Simple enough. But a litigating attorney will immediately "what-if" the contract to death. For example, he might insist on rewriting the above provision as follows:

The Fiscal Corporation agrees and guarantees to deliver to the Beetle Company, on or before December 1, 1988, one ton of Millaget Material meeting the specifications set forth in Exhibit 4 hereof. If The Fiscal Corporation fails to make such delivery in full on or before December 1, 1988, or fails in any respect to meet the specifications as set forth, Beetle Corporation shall have the undisputed right to purchase the Millaget Material from any other source and The Fiscal Corporation agrees to reimburse Beetle Corporation for any and all costs incurred in excess of what it would have paid had The Fiscal Corporation not defaulted in its obligations hereunder, which costs shall include any damages suffered because of delayed delivery, including but not limited to loss of production, lost sales, direct and indirect, returned goods, warranty costs, and all other expenses of every kind in any way related to the failure of The Fiscal Corporation to perform in accordance with this Agreement. Furthermore, The Fiscal Corporation agrees to hold Beetle Company harmless from any claims of loss from its customers, agents or suppliers in any way

continued on page 15-5

continued from page 15-4

```
related to the failure of The Fiscal Corporation to make
timely delivery hereunder or failure to meet the appli-
cable specifications. In the event of litigation between
the parties hereto that is in any way related to the
failure of The Fiscal Corporation to perform hereunder,
The Fiscal Corporation agrees to reimburse Beetle
Corporation for all costs, including but not limited to
attorneys' fees, incurred by Beetle Company in pursuit of
such litigation. Further The Fiscal Corporation...
```

The deal? It has died in the arms of the attorneys. In fairness, not all litigation attorneys will react in such a wild manner, but it is not unusual. And it is really not the fault of the litigator—his environment is polluted. The lesson is: Beware of allowing a litigation attorney to kill a business deal that would be good for both parties.

Step 5—Try It On

Having selected an attorney, consider it a trial, not a permanent, commitment. Rather than giving him a "pile" of things to do, give him one task and see how he performs, and what he charges, before giving him additional work. Build up slowly. Even better, if finances and other considerations permit, give the identical task to two or more attorneys and compare the results. This can be a fairly simple task and the results may well justify the extra cost.

It is a necessity that you know something about the task you are giving to the attorney, if you are to keep charges in check. If you ask the attorney to form a new corporation, be aware of the general steps and the fees involved (see the next chapter). It will save money. Sometimes even the simplest of clues can be revealing. For example, attorneys once used legal-size paper. It was even required by the courts. It is a damned nuisance and won't fit in the file cabinets of a business organization. If the attorney writes contracts on legal-size paper forget him.

Do not expect or rely on an attorney to structure a deal for you. That is a job for management. It is up to you to weigh the risks against the gains and to determine just what deal is acceptable and what deal is not. When you have drafted the agreement, or at least written down all of the terms of the agreement, let the attorney tell you what is wrong with it—but don't blindly believe all you hear. Attorneys are not a creditable substitute for thinking.

Contingent fees have a place in the system, as in negligence actions and the like. But by and large, they have no place in business agreements and you should not select an attorney that thinks in terms of contingent payments. A more usual arrangement is the payment of a retainer to an attorney.

My advice: Don't. The better attorneys do not want and will not accept a retainer. If your credit is so bad the attorney demands advance payment, you are going to have to make do with an inferior attorney. Capable attorneys do not have to do business with poor credit risks, and the offer of a retainer will not change them.

Chapter Sixteen

Forming and Maintaining a Corporation

There are several forms of business entities including: individuals doing business under their own names; individuals doing business under an assumed name; partnerships; limited partnerships; and corporations. Most larger businesses are corporations, because the owners of a corporation are not usually liable for the debts of the corporation. This is a necessary condition for acquiring capital from one not personally involved in managing the business. Partnerships among a number of individuals can carry dangerous liabilities—for debts of the partnership and even for debts or obligations of the individual partners. Various states have established statutory rules for partnerships, sometimes called a Limited Partnership, by which the liability of the investing partner is limited. Usually a General Partner is appointed to administer the affairs of the partnership. Such a partnership, if established and operated in accordance with the statutory requirements, will provide immunity for the investing partners from partnership obligations. However, since the corporation is by far the most usual arrangement for larger businesses, we will confine our remarks here to the corporate entity.

A corporation is a statutory entity that has many of the legal powers of an individual. In its own name, a corporation can sue or be sued; carry on business activities; hire employees; own tangible and intangible assets; etc. A corporation has three primary parts: the stockholders, the board of directors and the officers. It is important that every businessman understand the specific functions of each of these parts. This is true even for individuals operating an unincorporated business, for such companies must do business with corporations.

The stockholders are the owners of the business. When a corporation is established, the equity of the corporation is divided among a number of shares of stock that are issued to the investors in proportion to their investment in the corporation. A general protocol for operation of the company, called the "by-laws," is adopted by the stockholders. Sometimes these by-laws can be amended or changed by the board of directors, sometimes only by the stockholders. The ultimate power and control of every corporation lies in the hands of the stockholders.

The board of directors has responsibility for the overall operation of the company. The stockholders elect the board and have the power to remove board members. The board establishes the general policies of the company and, to a greater or lesser extent depending upon the particular corporation, various details of the operating procedures. The board of directors elects the officers of the corporation to handle the day-to-day affairs.

The usual officers in a corporation are president, secretary (or in quagmire states, the "clerk"), and treasurer. The functions of each officer are defined by the board of directors. The president is the one in charge of day-to-day operations under the directives of the board of directors. The secretary is charged with handling the paper work of the corporation, such as preparing minutes of stockholder and directors' meetings, sending out notices, preparing stock certificates, etc. The treasurer is charged with guardianship of the corporate finances. However, there are wide differences in the functions of the officers among different corporations.

Additional officers may include vice presidents, sometimes charged with a specific aspect of operations such as engineering, finance, production, sales, etc. There may also be assistants for each of the offices, such as assistant secretary, assistant treasurer, etc.

You do not need the services of an attorney to set up and maintain a corporation. The days when a corporation was a rigid structure with reams of rules for the precise keeping of records and holdings of meetings are gone. The various states have revised the corporate laws to allow great flexibility in the creation and maintaining of a corporation. Nevertheless, if you wish to have the benefits offered by a corporation, you must treat the business as a corporation, not as a proprietorship. We'll say more about this presently.

The specific requirements for forming a corporation vary from state to state. The easiest way to start is to request information and forms from the office of your local Secretary of State. This will tell you the fees and generally how to prepare the papers for filing.

Delaware is a popular state for incorporation, so we will use that as a practical example. If you are not a resident of Delaware, you must have an agent in the state who is empowered to accept service in the event the corporation is sued. In other words, if you incorporate in a particular state, the corporation can be sued in that state even if you conduct no other activities there. Such agents represent the corporation for a relatively modest annual fee. A list of acceptable agents in Delaware can be obtained by writing to the Department of State, Division of Corporations, P.O. Box 898, Dover, Delaware 19901. Similar lists for other states are available from the Secretary of State in that state. After obtaining the list of agents, you can then write to them to inquire about their annual fees and the "extra" fees for performing additional special functions. There is a wide disparity among the charges of the agents.

After selecting a local agent, the next step is to select the corporate name. The name must include an indication that the entity is a corporation. In many states, you could not, for example, call your corporation "The Bessie Company." You could call it "The Bessie Company, Inc.," or "The Bessie Company Corp.," or "Bessie Inc.," etc. You should find out just what corporate indicators are required in your state of incorporation. In Delaware, the permitted corporate indicators are "Association," "Club," "Company," "Corporation," Foundation," "Fund," "Incorporated," "Institute," "Limited," "Society," "Syndicate," "Union," or any of these abbreviations: "Co.," "Corp.," "Inc.," or "Ltd."

You can ask your agent to check on the availability of the name. This can usually be done by telephone. If the name is available, it can be reserved for thirty days without charge. "Availability" means that no other corporation has a prior registration of the same name or one sufficiently similar that it might cause confusion. If "Bessie Incorporated" is already incorporated in your state, you could not use the name "Bessie" even if you changed the other parts of the name. You could still incorporate in another state where the name has not been usurped, but this is not likely to be a practical solution, because before a foreign corporation (a corporation formed in another state) can do business in your state it must register there as a foreign corporation, and this will not be permitted if another local or foreign corporation has the same or a confusingly similar name.

The next step is to prepare the Certificate of Incorporation (sometimes the Articles of Incorporation). The following is a typical form ready for forwarding to the agent, along with the filing fee and the first annual charge for the agent:

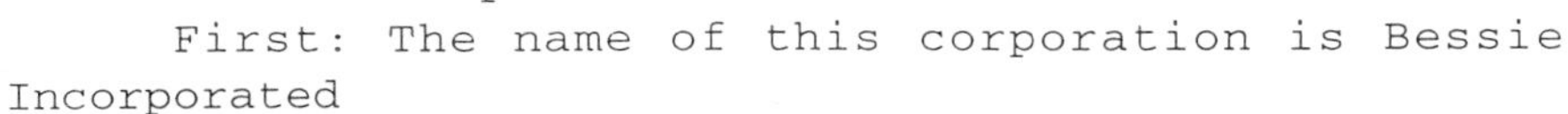

CERTIFICATE OF INCORPORATION OF BESSIE INCORPORATED

A Close Corporation

First: The name of this corporation is Bessie Incorporated

Second: Its registered office in the State of Delaware is to be located at [here insert the address of the Delaware agent you have selected]. The name of the registered agent is [name of registered agent].

Third: The nature of the business, and the objects and purposes proposed to be transacted and carried on, are to engage in any lawful act or activity for which corporations may be organized under the General Corporation Law of Delaware.

Fourth: The amount of total authorized capital stock of the corporation is divided into 3,000 shares of no par common [the maximum number of shares with minimum tax].

Fifth: The name and address of the incorporator is:

John Doe,
21 Vista,
Boulder City, Nevada 89005

Sixth: The powers of the incorporator are to terminate upon the filing of the Certificate of Incorporation. The name and mailing addresses of the persons who are to serve as directors until their successors are elected are as follows:

Mary Smith,
240 Tara Ct.,
Boulder City, Nevada 89005

John Smith,
240 Tara Ct.,
Boulder City, Nevada 89005

Seventh: All of the issued stock of the corporation, exclusive of treasury shares, shall be held of record of not more than thirty (30) persons.

Eighth: All of the issued stock of all classes shall be subject to the following restriction on transfer permitted by Section 202 of the General Corporation Law.

Each stockholder shall offer to the corporation or to other stockholders of the corporation a thirty (30) day "first refusal" option to purchase the stock of a stockholder electing to sell stock in the corporation.

Ninth: The corporation shall make no offering of any of its stock of any class which would constitute a "public offering" within the meaning of the Unites States Securities Act of 1933, as amended.

Tenth: Directors of the corporation shall not be liable to either the corporation or to its stockholders for monetary damages for a breach of fiduciary duties unless the breach involves: (1) a director's duty of loyalty to the corporation or its stockholders; (2) acts or omissions not in good faith or which involve intentional

continued on page 16-4

continued from page 16-3

```
misconduct or a knowing violation of law; (3) liability
for unlawful payments of dividends or unlawful stock pur-
chases or redemption by the corporation; or (4) a trans-
action from which the director derived an improper per-
sonal benefit.
      I, the undersigned, for the purpose of forming a
corporation under the laws of the state of Delaware do
make, file and record this Certificate, and do certify
that the facts stated herein are true; and I have accord-
ingly set my hand.
      Dated at Boulder City, Nevada June 30, 1987.
________________________________ John Doe, Incorporator
```

This may seem a bit crowded, but that is an advantage in states (including Delaware) where the recording fee is based on the number of pages.

Corporate Stock

The ownership of a corporation lies in the stockholders and is evidenced by stock certificates issued to the shareholders. There may be several classes of stock: The most usual is no-par value common stock. Common stock most often has voting power equal one vote per share. However, there may be more than one class of common stock. For example, a Class A stock may have voting rights, while a Class B stock, with exactly the same characteristics relative to corporate ownership, has no voting rights. Thus it is possible to have a corporation in which the Class B stockholders own, say, 95 percent of the corporation, but the entire corporation is controlled by the five percent of the outstanding stock held by the Class A stockholders.

A specific number of shares of each class is authorized in the Articles of Incorporation and more than that amount may not be issued without first amending the Articles of Incorporation. Provision may be made for conversion of one class of stock into another. For example, Class B stock might be convertible, at the option of the holder, into Class A stock on a share-for-share basis or any other specified ratio.

Another class of stock is called "preferred" because it usually has a preferred position with respect to dividends. For example, a corporation might issue preferred stock for $100 per share that carries a normal dividend of, say, $8.00 per share. Those dividends would ordinarily have a preference in that the dividends must be paid on the preferred stock before any dividends can be paid on the common stock. So someone investing in preferred stock could expect a return of eight percent on the investment, if the company is sufficiently profitable to pay the dividend out of profits.

Dividends on preferred stock may be either cumulative or non-cumulative. If the dividends are non-cumulative, a lost dividend is gone forever. The company may subsequently become profitable, pay the current dividend on the preferred stock and then pay dividends on the common stock without making up for the missed dividend. If the dividend is cumulative, all missed dividends on the preferred stock must be paid before any dividend on the common stock could be paid. Preferred stock may be convertible into common stock at the option of the holder, or the Board of Directors may have power to compel conversion under some pre-established formula. Preferred stock usually has no voting power. It is permissible for preferred stock to have voting power, but usually voting rights are limited to common stock. Different classes of stock may have different voting powers: For example, Class A common could have three votes per share, Class B common could have two votes per share and the preferred stock could have one vote per share.

There is great flexibility in establishing classes of stock, voting rights, and rights to dividends, so you can tailor your corporation to best meet the needs of your particular situation.

"Par Value" is an archaic concept that is still applied to stocks. Par value is the monetary value assigned to each share of stock in the Articles of Incorporation. Such stock must be issued for an amount of money, or other property, equal to at least the par value of the stock. If par value stock is issued by the corporation without such remuneration, the stock holder could be liable to creditors for the difference between the par value and the amount actually paid. Once the stock is issued, the par value of the stock bears no relationship to its actual value. "No Par Value" common stock has no stated valuation in the corporate charter. In practical terms, the difference in par value stock from no par value stock lies in the tax area. In some states, as in Delaware, the corporate tax may be less for par value stock than for no par value stock.

Annual taxes are usually based on the number of shares of authorized stock and whether the stock has a par value. At this writing in Delaware, the minimum annual tax on a company with 500,000 shares of authorized no par value common stock is almost $1770.55 If the stock has a par value, the minimum tax on the same amount of par value stock may be as little as $40.00. Before sending in your annual corporate tax to the state of incorporation, read the tax law carefully. Delaware has a bit of a scam in its tax notices. For example, the company with 500,000 shares of authorized stock having a par value of $0.01 per share receives an official notice in which the tax is calculated as $1770.55. The busy businessman might just send a check for the full amount. However, the fine print on subsequent pages of the tax notice describes a rather complex method of computing an alternate tax based on the assets of the corporation. If the corporation has few assets, the actual tax due may be only the minimum of $40.00. If you inadvertently pay the larger sum to the State of Delaware, you can, with some red tape, likely recover the over payment. If you intend to create a Delaware corporation and plan to issue more than 3,000 shares, consider making it par value stock, because the alternate tax computation method cannot be used for no par value stock. There is no logical reason for the legal distinctions drawn by the Delaware tax law—but logic is never a strong point among lawyers who write tax legislation.

The number of shares you will want to authorize depends upon the particular circumstances. Suppose only one or a few people are to be stockholders, then 10 or 100 shares might be sufficient. Usually some number of shares can be authorized at the minimum tax rate. In Delaware it is 3,000. The maximum might as well be authorized so that if needed in the future additional shares can be issued without amending the Certificate of Incorporation.

There may be a psychological reason for authorizing more shares. If a corporation, for example, intends to make stock options available to its employees and has only 100 shares issued, an employee getting an option for an amount of stock representing one percent ownership of the company receives an option for one share, which doesn't sound like much. If the ownership of the corporation is represented by 2,000,000 shares, then one percent ownership is represented by 20,000 shares. Sounds like a lot more! There is, of course, no difference, but many individuals may not be aware of that. Even if I do know the difference, I'd still rather show 100,000 shares in my portfolio than only one.

Assume now the Certificate of Incorporation has been filed and the selected corporate name has been reserved. The corporation will come into existence as of the day the Certificate is filed. Confirmation of the recording of the Certificate will not be received for some weeks. The next step is to hold an organization meeting of the stockholders. Typical actions taken at an organizational meeting are represented by the following set of minutes:

MINUTES OF ORGANIZATIONAL MEETING OF INCORPORATORS OF Bessie Incorporated

The first meeting of the Incorporators of the corporation was held on July 15, 1988 at Boulder City, Nevada. All [or a majority constituting a quorum] of the Incorporators were present:

John Doe
Mary Smith
John Smith

John Doe was elected chairman to conduct the meeting. Mary Smith was elected Secretary and directed to keep minutes of the meeting.

It was unanimously voted to issue the following no par common stock of the corporation (the "Stock"):

1000 shares of Stock to	John Doe.
500 shares of Stock to	Mary Smith.
500 shares of Stock to	John Smith.

The following directors were unanimously elected to serve until the next annual meeting and until a successor has been elected and qualified:

John Doe
Mary Smith
John Smith

It was noted for the record that the Certificate of Incorporation was filed in the Office of the Secretary of State on July 15, 1988. The certified copy of the Certificate of Incorporation was ordered to be inserted into the minute book when received.

The by-laws attached to these minutes were adopted by unanimous vote of the stockholders.

Each of the undersigned approves and adopts the foregoing minutes and waives notice of the meeting.

____
John Doe

____
Mary Smith

____
John Smith

In this example, the incorporators are the same as the stockholders, so the first meeting of the stockholders is in effect combined with the organizational meeting. If the stockholders are not the same as the incorporators, a meeting of the stockholders will be held to elect the directors and to adopt the by-laws. This and other actions of the corporation may be taken without an actual meeting. The minutes are signed by each of the appropriate parties and placed in the minute book. In general, whether or not an actual meeting is held, it is good practice to have the minutes signed by each of the voting parties. This is convenient for stockholders in a small corporation, but may become too burdensome in a larger corporation.

Next, we have a typical set of by-laws. Many elements of these by-laws are subject to change depending upon the particular operating procedures that are desired, but these can serve as a starting point for amendment.

BY-LAWS OF BESSIE INCORPORATED

ARTICLE I. OFFICES

The principal office of the corporation in the State of Nevada shall be located at 242 Tara Court, Boulder City, Nevada. The corporation may have such other offices, either within or without Nevada as the Board of Directors may designate or as the business of the corporation may require from time to time.

ARTICLE II. SHAREHOLDERS

SECTION 1. Annual Meeting. The annual meeting of the shareholders shall be held on the First Monday in the month of February in each year beginning with the year 1989, for the purpose of electing Directors and for the transaction of such other business as may come before the meeting. If the election of Directors shall not be held on the day designated herein for any annual meeting of the shareholders, or at any adjournment thereof, the Board of Directors shall cause the election to be held at a special meeting of the shareholders as soon thereafter as conveniently may be.

SECTION 2. Special Meetings. Special meetings of the shareholders, for any purpose, unless otherwise prescribed by statute, may be called by the President or by a majority vote of the Board of Directors.

SECTION 3. Place of Meeting. The Board of Directors may designate any place, either within or without Nevada, unless otherwise prescribed by statute, as the place of meeting of any annual or special meeting called by the Board of Directors. If no designation is made, or if a special meeting be otherwise called, the place of meeting shall be the principal office of the corporation in Nevada.

continued on page 16-8

continued from page 16-7

SECTION 4. Notice of Meeting. Written notice stating the place, day and hour of the meeting, and for special meetings, the purpose for which the meeting is called, shall unless otherwise prescribed by statute, be delivered not less than five nor more than ten days before the date of the meeting, either personally or by mail, by direction of the President, or the Secretary, or the persons calling the meeting, to each shareholder of record entitled to vote at such meeting. If mailed, such notice shall be deemed to be delivered when deposited in United States mail, certified return receipt requested, addressed to the shareholder at his address as it appears on the stock transfer books of the corporation.

SECTION 5. Closing of Transfer Books or Fixing of Record Date. For the purpose of determining shareholders entitled to notice of or to vote at any meeting of shareholders or any adjournment thereof, or shareholders entitled to receive payment of any dividend, or in order to make a determination of shareholders for any other purpose, the Board of Directors of the corporation may provide that the stock transfer books shall be closed for a stated period not greater than thirty days. If the stock transfer books shall be closed for the purpose of determining shareholders entitled to notice of or to vote at a meeting of shareholders, or shareholders entitled to receive payment of a dividend or distribution of capital, the date on which notice of the meeting is mailed or the date on which the resolution of the board of Directors declaring such dividend, as the case may be, shall be the record date for such determination of shareholders. When a determination of shareholders entitled to vote at any meeting of shareholders has been made as provided in this Section, such determination shall apply to any adjournment thereof.

SECTION 6. Voting Lists. The officer or agent having charge of the stock transfer books for shares of the corporation shall make a complete list of the shareholders entitled to vote at each meeting of shareholders or any adjournment thereof, with the address of and number of shares held by each. Such list shall be produced and kept open at the time and place of the meeting and shall be subject to the inspection of any shareholder during the meeting.

SECTION 7. Quorum. A majority of the outstanding shares of the corporation entitled to vote, represented in person or by proxy, shall constitute a quorum at a meeting of shareholders. If less than a majority of the outstand-

continued on page 16-9

continued from page 16-8

ing shares are represented at a meeting, a majority of the shares so represented may adjourn the meeting from time to time without further notice. At such adjourned meeting at which a quorum shall be present or represented, any business may be transacted which might be transacted at the meeting as originally noticed. The shareholders present at a duly organized meeting may continue to transact business until adjournment, notwithstanding the withdrawal of enough shareholders to leave less than a quorum.

SECTION 8. Proxies. At all meetings of shareholders, a shareholder may vote in person or by proxy executed in writing by the shareholder or by his or her duly authorized attorney in fact. Such proxy shall be filed with the Secretary of the corporation before or at the time of the meeting. No proxy shall be valid after six months from the date of execution, unless otherwise provided in the proxy.

SECTION 9. Voting of Shares. Subject to the provisions of Section 12 of this Article II, each outstanding share entitled to vote shall be entitled to one vote upon each matter submitted to a vote at a meeting of shareholders.

SECTION 10. Voting of Shares by Certain Holders. Shares standing in the name of another corporation may be voted by such officer, agent or proxy as the by-laws of such corporation may prescribe, or, in the absence of such provision, as the Board of Directors of such corporation shall determine.

Shares held by an administrator, executor, guardian or conservator may be voted by him, either in person or by proxy, without transfer of shares into his or her name. Shares standing in the name of a trustee may be voted by him, either in person or by proxy, but no trustee shall be entitled to vote shares held by him without a transfer of such shares into the name of the trustee.

Shares standing in the name of a receiver may be voted by such receiver, and shares held by or under the control of a receiver may be voted by such receiver without the transfer thereof into his name if authority to do so is contained in an appropriate order of the court by which such receiver was appointed.

A shareholder whose shares are pledged shall be entitled to vote such shares until the shares have been transferred from the name of the shareholder to another.

continued on page 16-10

continued from page 16-9

Shares of its own stock belonging to the corporation shall not be voted, directly or indirectly, at any meeting, and shall not be counted in determining the total number of outstanding shares at any given time.

SECTION 11. Informal Action by Shareholders. Unless otherwise provided by law, any action required to be taken at a meeting of the shareholders, or any other action which may be taken at a meeting of the shareholder, may be taken without a meeting if a consent in writing, setting forth the action so taken, shall be signed by all of the shareholders entitled to vote with respect to the subject matter thereof.

SECTION 12. Cumulative Voting. Unless otherwise provided by law, at each election for Directors every shareholder entitled to vote in such election shall have the right to vote, in person or by proxy, the number of shares owned by him for as many persons as there are Directors to be elected and for whose election he or she has a right to vote, or to cumulate his votes by giving one candidate as many votes as the number of such Directors multiplied by the number of his or her shares shall equal, or by distributing such votes on the same principle among any number of candidates.

ARTICLE III. BOARD OF DIRECTORS

SECTION 1. General Powers. The business and affairs of the corporation shall be managed by its Board of Directors.

SECTION 2. Number, Tenure and Qualifications. The number of Directors shall be not less than two or more than five as directed by the Board of Directors. Each Director shall hold office until the next annual meeting of shareholders and until a successor has been elected and qualified.

SECTION 3. Regular Meetings. A regular meeting of the Board of Directors shall be held, without other notice than this by-law, immediately after, and at the same place as, each annual meeting of the shareholders. The Board of Directors may provide, by resolution, the time and place for the holding of additional regular meetings without other notice of such resolution.

SECTION 4. Special Meetings. Special meetings of the Board of Directors may be called by or at the request of the President or any Director. The person or persons

continued on page 16-11

continued from page 16-10

authorized to call such a special meeting of the Board of Directors may fix the place for holding such meeting within Nevada.

SECTION 5. Notice. Notice of any special meeting of the Board of Directors shall be given at least five days previous thereto by written notice delivered personally or mailed by certified mail, return receipt requested, which notice shall be deemed to be delivered when deposited in the United States mail. Any Director may waive notice of any meeting. The attendance of a Director at a meeting shall constitute a waiver of notice for such meeting, except where a Director attends a meeting for the express purpose of objecting to the transaction of any business because the meeting was not lawfully called or convened.

SECTION 6. Quorum. A majority of the number of Directors fixed by these by-laws shall constitute a quorum for the transaction of business at any meeting of the Board of Directors, but if less than such a majority is present at a meeting, a majority of the Directors present may adjourn the meeting from time to time without further notice.

SECTION 7. Manner of Acting. The act of the majority of the Directors present at a meeting at which a quorum is present shall be the act of the Board of Directors.

SECTION 8. Action Without a Meeting. Any action that may be taken by the Board of Directors at a meeting may be taken without a meeting if a consent in writing, setting forth the action so to be taken, shall be signed before such action by a majority of the Directors.

SECTION 9. Vacancies. Any vacancy occurring in the Board of Directors may be filled by the affirmative vote of a majority of the remaining Directors though less than a quorum of the Board of Directors, unless otherwise provided by law. A director elected to fill a vacancy shall be elected for the unexpired term of his or her predecessor in office. Any directorship to be filled by reason of an increase in the number of Directors may be filled by the Board of Directors for a term of office continuing only until the next election of Directors by the shareholders.

SECTION 10. Compensation. By resolution of the Board of Directors, each Director may be reimbursed for expenses of attending any meeting and may be paid stated salary as

continued on page 16-12

continued from page 16-11

a Director or a fixed sum for attendance at each meeting of the Board of Directors or both. No such payment shall preclude any Director from serving the corporation in any other capacity and receiving compensation therefore.

SECTION 11. Presumption of Assent. A Director who is present at a meeting of the Board of Directors at which any action on any corporate matter is taken shall be presumed to have assented to the action taken unless his or her dissent shall be entered in the minutes of the meeting or unless he shall file his or her dissent with the person acting as secretary of the meeting before the adjournment of the meeting or within three days thereafter. Such right of dissent shall not apply to any Director who voted in favor of such action.

ARTICLE IV OFFICERS

SECTION 1. Number. The officers of the corporation shall be a President, Treasurer and Secretary, each of whom shall be elected by the Board of Directors. Such other officers and assistant officers as may be deemed necessary may be elected or appointed by the Board of Directors.

SECTION 2. Election and Term of Office. The officers of the corporation shall be elected by the Board of Directors to hold office until a successor has been elected by the Board of Directors, or the resignation of the officer, or until removed from office by a majority vote of the a Board of Directors.

SECTION 3. President. The President shall be the principal executive officer of the corporation and, subject to the control of the Board of Directors, shall supervise and control all of the business affairs of the corporation. He shall have the right to preside at all meetings of the Directors and shareholders. SECTION 4. Secretary. The Secretary shall: (a) keep the minutes of the proceedings of the shareholders and of the Board of Directors; (b) see that all notices are duly given in accordance with the provisions of these by-laws or as required by law; (c) be custodian of the corporate records and of the seal of the corporation; (d) keep a register of the post office address of each shareholder which shall be furnished to the Secretary by such shareholder; (e) sign with the President, certificates for shares of the corporation which have been authorized by the Board of Directors or the shareholders; (f) have general charge of the stock transfer books of the corporation; and (g) in general perform all duties incident to the office of Secretary

continued on page 16-13

continued from page 16-12

and such other duties as from time to time may be assigned to him by the President or by the Board of Directors.

SECTION 5. Treasurer. The Treasurer shall: (a) have custody of and be responsible for all funds and securities of the corporation; (b) receive and give receipts for money due and payable to the corporation, and deposit all such moneys in the name of the corporation in such banks or other depositories as shall be designated by the Board of Directors; and (c) in general perform all of the duties incident to the office of Treasurer and which may be assigned to him or her from time to time by the President or the Board of Directors.

SECTION 6. Salaries. The salaries of the officers shall be fixed from time to time by the Board of Directors and no officer shall be prevented from receiving such salary because he is a Director.

ARTICLE V. CONTRACTS, LOANS, CHECKS AND DEPOSITS

SECTION 1. Contracts. The Board of Directors may authorize any officer or officers, agent or agents, to enter into any contract or execute and deliver any instrument in the name of and on behalf of the corporation, and such authority may be general or limited to specific events.

SECTION 2. Loans. No loans shall be contracted on behalf of the corporation and no evidence of indebtedness shall be issued in its name unless authorized by a resolution of the Board of Directors. Such authority may be general or limited to specific areas or events.

SECTION 3. Checks, drafts, etc. All checks, drafts or other orders for the payment of money, notes or other evidence of indebtedness issued in the name of the corporation, shall be signed by such officer or officers or agent or agents of the corporation and in such manner as from time to time shall be determined by resolution of the Board of Directors.

SECTION 4. Deposits. All funds of the corporation not otherwise employed shall be deposited from time to time to the credit of the corporation in such banks or other depositories as the Board of Directors shall designate.

ARTICLE VI. CERTIFICATES FOR SHARES AND THEIR TRANSFER

SECTION 1. Certificates for Shares. Certificates representing shares of the corporation shall be in such

continued on page 16-14

continued from page 16-13

form as shall be determined by the Board of Directors. Such certificates shall be signed by the President and the Secretary or by such other officer or officers as shall be authorized by the Directors in conformity with applicable law, and sealed with the corporate seal. All certificates for shares shall be consecutively numbered or otherwise identified. The name and address of the person or other entity to which shares are issued, with the number of shares and date of issue, shall be entered on the transfer books of the corporation. All certificates surrendered to the corporation for transfer shall be canceled and no new certificates shall be issued until the former certificate for a like number of shares has been surrendered and canceled, except that in the case of a lost, destroyed or mutilated certificate a new one may be issued therefore upon such terms and indemnity to the corporation as the Board of Directors may prescribe.

SECTION 2. Transfer of Shares. Transfer of shares of the corporation shall be made only on the stock transfer books of the corporation by the holder of record thereof or by his legal representatives, who shall furnish proper evidence of authority to transfer, or by his duly authorized attorney, and on surrender for cancellation of the certificates of such shares. The person or other entity in whose name the shares stand on the books of the corporation shall be deemed by the corporation to be the owner thereof for all purposes.

ARTICLE VII. FISCAL YEAR.

The fiscal year of the corporation shall end on the last day of December of each year.

ARTICLE VIII. DIVIDENDS

The Board of Directors may from time to time declare, and the corporation may pay, dividends on its outstanding shares in the manner and upon the terms and conditions provided by law and its articles of incorporation, except that no such dividend shall be paid except from accrued profits.

ARTICLE IX. CORPORATE SEAL

The seal of the corporation shall be such as impressed on this page, subject to change at any time by the Board of Directors.

continued on page 16-15

continued from page 16-14

ARTICLE X. WAIVER OF NOTICE

Unless otherwise provided by law, whenever any notice is required to be given to any shareholder or Director of the corporation, a waiver thereof in writing, signed by the person entitled to such notice, whether before or after the time stated therein, shall be deemed equivalent to the giving of such notice.

ARTICLE XI. AMENDMENTS

These by-laws may be altered or amended or replaced by the Board of Directors at any meeting thereof.

I, Mary Smith, certify the foregoing by-laws were duly adopted by the shareholders of the corporation on July 15, 1988.

____

Secretary

The next step is a meeting of the Board of Directors to approve the by-laws and elect the officers of the corporation.

MEETING OF THE BOARD OF DIRECTORS OF BESSIE INCORPORATED

A meeting of the Board of Directors of the corporation was held on July 15, 1988 in Boulder City, Nevada. All of the Directors were present. By unanimous vote the following resolutions were adopted:

RESOLVED THAT the By-laws previously adopted by the stockholders of the corporation and placed in the corporate minute book be approved.

RESOLVED THAT the following officers of the corporation be elected: President: John Doe. Treasurer: John Smith. Secretary: Mary Smith.

RESOLVED THAT the initial salaries of the officers be established at the rates shown on Appendix A of these minutes.

The undersigned adopt and approve the foregoing minutes and waive notice of this meeting.

____

John Doe, Director

____

John Smith, Director

____

Mary Smith, Director

In the foregoing minutes reference is made to the officers' salaries on a separate appendix. This makes it convenient for removal when the minutes are to be shown to a party that should not be privy to individual salaries.

The usual decorations for a corporation such as a minute book, seal, and stock certificates can be procured from any of various suppliers. One such supplier is All-State Legal Supply Co., One Commerce Drive, Cranford, NJ 07016. It is my experience that one is better advised to purchase corporate outfits directly from such a supplier rather than through one of the authorized corporate agents.

Printed stock certificates are readily available as part of the corporate outfit. The information required for the printing of the certificates includes: the name of the corporation, the state of incorporation, the year of incorporation, and the total number of shares of each class authorized by the Articles of Incorporation. If more than one class of stock is authorized, printed certificates will be obtained for each class.

The stock records are kept by the Secretary of the corporation. The stock record will include the name and address of each stockholder and the number of shares held. When stock is to be issued, the Secretary will prepare a stock certificate and have it signed by the appropriate corporate officers, usually the President and either the Secretary or Treasurer. The Secretary is responsible for keeping a complete and current record of the stock held by each stockholder. When one stockholder transfers stock to another entity, the clerk will void the original stock and issue the new stock in the name of the new stockholder.

Each time a meeting of either the stockholders or the Board of Directors is held, the Secretary will send out appropriate notices and will prepare minutes of the meetings. In small corporations, it is a good practice to have the minutes signed by each stockholder or director as the case may be. The signatures may be preceded by a statement such as:

```
The undersigned approve the above minutes and waive
notice of this meeting,
```

In most states where the corporation is chartered or where it is registered to do business, the state requires the filing of an annual report listing certain information such as the names and addresses of the officers and directors.

Stock Purchase Agreements

If unregistered stock is sold, it is important to have a stock purchase agreement signed by each purchaser. This agreement should state the amount of stock being purchased, a recitation of the restrictions on transferability of the stock, a statement that the purchaser has evaluated the risks involved in the stock purchase and that he is financially able to withstand the loss of the investment, and reference to a stock restriction notice to be placed on the stock certificates. It is important that the agreement include a statement by the purchaser that the stock is being purchased for investment purposes and that the purchaser does not intend to sell the stock to others. The agreement may include a first right of repurchase by the company. The following is a more or less typical stock purchase agreement. (See also Chapter 7 where similar provisions are illustrated in connection with employee stock options.)

STOCK PURCHASE AGREEMENT

This is an Agreement, effective September 9, 1987, between Basic Technology, Inc., a Delaware corporation (the "Company"), and Prince Winsor II (the "Purchaser"). The parties agree as follows:

1. Sale of Stock. The Company agrees to sell and deliver herewith to the Purchaser Ten Thousand (10,000) shares of its common stock (the "Stock") for previously agreed compensation.

2. Restrictions on Transferability. No shares of Stock shall be transferred other than in accordance with the Securities Act of 1933, as amended, and in accordance with all other applicable state or federal laws or regulations.

In the event the Purchaser desires to sell or transfer any Stock and receives a bona fide offer, the Purchaser agrees to submit in writing to the Company the identity of the offeror and all details of the terms of such offer. The Company shall have ten (10) business days from the receipt of the terms of the offer to elect to acquire the Stock on identical terms. In the event the Company fails to exercise its purchase option, the Purchaser shall have the right, for a period of ten (10) business days after refusal of the option or the expiration of the option period, whichever is earlier, to sell the Stock to the original offeror on the identical terms submitted to the Company. With respect to any Stock not sold within the specified period, this provision shall remain in effect.

3. Legends on Stock Certificates. Each stock certificate issued by the Company shall bear an appropriate legend stating the restrictions on transfer of the stock.

4. Purchase for Investment. The Purchaser warrants and represents that he is purchasing the Stock for investment purposes and not with any view to resale or distribution thereof.

______________________________ Purchaser

The following legend, consistent with the above agreement, is suitable as a notice on each stock certificate.

NOTICE OF RESTRICTIONS

Any disposition of any interest in the securities represented by this Certificate is subject to restrictions, and the securities represented by this Certificate are subject to a right of first refusal contained in a certain agreement between the record holder hereof and the corporation, a copy of which will be mailed to any holder of this Certificate without charge within five (5) days of receipt by the corporation of a written request therefor.

The securities represented by this Certificate have not been registered under the Securities Act of 1933 and, accordingly, may not be offered for sale, sold or otherwise transferred except (i) upon effective registration of the securities represented by this Certificate under the Securities Act of 1933, or (ii) upon acceptance by the issuer of an opinion of counsel in such form and by such counsel, or other documentation, as shall be satisfactory to counsel for the issuer that such registration is not required.

Voting Trusts

Trusts are one of the most useful legal instruments available, but in general are beyond the scope of this book. A trust is an arrangement by which property is transferred with the intention that it be administered by a trustee for the benefit of another. For example, one could place the ownership of a piece of real estate in trust with the provision that all net income from the property be paid to a named individual. The trustee could be provided with the power to pay all taxes and expenses from the property income and to pay the remainder to the named individual. The trust must have a termination as trusts "in perpetuity" are not permitted. A stock voting trust must terminate within 10 years. This trust might provide that upon the death of the person creating the trust, the real estate is to be transferred by the trustee to another person, who may or may not be the same person who received the income from the real estate. A trust may be revocable or irrevocable. If the trust is irrevocable, it cannot be terminated or amended even by the person who established the trust. There are many reasons for trusts and often have to do with taxes and probate. If you want to set up a trust for any reason, you should first read a good book about trusts or consult an expert in this area.

The one who creates the trust is called the "trustor," "settlor," "grantor," or "creator." The trust is created for the benefit of a party called the "beneficiary" or, as the lawyers say, the "cestui que trust." The party administering the trust is the "trustee." The trustee is the legal owner of the trust property, but administers it for the benefit of the beneficiary.

Corporate stock may be placed in a voting trust with one party receiving the benefit of the stock while another has the right to vote the stock. This may be done by placing the stock itself in the trust and granting the right to vote the stock to the trustee. The owner of the stock may retain ownership of the stock while granting the right to vote to another party. The particular arrangement will depend upon the particular circumstances and the reasons for creating the voting trust.

Epilogue

More than one hundred years have come and gone since Charles Dickens so forcefully laid on the story of Jarndyce and Jarndyce, an inheritance case that lingered in the High Court of Chancery until the heirs were dead and the assets of the estate wasted by legal fees.

A fanciful tale, some may think. But no more fanciful, no more imaginary, no more improbable, than the present day web of legal activities that smothers our country under unrealized costs, direct and indirect. The total ransom extracted from society by the burgeoning legal business is beyond count.

There must be a limit to the specific density of lawyers that a nation can support and still manage at least a meager existence, but what that limit is, no one can say. Where lies the guilt for this tragedy? The obvious answer is the legal profession. And that is true. (If, with the advent of advertising ambulance-chasers, it may still be called a profession). But the individual members of that profession seem not to be conscious of the vast intrigue in which they are the major players.

We in the legal trade have a duty to pursue the answer—by encouraging clients to be reluctant to submit to legalese, by helping to demystify a sometimes intimidating profession —even if the result is a density lower than present reality.

And the case of Jarndyce and Jarndyce drones on in the High Court of Chancery.

Glossary

Contract Terms

A Priori

Lat. A Latin term best left to lawyers. It sort of means a term expressing a general or admitted truth from which certain effects must logically follow. If it is your draft, take it out and say what you mean.

Ab Initio

Lat. From the beginning. A contract may be void from the time it was entered into. The agreement is void ab initio.

Accord and Satisfaction

A term usually used when a contract is settled without exercising ones full legal rights. When the settlement agreement is signed, it is called an "accord and satisfaction".

Action

Usually refers to a suit or prosecution. One party to a contract may take "action" against the other.

Ad Valorem

According to value. An evaluation that is a percentage or other function of the value of the property. Usually used in contracts in referring to kinds of levies or taxes.

Affidavit

A written statement made under oath or otherwise certified to be true.

Agreement

An understanding between two or more parties. When meeting the legal requirements it becomes an "enforceable agreement". Used here as synonymous with "contract".

Arbitration

An unofficial procedure for investigating the facts related to a controversy and reaching a settlement. The proposed settlement may be binding or non-binding.

Articles of Incorporation

The document by which a corporation is formed under the laws of a particular state.

Assign

To turn over the rights to or some interest in property to another party. The document turning over the rights is an "assignment".

Boiler Plate

Contract provisions that are used repeatedly and may be considered a "standard" for use in an agreement.

Bona Fide or Bona Fides

Lat. In good faith; with integrity and honesty in dealing. The opposite of mala fides.

Breach

The violation of, or the failure to perform some provision of a contract.

By-Laws

The regulations or rules adopted by a corporation for governing the conduct of the corporation. The by-laws can be changed by either the Board of Directors or the stockholders, depending upon the restrictions in the Articles of Incorporation or in the by-laws themselves.

Certify

To vouch for a thing in writing; to make known or establish as a fact.

Consequential Damage

Damage that results as a consequence rather than directly from some failure to meet an obligation. A machine is guaranteed to produce 50 parts per minute. If it only produces 20 parts per minute, that is a direct damage under the guarantee. If the machine over-heats and burns down the factory, that is a consequential damage.

Consideration

Something of value in the eyes of the law that justifies a binding commitment on the part of the party receiving the consideration. Not to be confused with the motive for making a contract.

Contingent Fee

The fee paid to an attorney as a percentage of the proceeds of legal action or other proceeding. This fee is in lieu of an hourly or fixed charge established in advance.

Contract

A covenant or agreement between two or more parties to do or not to do certain things. The terms of the contract are expressed, either orally or in writing, and each party agrees to do or not do the recited things. An agreement.

Copyright

The exclusive right granted by the government to original literary property. Copyrights are registered with the Library of Congress.

Corporation

A legal entity formed by one or more persons. The corporation, formed under the laws of a particular state, is regarded as having a personality and existence distinct from that of its founders or owners.

Counterpart

A copy of an agreement that is executed by one or more of the parties to the agreement.

Covenant

A written pledge by one or more parties as to the truth of some statement or that some particular action will be taken.

Cum Grano Salis

Lat. The way to take business advice from an attorney.

DBA

A common abbreviation meaning "doing business as". The abbreviation is usually in lower case letters: "John Jones dba The Local Grocery Company".

De Facto

In fact or deed; actually. Words used to accept a past condition that may have been illegal or incomplete. May refer to a present condition as actually existing rather than just a paper plan.

Encumbrance

A burden, mortgage, lien, or any debt attached to either real or personal property.

Force Majeure

Fr. An irresistible or overpowering force. One may be forgiven, by the terms of an agreement, for failure to perform because of force majeure, an event that one was powerless to overcome - strikes, floods, riots, war, etc..

Grantor

The one who gives something. Frequently appears in trusts in which the one establishing the trust and transferring assets to it is called the "Grantor".

Indemnify

To save another harmless from loss or damage; to give security for the reimbursement in case of anticipated loss.

Independent Contractor

One who contracts to perform certain functions or deliver goods by his own methods and without being subject to the control of another party except as to the results. Many obligations attach to an employer that are not present when the same work is performed by an independent contractor.

Intellectual Property

Primarily refers to rights in products of mental activities. Copyrights and patents are the most usual examples. See Intangible Property.

Intangible Property

Property or a right that does not have a physical existence. It may refer to copyrights, patents, accounts receivable, rights of legal action, trade secrets etc.

Inter Alia

In the old days it meant "among other things". Now, when used in a contract, it means get a new attorney.

Ipso Facto

By the fact itself; by the mere fact.

Jurisdiction

The power of a court to enforce certain laws by enforcement or the award of remedies. See venue.

Lawyer

An individual lacking the self esteem to call himself an Attorney-at-Law or a Solicitor or even a Barrister.

Lessee

The party who rents and occupies property belonging to another. The one who holds property by lease from another.

Lessor

One who grants a lease.

Licensee

One who receives a license form another.

Licensor

One who grants a license to another.

Mala Fide

In bad faith. The opposite of bona fide.

Namely

A word importing things already included in the previous reference term. "Including" indicates something additional not included in the reference term. Using the word "including" to recite things inherently included in the reference term is a quick road to a Legal Omelet.

Net Lease

A lease that requires the tenant to pay all or a portion of the real estate taxes.

Net Net Lease

A lease that includes all of the charges of a net lease plus a charge for insurance on the building.

Net Net Net Lease

A lease under which the tenant pays all costs associated with the leased property including, taxes, maintenance, repairs, ground upkeep, snow removal, etc. Costs associated with maintaining the building structure are usually excluded.

Notary Public

A public officer with authority to certify signatures and statements, usually in connection with the transfer of real and personal property or agreements.

Offset

A deduction; a counterclaim; a contrary claim by which a given claim may be reduced or cancelled.

Party

One who undertakes an obligation under a contract and thus becomes a "party" to the agreement.

Personal Property

Things owned by an individual or by any entity that are not real property. Such things as a bank account, a chair, clothing, automobiles, and computers are personal property. Your house and lot are not personal property.

Pet Name

In written agreements it is convenient to refer to each of the parties by an alias (Licensor, Licensee, Joe, Buyer, Seller, etc.). The selected alias is a "pet name".

Power of Attorney

An instrument authorizing another to act as one's agent or on one's behalf. The person authorized need not be a lawyer.

Premises

That which is put before. In a contract, the expression "in consideration of the premises", means "in consideration of the things stated before".

Prima Facie

Lat. At first sight; on the face of it; presumably; so far as it can be judged from appearances.

Prime Rate

The lowest interest rate charged by a bank to its best customers.

Pro Rata

Proportionately; according to a certain rate; in equal ratios.

Proprietary

A reference to ownership. Often used in connection with intellectual property, such as "proprietary information".

Reduction to Practice

A term usually used in connection with inventions denoting the actual building and operation of the device or method embodying the invention. The filing of a patent application is sometimes referred to as a "constructive reduction to practice".

Retainer

An amount of money paid to the attorney in advance.

Representation

A statement in an agreement that a certain fact or circumstance is true. See warranty.

Royalty

A payment made for the use of a thing or a right. A payment for a license under a patent is a royalty.

Said

An over-used word meaning the same as before; in Legal Omelette terms, "aforesaid".

Security Interest

An undivided ownership interest in a thing. A security interest is often granted to secure the payment of a debt.

Subrogation

The substitution of one person (or thing) in the place of another with respect to rights, claims, or securities. For example, a person may by agreement give up certain rights and an insurer of that person may be asked to subrogate its rights so that the rights of the insurer do not exceed those of that person.

Survival of Terms

This usually refers to certain provisions or terms that continue to be effective even after the agreement expires or is terminated.

Trade Secret

A plan, process, tool, mechanism, compound or other proprietary information that is known only to its owner and those having a confidential obligation to the owner.

Trust

A right of property held by one entity for the benefit of another. The owner of property who puts it in trust, loses legal title to that property. A contract may provide that a party hold property "in trust" for some particular disposition. The party holding the property becomes a "trustee" and has certain legal obligations in connection with care of the property.

Trustee

The one who holds the legal title to the trust property and administers the assets of the trust, for the benefit of the beneficiary or beneficiaries, in accordance with a document that established the trust, sometimes called "A Declaration of Trust".

Trustor

An old fashioned word referring to the one who establishes the trust. A grantor, donor, creator or founder of a trust.

Uniform Commercial Code

A set of laws adopted by the various states, with some variations, to generate an almost uniform set of laws to govern business transactions.

Venue

The place or area where the court has jurisdiction. Venue refers to geographical location, jurisdiction to the authority of the court.

Vested Interest

A present right or title to a thing that carries with it the right to sell or trade it, even though the right to actual possession may be postponed to some future time. This is different from a "future right".

Warranty

An undertaking or stipulation that certain facts are as stated.

Ze End

Lat. That is all.

Index

ORDER DIRECTLY FROM THE OASIS PRESS®

THE OASIS PRESS® ORDER FORM

Call, Mail, Email, or Fax Your Order to: PSI Research, 300 North Valley Drive, Grants Pass, OR 97526 USA
Email: psi2@magick.net *Website:* http://www.psi-research.com
Order Phone USA & Canada: +1 800 228-2275 *Inquiries & International Orders:* +1 541 479-9464 *Fax:* +1 541 476-1479

TITLE	✓ BINDER	✓ PAPERBACK	QUANTITY	COST
Bottom Line Basics	❑ $39.95	❑ $19.95		
The Business Environmental Handbook	❑ $39.95	❑ $19.95		
Business Owner's Guide to Accounting & Bookkeeping		❑ $19.95		
Buyer's Guide to Business Insurance	❑ $39.95	❑ $19.95		
Collection Techniques for a Small Business	❑ $39.95	❑ $19.95		
A Company Policy and Personnel Workbook	❑ $49.95	❑ $29.95		
Company Relocation Handbook	❑ $39.95	❑ $19.95		
CompControl: The Secrets of Reducing Worker's Compensation Costs	❑ $39.95	❑ $19.95		
Complete Book of Business Forms		❑ $19.95		
Customer Engineering: Cutting Edge Selling Strategies	❑ $39.95	❑ $19.95		
Develop & Market Your Creative Ideas		❑ $15.95		
Doing Business in Russia		❑ $19.95		
Draw The Line: A Sexual Harassment Free Workplace		❑ $17.95		
The Essential Corporation Handbook		❑ $21.95		
The Essential Limited Liability Company Handbook	❑ $39.95	❑ $21.95		
Export Now: A Guide for Small Business	❑ $39.95	❑ $24.95		
Financial Management Techniques for Small Business	❑ $39.95	❑ $19.95		
Financing Your Small Business		❑ $19.95		
Franchise Bible: How to Buy a Franchise or Franchise Your Own Business	❑ $39.95	❑ $24.95		
Friendship Marketing: Growing Your Business by Cultivating Strategic Relationships		❑ $18.95		
Home Business Made Easy		❑ $19.95		
Incorporating Without A Lawyer (Available for 32 states) SPECIFY STATE:		❑ $24.95		
Joysticks, Blinking Lights and Thrills		❑ $18.95		
The Insider's Guide to Small Business Loans	❑ $29.95	❑ $19.95		
InstaCorp – Incorporate In Any State (Book & Software)		❑ $29.95		
Keeping Score: An Inside Look at Sports Marketing		❑ $18.95		
Know Your Market: How to Do Low-Cost Market Research	❑ $39.95	❑ $19.95		
Legal Expense Defense: How to Control Your Business' Legal Costs and Problems	❑ $39.95	❑ $19.95		
Location, Location, Location: How to Select the Best Site for Your Business		❑ $19.95		
Mail Order Legal Guide	❑ $45.00	❑ $29.95		
Managing People: A Practical Guide		❑ $21.95		
Marketing Mastery: Your Seven Step Guide to Success	❑ $39.95	❑ $19.95		
The Money Connection: Where and How to Apply for Business Loans and Venture Capital	❑ $39.95	❑ $24.95		
People Investment	❑ $39.95	❑ $19.95		
Power Marketing for Small Business	❑ $39.95	❑ $19.95		
Profit Power: 101 Pointers to Give Your Business a Competitive Edge		❑ $19.95		
Proposal Development: How to Respond and Win the Bid	❑ $39.95	❑ $21.95		
Raising Capital	❑ $39.95	❑ $19.95		
Retail in Detail: How to Start and Manage a Small Retail Business		❑ $15.95		
Secrets to Buying and Selling a Business		❑ $24.95		
Secure Your Future: Financial Planning at Any Age	❑ $39.95	❑ $19.95		
The Small Business Insider's Guide to Bankers		❑ $18.95		
Start Your Business *(Available as a book and disk package – see back)*		❑ $ 9.95 (without disk)		
Starting and Operating a Business in...series *Includes FEDERAL section PLUS ONE STATE section*	❑ $29.95	❑ $27.95		
PLEASE SPECIFY WHICH STATE(S) YOU WANT:				
STATE SECTION ONLY (BINDER NOT INCLUDED) SPECIFY STATE(S):	❑ $8.95			
FEDERAL SECTION ONLY (BINDER NOT INCLUDED)	❑ $12.95			
U.S. EDITION (FEDERAL SECTION – 50 STATES AND WASHINGTON DC IN 11-BINDER SET)	❑ $295.95			
Successful Business Plan: Secrets & Strategies	❑ $49.95	❑ $27.95		
Successful Network Marketing for The 21st Century		❑ $15.95		
Surviving and Prospering in a Business Partnership	❑ $39.95	❑ $19.95		
TargetSmart! Database Marketing for the Small Business		❑ $19.95		
Top Tax Saving Ideas for Today's Small Business		❑ $16.95		
Which Business? Help in Selecting Your New Venture		❑ $18.95		
Write Your Own Business Contracts	❑ $39.95	❑ $24.95		
BOOK SUB-TOTAL (FIGURE YOUR TOTAL AMOUNT ON THE OTHER SIDE)				

OASIS SOFTWARE Please check Macintosh or 3-1/2" Disk for IBM-PC & Compatibles

California Corporation Formation Package ASCII Software	☐	☐	$ 39.95		
Company Policy & Personnel Software Text Files	☐	☐	$ 49.95		
Financial Management Techniques (Full Standalone)	☐		$ 99.95		
Financial Templates	☐	☐	$ 69.95		
The Insurance Assistant Software (Full Standalone)	☐		$ 29.95		
Start A Business (Full Standalone)	☐		$ 49.95		
Start Your Business (Software for Windows™)	☐		$ 19.95		
Successful Business Plan (Software for Windows™)	☐		$ 99.95		
Successful Business Plan Templates	☐	☐	$ 69.95		
The Survey Genie - Customer Edition (Full Standalone)	☐		$149.95		
The Survey Genie - Employee Edition (Full Standalone)	☐		$149.95		
SOFTWARE SUB-TOTAL					

BOOK & DISK PACKAGES Please check whether you use Macintosh or 3-1/2" Disk for IBM-PC & Compatibles

The Buyer's Guide to Business Insurance w/ Insurance Assistant	☐		☐$ 59.95	☐$ 39.95		
California Corporation Formation Binder Book & ASCII Software	☐	☐	☐$ 69.95	☐$ 59.95		
Company Policy & Personnel Book & Software Text Files	☐	☐	☐$ 89.95	☐$ 69.95		
Financial Management Techniques Book & Software	☐		☐$ 129.95	☐$ 119.95		
Start Your Business Paperback & Software (Software for Windows™)	☐			☐$ 24.95		
Successful Business Plan Book & Software for Windows™	☐		☐$125.95	☐$109.95		
Successful Business Plan Book & Software Templates	☐	☐	☐$109.95	☐$ 89.95		
BOOK & DISK PACKAGE TOTAL						

AUDIO CASSETTES

Power Marketing Tools For Small Business	☐ $ 49.95		
The Secrets To Buying & Selling A Business	☐ $ 49.95		
AUDIO CASSETTE SUB-TOTAL			

OASIS SUCCESS KITS Call for more information about these products

Start-Up Success Kit	☐ $ 39.95		
Business At Home Success Kit	☐ $ 39.95		
Financial Management Success Kit	☐ $ 44.95		
Personnel Success Kit	☐ $ 44.95		
Marketing Success Kit	☐ $ 44.95		
OASIS SUCCESS KITS TOTAL			

COMBINED SUB-TOTAL (FROM THIS SIDE)

YOUR GRAND TOTAL

SUB-TOTALS (from other side)	$
SUB-TOTALS (from this side)	$
SHIPPING (see chart below)	$
TOTAL ORDER	$

If your purchase is:	Shipping costs within the USA:
$0 - $25	$5.00
$25.01 - $50	$6.00
$50.01 - $100	$7.00
$100.01 - $175	$9.00
$175.01 - $250	$13.00
$250.01 - $500	$18.00
$500.01+	4% of total merchandise

SOLD TO: *Please give street address*

NAME:

Title:

Company:

Street Address:

City/State/Zip:

Daytime Phone: Email:

SHIP TO: *If different than above, please give alternate street address*

NAME:

Title:

Company:

Street Address:

City/State/Zip:

Daytime Phone:

PAYMENT INFORMATION: *Rush service is available, call for details.*

International and Canadian Orders: Please call for quote on shipping.

☐ CHECK Enclosed payable to PSI Research

Charge: ☐ VISA ☐ MASTERCARD ☐ AMEX ☐ DISCOVER

Card Number:

Expires:

Signature:

Name On Card:

Insta06/97

Call toll free to order 1-800-228-2275 PSI Research 300 North Valley Drive, Grants Pass, OR 97526 FAX 541-476-1479

Use this form to register for an advance notification of updates, new books and software releases, plus special customer discounts!

Please answer these questions to let us know how our products are working for you, and what we could do to serve you better.

Write Your Own Business Contracts

This book format is:
☐ Binder book
☐ Paperback book
☐ Book/Software Combination
☐ Software only

Rate this product's overall quality of information:
☐ Excellent
☐ Good
☐ Fair
☐ Poor

Rate the quality of printed materials:
☐ Excellent
☐ Good
☐ Fair
☐ Poor

Rate the format:
☐ Excellent
☐ Good
☐ Fair
☐ Poor

Did the product provide what you needed?
☐ Yes ☐ No

If not, what should be added?
____
____
____
____

This product is:
☐ Clear and easy to follow
☐ Too complicated
☐ Too elementary

Were the worksheets (if any) easy to use?
☐ Yes ☐ No ☐ N/A

Should we include?
☐ More worksheets
☐ Fewer worksheets
☐ No worksheets

How do you feel about the price?
☐ Lower than expected
☐ About right
☐ Too expensive

How many employees are in your company?
☐ Under 10 employees
☐ 10 - 50 employees
☐ 51 - 99 employees
☐ 100 - 250 employees
☐ Over 250 employees

How many people in the city your company is in?
☐ 50,000 - 100,000
☐ 100,000 - 500,000
☐ 500,000 - 1,000,000
☐ Over 1,000,000
☐ Rural (Under 50,000)

What is your type of business?
☐ Retail
☐ Service
☐ Government
☐ Manufacturing
☐ Distributor
☐ Education

What types of products or services do you sell?
____
____
____

What is your position in the company?
(please check one)
☐ Owner
☐ Administrative
☐ Sales/Marketing
☐ Finance
☐ Human Resources
☐ Production
☐ Operations
☐ Computer/MIS

How did you learn about this product?
☐ Recommended by a friend
☐ Used in a seminar or class
☐ Have used other PSI products
☐ Received a mailing
☐ Saw in bookstore
☐ Saw in library
☐ Saw review in:
☐ Newspaper
☐ Magazine
☐ Radio/TV

Where did you buy this product?
☐ Catalog
☐ Bookstore
☐ Office supply
☐ Consultant

Would you purchase other business tools from us?
☐ Yes ☐ No

If so, which products interest you?
☐ EXECARDS® Communications Tools
☐ Books for business
☐ Software

Would you recommend this product to a friend?
☐ Yes ☐ No

Do you use a personal computer?
☐ Yes ☐ No

If yes, which?
☐ Macintosh
☐ IBM/compatible

Check all the ways you use computers?
☐ Word processing
☐ Accounting
☐ Spreadsheet
☐ Inventory
☐ Order processing
☐ Design/Graphics
☐ General Data Base
☐ Customer Information
☐ Scheduling

May we call you to follow up on your comments?
☐ Yes ☐ No

May we add your name to our mailing list? ☐ Yes ☐ No

If you'd like us to send associates or friends a catalog, just list names and addresses on back.

Is there anything we should do to improve our products?
____

Just fill in your name and address here, fold (see back) and mail.

Name ______________________________
Title ______________________________
Company ______________________________
Phone ______________________________
Address ______________________________
City/State/Zip ______________________________
E Mail Address (Home) ______________ (Business) ______________

PSI Research creates this family of fine products to help you more easily and effectively manage your business activities:
The Oasis Press®
PSI Successful Business Library
PSI Successful Business Software
EXECARDS® Communication Tools

3/97

If you have friends or associates who might appreciate receiving our catalogs. please list here. Thanks!

Name____________________ Name____________________

Title____________________ Title____________________

Company____________________ Company____________________

Phone____________________ Phone____________________

Address____________________ Address____________________

Address____________________ Address____________________

FOLD HERE FIRST

NO POSTAGE NECESSARY IF MAILED IN THE UNITED STATES

BUSINESS REPLY MAIL

FIRST CLASS MAIL PERMIT NO. 002 MERLIN, OREGON

POSTAGE WILL BE PAID BY ADDRESSEE

PSI Research
PO BOX 1414
Merlin OR 97532-9900

FOLD HERE SECOND, THEN TAPE TOGETHER

Please cut along this vertical line, fold twice, tape together and mail.